Alfred Hitchcock's High Vernacular:

THEORY AND PRACTICE

Alfred Hitchcock's High Vernacular

THEORY AND PRACTICE

◇　　◇　　◇

Stefan Sharff

◇

COLUMBIA UNIVERSITY PRESS

NEW YORK

Columbia University Press
New York   Oxford
Copyright © 1991 Columbia University Press
All rights reserved

Library of Congress Cataloging-in-Publication Data
Sharff, Stefan.
Alfred Hitchcock's high vernacular : theory and practice
/ Stefan Sharff.
p. cm.
ISBN 0-231-06914-6
1. Hitchcock, Alfred, 1899–   —Criticism and interpretation.
2. Cinematography.   I. Title.
PN1998.3.H58S48   1991
791.43'0233'092—dc20
90-2515
CIP

Printed in the United States of America

c 10 9 8 7 6 5 4 3 2 1

Contents

◇ —————————————— ◇

Preface

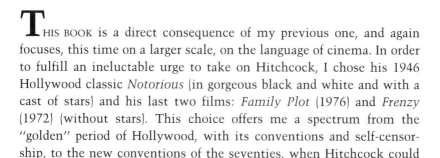

THIS BOOK is a direct consequence of my previous one, and again focuses, this time on a larger scale, on the language of cinema. In order to fulfill an ineluctable urge to take on Hitchcock, I chose his 1946 Hollywood classic *Notorious* (in gorgeous black and white and with a cast of stars) and his last two films: *Family Plot* (1976) and *Frenzy* (1972) (without stars). This choice offers me a spectrum from the "golden" period of Hollywood, with its conventions and self-censorship, to the new conventions of the seventies, when Hitchcock could perform more freely. As it turned out, he was the great master in both periods. All three films, in the opinion of this writer, are masterly.

I should like to forewarn the reader that as this book is wholly concerned with structure, there will be hardly any commentary on the narrative, the acting, or any other aspect of these films not related to cinema language.

I am much indebted to Professor Frank Kermode for his comments on portions of the manuscript as well as to Professor Julian Hochberg for his pertinent criticism and suggestions. I would like to extend my special gratitude to my wife, Laura Foley, for her patient help in editing the text, always watching for logic and clarity.

Alfred Hitchcock's High Vernacular:

THEORY AND PRACTICE

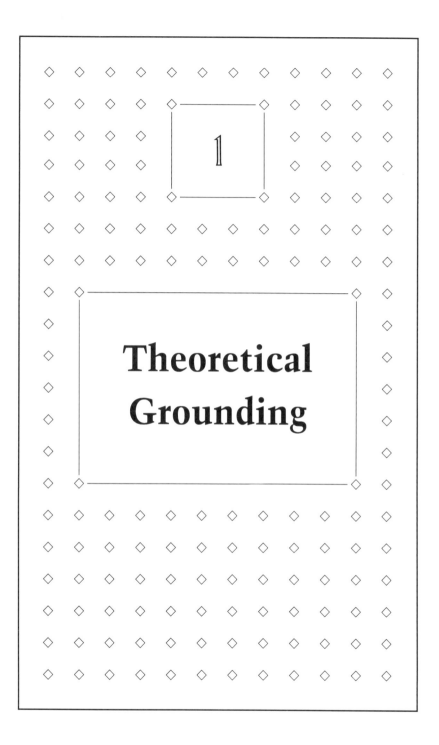

1

Theoretical Grounding

H ITCHCOCK is admired foremost as a master of cinematic form; yet, ironically, his forms have hardly been fully understood. Cinematic structures in general are an enigma to a great number of filmmakers. One hears, here and there, accolades for specific shots in Hitchcock films, such as the "fantastic high angle" in *The Birds*, the "spectacular dolly" in *Frenzy*, and the "soaring crane shot" in *Notorious*. What is missed is an awareness that Hitchcockian shots, however memorable, do not work each by themselves but, rather, are an integral part of his complex harmonies, interwoven, orchestrated, and meticulously choreographed in a rich and elegant cinema "language." One shot, like an utterance in speech, is but one link, at times a very significant link, in a continuous chain of cinematic performance.

This book stands on the proposition that there is a film language, and that it is in a state of sufficient maturity to be theoretically and philosophically defined and scrutinized.* Granted, legions of theorists both in France and here have explored this realm, notably the pioneering Christian Metz in his *Film Language*. Due credit should also be given to other studies that emphasize Hitchcock's structures, like Bill Rothman's, Raymond Belour's, Robin Wood's, as well as Bordwell's, Thompson's, and Staiger's. Yet, the focus here is different, since I am discussing the craft on a level at which the director has to cope from shot to shot throughout a film.

I developed my methodology over a period of thirty years, as a former student of Eisenstein, to begin with, then as an active filmmaker and teacher of cinema at Columbia University. During the years of research I found the need for some new classifications and terms. I isolated eight models of structure most frequently repeated in films of

---

*Perhaps a disclaimer is in order: I do not aim for a precise linguistic analogy. Shots are not words and film does not have noun-verb structures.

quality.* Those models or elements of structure, characteristic of and often unique to cinema, become, in the hands of the film director, the devices for narrative strategy and cinesthetic form. A succession of images, properly arranged within the specific elements of structure, bring to mind the principles of organization known in music and in language. The viewers' ability to decipher cinematic structures on a continuum resembles the human, innate faculty for language. However, unlike language, with its metaphoric vocabulary (metaphoric "labels for things"), cinema's vocabulary is taken from life, mirror-like. When we scan the world (in real life) we see things at random, unless we look for something. The latter is precisely what cinema does: it looks for something, it is always story bound. The organization of the information has to be cinema specific. The film language is "looking" in a specific way, penetrating the space around in search of meaning.

Let me now present, in a more condensed form, a list of the elements with brief descriptions; later I shall continue expanding on the nature of these structures with practical examples and analyses from Hitchcock films.

1. Separation: fragmentation of a scene into single images, seen in alternation, A, B, A, B, A, B, etc. Separation is a particularly strong element in cinema and, as is the case with all elements, it has a number of rules of performance: the scene usually, but not always, starts with a full exposition, wherein all participants are seen in one frame, together; the ensuing single images should not be of the same size (but more or less constant), in order to create the sense of perspective; participants in the single images are in visible eye contact with each other; and at the end of the scene there usually is a resolution consisting, again, of a fully populated frame as in the introduction. In a well-constructed separation scene the images seen one at a time give the unmistakable impression of being in more intimate contact with each other than would be the case in a more "realistic" arrangement, with the participants all the time in one frame. The minimum number of singles needed to wind up a dramatically viable relationship is three to four shots for each participant. In general usage the norm for sep-

---

*Stefan Sharff, *The Elements of Cinema: Toward a Theory of Cinesthetic Impact* (New York: Columbia University Press, 1982), p. 2.

aration is about twelve to eighteen shots. Hitchcock, as we shall see, sustains, with great success, much longer scenes using this element. Moreover, he introduces many innovations and variants, dispensing, at times, with the need for an introduction and/or resolution.

The element of separation draws the viewer into a more active participation in the film by forcing him to unify the fragmented parts, to occasionally act for the A when the B is on the screen and to anticipate reactions of those who in turn (the A or the B) are about to come on the screen. Hitchcock is able to maneuver the above in a masterly way.

2. Parallel Action: two or more narratives running simultaneously or consecutively; an ideal vehicle for chases, rescues, and crime dramas and, as we shall see, a method for breaking a naturalistic linearity.

3. Slow Disclosure: gradual introduction of information. As a method it can be applied to one scene or to a whole narrative; basically it is a way of avoiding a simplistic and over-expository flow of information.

4. Familiar Image: repetition of certain images that thus become familiar and are used as the means of keeping together a fragmented continuity. Familiar Image may also be a minor figure in the drama. On the other hand, if it is one of the protagonists the familiar image becomes a significant one to boot: a strong and immaculately presented pictorial structure (as Daniel Bell defined it for the plastic arts). Occasionally the familiar image is the onlooker through whose line of vision we see the action or part of it.

5. Moving Camera: an element of structure that is diametrically opposite to fragmentation. It carries a completely different rhythm and energy; while in some sense more realistic since it shows real time (the action lasts on the screen the same time as it does in life), the moving camera is prone to stylization and often takes liberties with reality (to a point of sometimes calling attention to the existence of the camera). Most importantly, the moving camera introduces a new kind of dramatics by exploring and penetrating the cinematic space.

6. Multiangularity: unlike the fragmentation into singles in the element of separation, this element of structure conveys information in all sizes and in contrasting angles and compositions; it is the most common structure in cinema, responsible for the creation of the illusion of three-dimensionality on the flat screen.

7. Master Shot Discipline: a more traditional structure, mainly cul-

tivated in Hollywood, less frequent in contemporary cinema. It is useful in situations where most of the information is linear and is carried via extensive dialogue scenes.

8. Orchestration: since most of the elements mentioned above often interlock and are used in various combinations, the orchestration has to attend to the arrangement, distribution, and modality over the larger geography of the narrative. For example, orchestration is responsible for making sure that scenes succeed each other with proper and elegant transitions, so very important in cinema; that the principle of "trigger-release" between high and low points in drama is adhered to; that symmetries are evident; and, most importantly, that the cinematic space is honed with finesse and not wasted on trivialities.*

Fortunately for the study of quality cinema, we benefit from an impressive filmography of the great masters who, from the early twenties, intuited cinema's possibilities and, by leaps and bounds, arrived at the basic elements of structure. As they went on they introduced more and more complexities until cinema started behaving like a real art form. In my previous book, *Elements of Cinema* (1982), I pinpointed specific elements of structure with examples from scenes from various films. Here I shall use three full-length features by Alfred Hitchcock to show how a solid architecture of cinematic elements is sustained over three large canvases: *Notorious, Frenzy,* and *Family Plot.*

What should the reader expect from this study? For one, a preliminary set of systematically related generalizations that are anchored in a singular, open-ended cinema "language." When practiced with skill a language can lead to new cinematic solutions, often solidifying and extending the range of that language. The important function here is to clarify and bring forth an understanding of cinematic structures as unique narrative and aesthetic building blocks in cinema. Quite predictably, theoretical questions initially arise in the context of some practical encounter. One should not lose sight of the fact that cinema is still a developing art; trial and error experiments often lead to some revealing discoveries, thus contributing to the enrichment of the "lan-

---

*Curiously enough, Wittgenstein's notion of "logical space . . . as an interplay between structures of necessary connection . . . consisting solely of objects concatenated in a determinate way" fits excellently to the nature of cinema with its nexus of images chosen in a determinate way.

guage." Accordingly, most theoretical statements here are, at bottom, statements about relations that hold between rules and the resulting vibrancy of expression; in sum, they are about the potential of cinema as an art form. My concern is to attend to the vibrancy of expression that Hitchcock labored to achieve.

I chose Hitchcock for the focus of this study because I believe him to be one of the great masters, a man who persistently experimented with new forms, who always sought new ways. While an artist of considerable purity, he was not an extremist and was able to attain enormous popular appeal. This fact alone may be the beginning of proof that an elegant cinema "language" can reach and gratify a mass audience.

As I proceed, a major task will be to attend to a cluster of questions, often parading as one, namely: what is cinema? Or perhaps, reversing the angle of vision, first by asking, what is cinema not?

Cinema is not and should not attempt to be the novel.

Both do have points in common, both are modes of story-telling and can artistically sustain fictionality in a realistic setting. But that is where the relationship ends, more or less. Each has a different road to climb and uses different methods and techniques to achieve its effect. Most efforts to popularize the great novelistic heritage via films fail artistically.

Furthermore, cinema is not theater and therefore should not imitate the stage. This is the most pressing problem since in the last few decades film has more and more shifted to the verbal and theatrical mode from the basically visual, producing a hybrid that brought us, among other trends, the so called "talking heads." Theater and cinema both have their own means of expression, not necessarily compatible.

Also, cinema is not just photography, or "editing," nor is it a display of technical tricks; it is not a verité slice of life, nor is it a conglomerate of the arts. As Lessing so astutely said in his argument against pictorial poetry and allegorical painting (in *Laocoön*): "Both were doomed to fail because their aims were in contradiction to the fundamental properties of their medium." The filmmakers who are cognizant of and committed to the "fundamental properties of their medium" have an important obligation: to cultivate those properties, to develop in the viewing public a sensitivity to the elegance of cinema "language" and, at the same time, to educate the critical community toward a consideration that quality in cinema is not derived from the novelistic and theatrical elements only.

Inasmuch as I distinguish here between "movies" as pop, and "cinema" as art, such a distinction requires at least a brief look at the perception of film viewing as an idiom of some singularity. Film as a realistic depiction of a known world is by necessity figurative and mainly related to vision, consequently dependent on visual experience. The latest findings in the psychology of visual perception tell us, convincingly enough, that vision is now considered to be a mental reconstruction of reality, rather than mere sensory apprehension. Such a mental reconstruction can be passive, as in the movies, or a complex and active one, as in cinema. The difference, as a rule, is in the language, the quality of the tale, the ethical "afterimage," and the artistic import it carries. The passive viewing of movies takes place mostly as a response to explicit, mostly linear, presentations of easily decipherable reality.

The category of viewing most pertinent to this study, the active-creative one, is in response to structured cinema. The mechanics of active viewing are put in motion by cinema's built-in hermeneutic specialization. A larger reality broken up into small units (shots) requires continuous contextualization: a house, a face, a clock, or any other fragment forces the viewer into a search for the context, for sequences of meaning, often involving a mental winding back to reprocess plurisignifications or false assumptions. The film chain, the succession of shots, is central and singular in cinema, equal in importance to the succession of words in written language. Dryden's remarks about Virgil (whose *Aeneid* he translated) are perfectly applicable to cinema structure: "His (Virgil's) words are not only chosen, but [so are] the places in which he ranks them. . . . He who removes them from the station wherein their master set them spoils the harmony. . . . They must read in order as they lie."

The elements of cinema language came into being piecemeal, uncoordinated at first. Accordingly, my terminology needs to be hedged round with necessary qualifications to give it a semblance of precision. I assume that in addition to the glossary here my method of analysis places those elements in context and illustrates them as "examples in action." One should keep in mind that the anatomy of perceiving a cinematic text is, in important ways, different from the one in written language. The meaning of a shot with its baggage of pictorial information depends on its contextual vicinity (shots preceeding and succeeding), on its duration on the screen, which may allow eye scanning and give thinking time, and, in addition, on the intensity of the graphic impact. A longer duration shot may provoke (in the viewer) a speculative story-building process of a different kind from the one of shorter duration shots. The next two shots will round up the necessary triad, ripening those speculations into a story hypothesis, however tentative, while the following series of shots will either confirm the viewer's speculations or force him to shift to another track. The artist/filmmaker can maneuver the chain to serve his dramatic needs by playing on or against the viewers' expectations. Indeed, with all its attachment to reality, cinema produces a speculative and tentative matrix that with the proper narrative strategy can afford to break out of the naturalistic constraints toward a meaningful ambiguity.

While analyzing the Hitchcockian material, I shall refer to patterns that are repeated by him, and can therefore become ground for generalizations of theoretical importance. In this way I will be accumulating, as I go, blocks of theoretical material.

Starting with *Notorious* (1946) I see Hitchcock's entry into cinema's full expressiveness, its "high vernacular"—to borrow, from the literary world, Frank Kermode's apt expression.* I shall pay special attention to this high vernacular, in itself a precondition for a well functioning cinema, like Hitchcock's, particularly when sequences of meaning in a film pile up into larger and at times complex units.

I am aware that the above attempts for brief summaries may obscure a host of problems that have kept theorists busy for decades. However, and without the slightest claim of exhausting the subject, I shall limit myself to the problems of the architecture of the cinematic text and to an account of the modes of cinematic "discourse," its conventions, and elements of organization producing meaning. I will not attempt to interpret them but will search for the structures which enable them to have the meaning they do. And, since I am analyzing mainly an artistic process, I will be on the lookout for cinesthetic patterns that soar above the restrictions of raw reality.

The questions I have already posed and the way I have posed them

---

*During a conversation with Hitchcock in 1975 he told me that *Notorious* was his crowning work, where he put together all he learned from his previous explorations.

focus primarily on cinema as a system operating strictly within the "fundamental properties of its medium." And although cinema developed elements of structure echoing those in the other arts, the forms and functions they take here are significantly different and again unique to the medium. Parallel action, symmetry, rhythm, to mention only a few, are present in the other arts, notably in the novel and in music, but their application is quite different in each. And here again Hitchcock the purist watches that the difference is inherently advantageous, that the uniqueness is not, by chance, compromised. As we shall see later, his parallel actions (as, for example, in *Family Plot*) are radical; his symmetries are ever present not only in his "grand designs" of large narrative units but often as sub-symmetries in the smallest units of structure; as for rhythm, he invented new forms like the waves of high and low shots succeeding each other with staccato beats of their own. His major contributions are in most cases toward the enlargement of the cinematic vocabulary, open to imitation, absorbable for general usage, and are not examples of Hitchcock's individual style, even though they may at first appear so.

2

Notorious

1946, Black and White

To discuss the film I will have to undertake, first, the tedious task of describing the plot, however crudely and summarily. The story in *Notorious* is basically linear, yet ingeniously complicated by strategically placed parallel actions and a narratively central love story.

The attractive Alicia Huberman (Ingrid Bergman) is the daughter of an ex-SS big shot who has just been sentenced, in a Miami court, to life imprisonment for spying against the United States. Wanting to forget it all, she takes to the bottle. Devlin (Cary Grant), an American intelligence agent, manages to convince her to become an American spy, and to fly to Rio on assignment. A predictable attraction soon develops between Alicia and Devlin, but Devlin's jealousies and suspicions cloud the love affair. In Rio, Alicia is given odious instructions by Captain Prescott (Louis Calhern), the field chief, to renew contact with Alex Sebastian (Claude Rains), an ex-beau of hers whom she had known through her father, and who is presently a wealthy industrialist. His mansion, as Alicia soon learns, is the hub of a major Nazi research center for rearming Germany, and is controlled by an old Gestapo-type, Eric Matisse. Alicia reports regularly to Devlin. Their love affair is further complicated when Alex Sebastian falls in love with her and proposes marriage. Alicia is caught in a dilemma between her duty as a spy—to accept the marriage proposal—and her love for Devlin—which anyway she is not sure is requited. Hesitating, she nevertheless agrees to marry Sebastian. Alicia soon finds out that the Germans are hiding something important in Sebastian's wine cellar. In order to unravel the mystery, Alicia arranges to have a huge party at the mansion; Devlin, posing as a journalist, is also invited. In a daring, suspenseful move, she steals the key to the wine cellar from her husband's key chain. At the peak of the party Alicia and Devlin, in the most nerve-wracking scene in the film, manage to enter the cellar and, thanks to an accidental fall of one of the wine bottles, find that the bottle contains a black sand—not wine; we find out later that this sand is enriched uranium. The pair of spies are nearly caught by Sebastian and the servant Joseph. Devlin, to cover up the incident, takes Alicia around and kisses her. However, Sebastian soon realizes, to his mortification, that his wife is an American spy. He and his mother (Madame Constantine) plot together to poison Alicia in slow doses so that she may appear to die of natural causes; they must cover up the scandal to save Sebastian from his Nazi supervisors. Alicia, ill, is put away in her room, telephone disconnected. Devlin, in the meantime, having lost contact with her, ventures to the mansion in person. Finding her sick, learning that she is being poisoned, he attempts to save her from her husband-turned-captor. On their way down the giant staircase they are confronted by Sebastian and his mother; but with Eric, the Gestapo-type, watching from downstairs, Sebastian cannot stop them from leaving. At the end he, in turn, tries to escape with the couple, but Devlin refuses to help. Eric calls him back to the house. The car with Alicia and Devlin moves away. Sebastian defeatedly walks up the steps to the mansion as if for an execution. And indeed Eric is waiting at the door. They enter. The door closes. Fade out.

As one can see, the story is a combination spy drama and love tale. Written by Ben Hecht on the heels of World War II, it quite predictably classified Germans as the bad guys. The moral weight of the film is on the side of the obviously good, against the Nazis. In addition, love wins, as do the interests of the United States.

The structure of the film is superb. The penchant here is toward close shots and, accordingly, an increasingly important presence is the element of separation, mostly in single A, B, A, B, A, B shots. The latter yield the significant images, so charismatic and plentiful in this film. Most of the pictorial information is introduced gradually via the element of slow disclosure, thus avoiding immediate or full exposition. Hitchcock lays out his iconography, without delay, in the first few scenes of the film, in order to ease in the elements of structure he uses, as well as to educate the viewer in his methods. Moving camera, for instance, is used at first in a mild form, as a plant, to be gradually increased in intensity during the climactic scenes, later in the film, with a brilliance and originality hardly seen before.

The dissolves, plentiful in *Notorious*, should be read as a mark of the times rather than of some distinct structural importance. Directors used them widely in the films of the forties and fifties as standard transitions and abandoned them in the next decade as the trends changed.

Scene I. Starts with a series of slow disclosures via moving camera. Shot 1: close-up of a flashing press camera, then a pan to faces of reporters, continuing to another group of reporters in medium shot and up to a sign: District Court; then to a double door, ever so slightly open, affording a limited view of the courtroom. As the camera rests we see the back of the defendant, his lawyer and the judge, all in long shot. We hear (voice over) that the defendant Huberman is found guilty of treason and sentenced to twenty-five years in jail.

So far the scene has no cuts; nevertheless, it is moving fast, since the floating camera changes quickly the size, content, and graphics of the pictorial configurations.

Shot 2: cut to door opening, reporters rushing forward. Presently Miss Huberman (Ingrid Bergman) comes out of the courtroom; the floating camera follows her as she walks in a low, dramatic medium shot—so far the first appearance of a significant image in the film. Hitchcock is able by perfect framing and pacing to imbue it with such strength that it stands out prominently, with a touch of stylization, slightly tampering with reality, but not sufficiently so to break out of the context. Such an image surely promises to carry an after-image, as this one does. Reporters, crowding, bombard her with questions about her father's conviction; she is imperially silent as she passes; camera pans to two types, most likely FBI agents; we hear instructions to watch her in case she tries to leave town. While we see them the image of Miss Huberman dominates, even though she is by now off screen.

Scene 2. Dissolve to an exterior long shot of a house; we see a detective on the sidewalk; dissolve to the same at night; dissolve to interior of the house, a noisy party is in progress.

In contrast to the previous scene, so busy pictorially, this one has no cuts whatsoever; the camera pans slowly, covering only a minimal area of the room, with action taking place also outside of the frame. Miss Huberman is the busy hostess.

A major innovation in this scene is the use of the element of slow disclosure in a much stronger form, in contrast to the way it was presented in the previous scene. The subject of the slow disclosure is a mystery man seated in the foreground always with his back to the camera; his identity will not be known until the next morning, in the next scene. Presently we hear drunken noises and conversations while Alicia, running in and out of frame, is filling glasses, conversing, offering drinks, and flirting with the mystery man. She informs him that she is followed by agents everywhere she goes, like a "marked woman." An older gentleman invites her to join him on a cruise to Havana. Hard drinking continues. Miss Huberman sits down facing the mystery man (still with his back to the camera). She likes him; she tells him so. She is drunk, like the rest of the crowd.

In a sudden change of mood she asks everyone to leave, "the party is over." Camera moves in closer to the back of the head of our mystery man, framed slightly on the right of center. Fade-out—end of Scene 2.

Scene 3. Daylight; interior (Shot 1): fade-in to a medium close-up of the back of the head of the mystery man as before, but this time in daylight; camera starts moving around the figure disclosing at last the face of Devlin (Cary Grant). After a long delay the viewer is given the physiognomy of a famous star, a significant factor in this variant of slow disclosure. The camera pulls back to also disclose Miss Huberman, at the same table, having a last drink with Devlin. Both are drunk, among a dozen empty bottles. Cut (shots 2 to 9) to a medium close-up of Devlin on a diagonal from Miss Huberman whose head is in the foreground; he horses around, draining a few drops of whiskey out of an empty bottle. Seven similar shots follow, each alternating from Devlin to Miss Huberman, and back to Devlin, etc. They converse and occasionally flirt. A near kiss passes without really happening. (Still to come are the narrative disclosures of who Devlin is and what his game is in this drama.) Miss Huberman wants to go for a drive. They get up, camera follows. Cut (shot 10) to a medium shot as they come out to a garage. She can hardly stand on her feet, yet decides to do the driving. Devlin ties a scarf around her waist; again they nearly kiss. Dissolve. The above seven over-the-shoulder shots on a diagonal, A, B, A, B, afford a pause of sort; this form, usually reserved for dialogue scenes, as it is here, reads dramatically neutral. Hitchcock's strategy is to give a release prior to the trigger in the next scene. In addition, both trigger and release, as in many of Hitchcock's films, are interwoven with humor.

Scene 4. The moving camera is replaced by cuts. Dissolve (shot 1, brief) to a long shot of a road with palm trees; an open convertible

automobile is racing forward, crossing visibly, for an instant, the middle line of the road. Dissolve (shot 2, brief) to a medium shot of the windshield; Miss Huberman is at the wheel, Devlin in the passenger seat. Prelude to separation. Cut (shot 3) to a higher medium shot of the two (without windshield in view); she: "How am I doing?" Devlin: "Not bad." Cut (shot 4) to road with radiator cap in foreground as the car sways from one side of the road to the other. Cut (shot 5) to the same two-shot as in shot 3; she: "Scared?" Devlin: "No." She: "You're not scared of anything." Cut (shot 6) to a close-up of Devlin; actual separation element begins. Devlin: "Not too much." Cut (shot 7) to an extreme close-up of Devlin's hand just about to reach the steering wheel. Cut (shot 8) to a close-up of Miss Huberman straining to look at the road as her hair is getting into her eyes. Cut (shot 9) to the road (as in shot 4), radiator cap indicating car's volatile movements; the view is obscured by hair. Cut (shot 10) to a close-up of Miss Huberman: "Fog gets me." Cut (shot 11) to a close-up of Devlin: "It's your hair in your eyes." Cut (shot 12) to a frontal two-shot (as in shot 3) of longer duration. A pause in the separation. She clears away her hair; they both smile and humor each other. They talk about the speedometer; she wants to reach eighty mph to wipe out his grin: "I don't like gentlemen grinning at me." Cut (shot 13) to a close-up of Devlin smiling, then as he looks ahead his face grows tense. Cut (shot 14) to the familiar shot

of the road with radiator cap; car is fast and unsteady. Note the sequence: in shot 13 we see the onlooker (Devlin) worried, in shot 14 we
see the reason (the road), in shot 15 we will see that he acts upon it.
Cut (shot 15) to a close-up of Devlin's hand (as in shot 7) about to grab
the steering wheel, then letting it go. Cut (shot 16) to the familiar two-
shot of Devlin and Miss Huberman, this time of longer duration. Behind them in the distance we see a single light, evidently a motorcycle.
Soon we hear a siren. Devlin: "A cop." Miss Huberman seems not to
know, then: "What?" Devlin: "A policeman is chasing us."

Cut (shot 17) to a close-up of the rearview mirror as Devlin's hand
adjusts it to frame better on the motorcycle approaching them. Cut
(shot 18) to a two-shot as the policeman reaches and passes them. Cut
(shot 19) to a medium two-shot of Devlin and Miss Huberman, both
in profile (note the change of set-up from frontal position to the profile)
as policeman enters frame, riding along the car. Cut (shot 20) to a close-
up of Devlin: "He wants to speak to you." Cut (shot 21) to a close-up
of Miss Huberman: "Drunken driving . . . second offense. I'll go to
jail." Car stops. Cut (shot 22) to the familiar two-shot in profile (as in
shot 19), the policeman has just left the frame. Miss Huberman: "Old
family jail—who cares." She reaches for the hand brake. Cut (shot 23)
to the policeman dismounting the motorcycle, taking off his glasses
and moving toward the driver's side of the car. Cut (shot 24) back to
the medium two-shot of Devlin and Miss Huberman in profile (as before); the policeman enters frame and addresses her: "Having a good
time, aren't you?" Miss Huberman mumbles out some abuse. This longer
duration shot is a perfect release after the tension created by the preceeding series of short ones. Cut (shot 25) to the familiar close-up of
Devlin. He takes out his identification card; camera follows the ID as
he hands it to the policeman, ending in a close-up of the latter, as the
policeman reads it. Cut (shot 26) to the familiar close-up of Miss
Huberman as the ID passes in front of her (on the way back to Devlin).
She looks at it in her drunken stupor, not comprehending. Devlin's
hand takes it out of frame. Miss Huberman looks up in the direction
of the policeman. Here again we see (or it is implied we see) only through
the onlooker (Miss Huberman is the only one in frame). Cut (shot 27)
to a close-up of the policeman that is tighter than before: "Sure you
can handle it?" He looks in the direction where Devlin is assumed to

be, salutes and steps out of frame (to his motorcycle, no doubt). Cut (shot 28) to the familiar close-up of Miss Huberman as she turns to where Devlin is. Cut (shot 29) to a new high two-shot of Devlin and Huberman. She asks: "Where is the ticket, he didn't give me a ticket . . ." (we hear the motorcycle leaving). "I saw the policeman saluting you . . . You're a cop!" A fight ensues. Devlin wants to take over the driving. Miss Huberman hits him on the wrist. The struggle is not devoid of humorous overtones. Finally Devlin manages to move her over and, while struggling (his back is to the camera), he seems to have hit her hard enough to knock her out. He settles down at the wheel, center frame. Fade out. This is the longest duration shot so far (1 min., 18 sec.) and at the end, quite obviously, a release from the tension.

By now, as the iconography unfolds, we have observed the following elements of structure: slow disclosure, moving camera, separation and, in addition, the subliminal force of trigger release. The latter, as it turns out, is an important gun in Hitchcock's arsenal. I must mention also the appearance of profile shots (shots 19 and 22). As we shall see later, profiles are assigned a significant role in this film, a sort of cinematic turn of phrase by Hitchcock (perhaps a "secret" of his) especially as they are unexpected, and startling. It can be said that profiles when well placed are an interesting form of reality, somewhere at the edge of our perceptual experience.

While examining closer the car-driving scene (scene 4) one cannot help admiring its simplicity as well as its effectiveness. Hitchcock evidently was fascinated and challenged by the subject since a variant of it exists in each of the three films under review here: in *Frenzy*, the potato truck riding at night; in *Family Plot*, the downhill drive without brakes. The car-driving scene in *Notorious* is a classical example of a perfect arrangement: the chain of 29 shots is composed in fact of only 6 shots repeated several times; they are placed with such precision that the assemblage comes to life magnificently, more by means of the "language" than by subject alone. The six basic shots are:

A. Medium two-shot of Devlin and Miss Huberman in 3 variants, repeated 10 times each

B. Close-up of Devlin repeated 5 times, in separation

C. Close-up of Miss Huberman repeated 5 times, in separation

D. Close-up of Devlin's hand reaching for the wheel, repeated 2 times
E. Medium shot of road, with radiator cap in foreground, repeated 3 times
F. Policeman; twice in close-up, once in a three-shot

The actual chain of shots after the introductory shot of the road is in the following order: A, A, E, A, B, D, C, E, C, B, A, B, E, D, A, a shot of the rear view mirror, then A, A, B, C, A, F, A, B, C, F, C, A (high). As we can see, the two-shot (A) of Devlin and Miss Huberman dominates, as it is repeated ten times. The road shot with the radiator (E), the only shot that shows how the car swerves, also becomes a delayed "mini" slow disclosure. It is repeated briefly 3 times. Devlin's hand reaching for the wheel (D), a companion to the previous shot (E), is repeated twice. The close-ups of Devlin and Miss Huberman in separation (B and C), repeated five times each, also function as comic relief.

It should be noted that most of the shots in this scene contain the "cuts on action," where a movement, let's say of a hand, a turn of the face, or a gaze, continues with the same inertia from one shot to the next. For example, Devlin looks up to the rearview mirror; he starts to move his hand up in the medium shot. Cut to his finger in close-up as it reaches the mirror and adjusts it. By this method Hitchcock achieves a fluidity in spite of a severely fragmented continuity, thus "hypnotizing" the viewer into real time, consequently leaving the impression of a much longer event than it really is on the screen. It is also interesting how reality is treated here. The car is never shown explicitly, except in the first shot when the viewer is not yet certain that indeed it is *the* car. Real suspense comes via the radiator cap (E), hardly an overstatement. The placement of these shots in the chain is of paramount importance. As in the quotation from Dryden about Virgil, they must remain in the places where Hitchcock ranks them . . . "they must read in order as they lie." In some small way this scene is a model of how to construct an event of this genre. Hitchcock has shown here how cinema can come to terms with reality and, what is more, how it can attempt to make sense of reality instead of remaining a mere mirror to it.

In the car-driving scene Hitchcock achieves both suspense and humor with the utmost economy, without pedantic exposition, and he thus touches upon the essence of the situation. In the next scene, with an almost avant-guardist audacity, Hitchcock reaches for forms seldom seen in realistic films.

Scene 5. Fade-in (shot 1) to long shot of Miss Huberman sleeping on a couch (brief). Cut (shot 2) to a close-up of Miss Huberman's face in a lying position, a glass with an effervescent liquid in front of her; she opens her eyes upon hearing a voice (Devlin offscreen): "You better drink it." Cut to (shot 3) a slanted long shot (45° list to the right) of Devlin in a doorway (1 1/2 sec.). Cut to (shot 4) the same close-up of Miss Huberman as she looks up, grunts, mumbles, and starts drinking from the glass, hesitatingly. Offscreen voice (Devlin): "Go on, drink it, finish it." She drinks and looks up (longer duration shot—37 sec.). The above four shots are already part of an ongoing separation which began at the start of Scene 5 without the benefit of a customary introduction (the two participants are not in the same frame). Cut to (shot 5) the same slanted shot of Devlin in the doorway (as in shot 3); he steps forward (1 1/2 sec.). Cut to (shot 6) the close-up of Miss Huberman (same as shot 4) (1 sec.). Cut to (shot 7) a medium shot of Devlin walking, his figure actually pivoting to a 160° list. Cut to (shot 8) the same close-up of Miss Huberman turning her face, as she follows Devlin's approach; his shadow glides over her face (1 1/2 sec.). It should be noted that this passing shadow in a way replaces the omitted introduction to the separation. Cut to (shot 9) a low medium close-up of Devlin, by now upside down, as if hovering over her. He says: "Feeling better?" Cut to (shot 10) the same close-up of Miss Huberman as she attempts to lift herself; camera moves back to a medium close-up of Miss Huberman: "What do you care how I feel . . . You cop . . . What's your angle?" (30 sec.). Cut to (shot 11) a medium close-up of Devlin this time *right side up*. He asks: "What angle?" [sic]. The last two shots (10 and 11) are designed to unwind the impact of the turning and upside down figure of Devlin.

In this episode Hitchcock hints at Miss Huberman's point of view in a drunken state. But the upside down shots represent such new and original phrasing that they nakedly call attention to themselves far beyond the narrative needs of the moment, yet there is nothing loose or gratuitous in Hitchcock's strategies. The effect works on several hierarchies: on the purely formal one it exposes the mechanics of cinema, not unlike the way some paintings expose their painterliness; on the narrative one, more importantly, it jolts the viewer out of a pedantic

her eyes are riveted on him with great intensity, as if she is actually looking into her own future. This significant image of her looking in such a way is repeated in the film in several climactic scenes.

Such sudden and unexpected images are used by Hitchcock judiciously, as we shall see, mostly at the end of scenes. Here again he reaps the benefit of not using master shots or any other expository shot as introductions to separations. As a result, the viewer is kept in the dark as to the exact positioning of the characters, freeing the director to move them as he wishes to form his own emphasis. In this instance one would have to assume, although we have not seen it, that Devlin was sitting across from Miss Huberman in such a position that in order to reach the door he had to go around her following an S-shaped path as he did (first behind, then in front). Thus an imaginary "logical space" is created, and the unexpected imagery, in turn, becomes doubly gratifying.

The scene continues with (shot 35) a medium long shot of Devlin opening the door and leaving; again a strong hint of closure, but, since Miss Huberman is central to the story, one more shot (36) was needed: a medium close-up of Miss Huberman looking (at the door), then sudan almost avant-guardist audacity, Hitchcock reaches for forms seldom seen in realistic films.

Scene 5. Fade-in (shot 1) to long shot of Miss Huberman sleeping on a couch (brief). Cut (shot 2) to a close-up of Miss Huberman's face in a lying position, a glass with an effervescent liquid in front of her; she opens her eyes upon hearing a voice (Devlin offscreen): "You better drink it." Cut to (shot 3) a slanted long shot (45° list to the right) of Devlin in a doorway (1 1/2 sec.). Cut to (shot 4) the same close-up of Miss Huberman as she looks up, grunts, mumbles, and starts drinking from the glass, hesitatingly. Offscreen voice (Devlin): "Go on, drink it, finish it." She drinks and looks up (longer duration shot—37 sec.). The above four shots are already part of an ongoing separation which began at the start of Scene 5 without the benefit of a customary introduction (the two participants are not in the same frame). Cut to (shot 5) the same slanted shot of Devlin in the doorway (as in shot 3); he steps forward (1 1/2 sec.). Cut to (shot 6) the close-up of Miss Huberman (same as shot 4) (1 sec.). Cut to (shot 7) a medium shot of Devlin walking, his figure actually pivoting to a 160° list. Cut to (shot 8) the same close-up of Miss Huberman turning her face, as she follows Devlin's approach; his shadow glides over her face (1 1/2 sec.). It should be noted that this passing shadow in a way replaces the omitted introduction to the separation. Cut to (shot 9) a low medium close-up of Devlin, by now upside down, as if hovering over her. He says: "Feeling better?" Cut to (shot 10) the same close-up of Miss Huberman as she attempts to lift herself; camera moves back to a medium close-up of Miss Huberman: "What do you care how I feel . . . You cop . . . What's your angle?" (30 sec.). Cut to (shot 11) a medium close-up of Devlin this time *right side up*. He asks: "What angle?" [sic]. The last two shots (10 and 11) are designed to unwind the impact of the turning and upside down figure of Devlin.

In this episode Hitchcock hints at Miss Huberman's point of view in a drunken state. But the upside down shots represent such new and original phrasing that they nakedly call attention to themselves far beyond the narrative needs of the moment, yet there is nothing loose or gratuitous in Hitchcock's strategies. The effect works on several hierarchies: on the purely formal one it exposes the mechanics of cinema, not unlike the way some paintings expose their painterliness; on the narrative one, more importantly, it jolts the viewer out of a pedantic realism, making him or her receptive to a drastic change of venue for Miss Huberman; for, as we shall see, she agrees in less than two minutes to become an American agent, having started the scene as a belligerent cop hater. Such a quick metamorphosis would be impossible to accomplish so swiftly in a realistic set-up. This strategy permits Hitchcock to delete chunks of narrative justifications and to proceed, head on and without a hitch, through what is potentially an unbelievable situation.

On another level, the above strategy is also a precursor to a symmetry of a similar pattern toward the end of the film. Hitchcock's stylistic "secret" works there in the same way, perhaps even more significantly, by using again a heavily distorted reality, as seen by Miss Huberman under the influence of poison; shortly after, Devlin is able, also in less than two minutes, to deliver her single-handedly out of a nest of enemies, who watch helplessly as the two protagonists escape to safety. We shall see later how Hitchcock uses this secret with great success, each time bringing, in a determinate way, the narrative line to the very edge of veracity.

Now let me return to the analysis of Scene 5 (interrupted at the end of the upside down shots, 11 and 12). The rest of the scene continues as it started, within the element of separation, for a total of 23 shots, all of them exchanges between Devlin and Miss Huberman. Devlin proposes that Miss Huberman join the "agency" and work against the German ex-Nazis now operating in Rio de Janeiro, Brazil. She protests with shouts and vulgarities, again calling him a dirty cop. Devlin puts on a recording of a conversation between Miss Huberman and her father (surreptitiously recorded by the "agency"). In the recording we hear her refusing her father's proposal that she become a German spy against the United States. We hear her voicing a love for this country and a repugnance toward her father's Nazi ideas. Devlin presses on. Miss Huberman listens, coming in and out of frame (while dressing). The separation is finally resolved in shot 23, with great skill and a feel for the cinesthetic. Shot 23 starts with an empty frame; in the near background is a doorway to a bedroom (Hitchcock likes to use frames of doorways and windows within the "movie frame"). Miss Huberman enters the frame of the doorway in medium long shot, combing her hair; the recording is still heard; she listens. Devlin enters the same frame from the back, we assume from where the record player is; an offscreen voice from the record is saying "I love this country." Devlin leans against the door. Camera moves in closer to a medium two-shot. Devlin: "What do you say?" We feel a sense of an upcoming closure. (Background music starts.) Yet Hitchcock likes to delay it; as in musical compositions where finales come in stages, he too likes to lead the viewer through several stages of apparent endings and finally into the real one.

The scene continues for another ten shots. Cut to (shot 24) a medium close-up of Miss Huberman. She bursts out with a tirade about how she wants to live her own life, among her own people, as gaily as she can manage. Devlin sits down. We hear a knock at the entrance door. Cut to (shot 25) a medium close-up of the door as it opens. The face of the elderly Commodore from the party of the night before peeps in to remind Alicia (Huberman) that they are sailing this morning for Havana. This shot starts a seven-shot, two-to-one separation between Miss Huberman and Devlin in one frame (a) and the Commodore at the door in the other (b). It is a humorous interlude intruding upon a tense situation. The Commodore leaves, but momentarily reappears to remind Alicia to be at the Hotel Pierre at nine in the morning. Miss Huberman agrees to be there. Cut back to (shot 31) the Commodore as he leaves; door closes. Cut to (shot 32) a close-up of Devlin sitting; he asks: "What about it? Plane for Rio leaves tomorrow morning." Cut to (shot 33) a close-up of Miss Huberman (longer duration) who, after a long, intense pause says: "All right! You better tell him" (meaning the Commodore). Thus her agreeing to go with Devlin is the narrative apogee of the scene; the cinematic one, a most elegant and original resolution to the separation and the scene, will ensue in the next two shots.

Cut to (shot 34) a close-up of Devlin sitting; he gets up; camera moves with him, and, on the way, unexpectedly comes upon a close shot of Miss Huberman in the foreground, as Devlin is passing *behind* her. The separation in this scene is thus resolved the moment Devlin passes behind Miss Huberman. He then passes again, this time in front of her. The most striking aspect of this finale is the suddeness with which these images appear (in a situation that otherwise seems to be calm and without turbulence). To achieve such an effect Hitchcock had to devise an elaborate mise-en-scène with Miss Huberman as the central and significant image. As Devlin comes in and out of frame,

her eyes are riveted on him with great intensity, as if she is actually looking into her own future. This significant image of her looking in such a way is repeated in the film in several climactic scenes.

Such sudden and unexpected images are used by Hitchcock judiciously, as we shall see, mostly at the end of scenes. Here again he reaps the benefit of not using master shots or any other expository shot as introductions to separations. As a result, the viewer is kept in the dark as to the exact positioning of the characters, freeing the director to move them as he wishes to form his own emphasis. In this instance one would have to assume, although we have not seen it, that Devlin was sitting across from Miss Huberman in such a position that in order to reach the door he had to go around her following an S-shaped path as he did (first behind, then in front). Thus an imaginary "logical space" is created, and the unexpected imagery, in turn, becomes doubly gratifying.

The scene continues with (shot 35) a medium long shot of Devlin opening the door and leaving; again a strong hint of closure, but, since Miss Huberman is central to the story, one more shot (36) was needed: a medium close-up of Miss Huberman looking (at the door), then sud-

denly noticing the silk scarf Devlin had wrapped around her waist the night before; fade-out.

Scene 6. Fade-in (shot 1): airplane in flight over mountainous terrain. With a terseness typical of cinema, this brief shot alone moves the plot quickly ahead: Miss Huberman has left Miami and is now on a plane on her way to an unknown future in Rio. Dissolve (shot 2) to the interior of the airplane; camera dollies into a medium shot of Miss Huberman at a window seat. She looks around. Cut to (shot 3) a medium two-shot of Devlin in the back of the plane talking to an impressive-looking gentleman (Louis Calhern); we soon find out that he is Captain Prescott, the head of intelligence, and Devlin's boss; they exchange some information and Devlin gets up, saying: "I'll tell her." He walks forward between rows of seats, the camera moving ahead, framing him in a low medium close-up. He looks penetratingly handsome and, despite the brevity of the shot (4 sec.), it becomes unmistakably clear that Devlin is destined to be the love object. Note that the above shot (3) has a moving camera, a mode Hitchcock keeps injecting into scenes structured basically with separation; thus, two rhythmically opposed elements (separation produces a staccato rhythm while moving camera is legato) are next to each other in an effective yet contrapuntal correlation. The element of the moving camera is kept alive for another and very good reason: as we shall see, Hitchcock will use it in a most spectacular way in the climactic scenes of the film.

Continuing with shot 3: Devlin walks over to Miss Huberman and sits down; camera adjusts to a two-shot. Devlin tells her that he received news of her father. Cut to (shot 4) a close-up of Miss Huberman who inquires what kind of news . . . ? (beginning of a nine-shot separation). Cut to (shot 5) a close-up of Devlin who informs her that her father has committed suicide in his cell, by taking poison. Cut to (shot 6) a close-up of Miss Huberman who listens and reacts to the news in what might be the most virtuoso performance in the film, delicately underplayed, thoughtful, and superbly controlled. In this Hitchcock helps her by framing her in a most complimentary close shot; she looks exceptionally lovely, and even tempting. She also gets screen preference: her shots, 4, 6, and 8 are of longer duration, while Devlin's are very brief, merely a second or so. Most importantly, another contrapuntal arrangement is at work: the pictorial information is sensual while the dialogue contains the tragic news of her father's death. Inasmuch as we expect by now a love affair, the logic of it would justify the decision to show Devlin and Miss Huberman the way Hitchcock does. Still, to juxtapose this with the news of her father's death is, to say the least, daring. As a result, the scene acquires a level of complexity that lifts it above the safe correlations made between elements of form and dialogue in a majority of films. I shall later return to this problem since it touches upon the most fundamental aspects of directorial decisions, such as where to place the camera, and what pictorial modality is needed at this or that point in the drama.

Scene 6 is coming to an end. Devlin in a close shot says: "We're coming to Rio." Cut to (shot 10) a close-up of Miss Huberman turning to the window; we see the bay of Rio, with islands and the famous monument; camera moves to the window across the aisle. Cut to (shot 11) Devlin in a close-up as Miss Huberman, leaning over, "penetrates" his frame in close-up profile, resulting in a "condensed" two-shot, medallion like. She looks at the view outside; Devlin, in the intimacy of this tight shot, looks at her admiringly, a most ingenious framing for the finale of the scene. Dissolve.

Scene 7. Five dissolves follow one after another, as in an old-fashioned montage: a view of the plane, buildings in Rio, a street, an exterior café, a long shot of Devlin and Miss Huberman at a table, then a closer shot of the same. This flood of dissolves somehow discharges the intimacy built up so far and starts a new chapter in the story. The café scene takes another narrative tack by setting seeds of doubt among the would-be lovers, a theme that will weave in and out throughout the rest of the drama. Devlin, the agent, keeps a tight protective shield around him, against any emotional involvement, or at least he tries to. Now he has doubts about Miss Huberman's resolve to give up alcohol; she in turn begs him to relax, to enjoy life. Devlin is cynical to the end. Miss Huberman, finally discouraged, orders, in spite of herself, a double Scotch. The dialogue is sharp and precise, the performances, as always here, superb, yet the cinema language is minimal, devoid of flight: the initial two-shot of Devlin and Miss Huberman at the table is followed by six consecutive over-the-shoulder shots, A, B, A, B, then a very short separation (2 shots) back to four over-the-shoulder shots and again a separation (7 shots). The over-the-shoulder A, B, A, B shots are the weakest links in cinema language, used mainly in scenes with lengthy dialogue. Hitchcock is quite justified in using them here, since dialogue indeed predominates in this scene. But, in addition, an important factor in the decision is the rhythm of scene sequences. In this case Scene 7 is a flat point before a lift; the next to follow is a love scene; a cycle of release, trigger.

Scene 8. Dissolve to an exterior long shot (shot 1) of a car; two figures walk away from it; dissolve to (shot 2) a medium close shot of the two as Miss Huberman asserts with bitterness that Devlin most

likely doesn't want to be involved with an alcoholic, a no good. . . .
Devlin grabs her and kisses her passionately (brief shot, brief scene).

Scene 9. Dissolve to a long shot of an imposing building (we learn
later that it is the U.S. Embassy). The shot of the embassy is of longer
duration, thus somehow discharging the impact of the kiss. Dissolve
to (shot 2) a slow disclosure medium shot of Captain Prescott (the chief
of intelligence) speaking as camera backs up to reveal a round table
meeting of a group of officials. Prescott: "Gentlemen, I assure you she's
a perfect type for the job"; it is easy to assume that they discuss Miss
Huberman's suitability for the assignment.

Scene 10. Dissolve to an exterior long shot of the beach; dissolve to
a car turning a corner; cut to a long shot of Devlin and Miss Huberman
exiting the car and entering a building (away from the camera); dissolve
to an opposite movement of the two, entering an apartment (toward
camera). Devlin moves on to a balcony. Cut to a high medium shot of
Miss Huberman joining him; a long stretch of beach is seen below in
the background. Cut to a closer shot as they start kissing; camera very
slowly moves in to a tighter shot; they continue kissing and talking,
mostly small talk about having dinner not at a restaurant but on the
balcony, she has a chicken in the ice box, etc. After 90 seconds they
move from the balcony to the room, camera follows in the same tight
two-shot, keeping them in profile. Devlin has to call his office for mes-
sages. The kissing continues as he waits by the phone. There is a mes-

sage for him to come immediately to the embassy. They don't break up the intimacy; she's not upset, she is too happy; they both walk to the door; camera floats with them. She asks him to bring some wine when he returns, to celebrate; they kiss again before Devlin slips out of the door. Alicia closes the door cautiously; her cheek rests on it; camera adjusts to a closer shot. The above scene has *no* cuts (since the balcony kiss) and lasts 2 minutes, 40 seconds; the impression left is of a much shorter time. Its most striking aspect is the immaculate execution of the camera movement through the complex blocking (room, balcony, phone, door).

One cannot help admiring Hitchcock for his decision to stage the first love scene in the film without any cuts; it establishes the moving camera as a principal stylistic element in this film. And, since the moving camera sustained for longer duration introduces real time to a screen narrative that otherwise has built-in deletions and compressions (via cuts, dissolves, and other devices), the juxtaposition of the former with the latter creates here a charismatic mix with a truly lyrical effect.

Scene 11. Dissolve to the exterior of the U.S. Embassy (familiar image): the scene is structured on a pole opposite to the previous one: opposite movement, slow disclosure, intense fragmentation. Shot 1 is a long shot of Devlin's car pulling in front of the Embassy as it arrives from right to left; in the previous scene Devlin exited Alicia's apartment to the right; Alicia, in the last shot of the scene, was facing right; here Devlin moves to the left. Hitchcock uses such opposites with precision, in each instance energizing scene-to-scene transitions. Another part of the opposite pole is the structure of frequent cuts; the lyrical Scene 10, with its moving camera and no cuts, is followed here by one with extra frequent cuts, far beyond the need to communicate the given situation: shot 1, Devlin's car arrives, stops; shot 2, closer shot of the side of the car, Devlin is about to exit; shot 3, reverse side of car, low angle medium shot of Devlin leaving car with a bottle of champagne in hand. In fact, a simple shot of Devlin arriving and getting out of his car would suffice. However, the extra shots visibly intensify a certain nervousness in the air, a precursor of bad tidings soon to come. The next shot pinpoints that nervousness: dissolve, close shot of the bottle of champagne on a table, fingers tapping (start of slow disclosure); camera moves along man's arm, finally revealing in medium close-up the face of Devlin; he's at the end of a sentence: "I don't know if she'll do it." Offscreen voice injects: "What do you mean she'll not?" Devlin visibly disturbed: "I did not know what the job was until this moment." Cut to (shot 6) a full long shot of three men in the middle of a conference (full disclosure).

Note that the dissolve from shot 4 to 5 (close-up of bottle) hides a sizable deletion, always an important cinematic move; Hitchcock has over-elaborated the first four shots (Devlin's arrival by car), then deleted a chunk of time and action (Devlin's actual entry to the Embassy and the beginning of the conversation), and finally disclosed the conference already in progress, all of it indicating a determined strategy.

In the long shot (6) the three men in conference are: Devlin on the left, Prescott (his is the offscreen voice) sitting at the table in a cloud of cigarette smoke, and a third man, not identified, leaning on the ledge of a large window. Presently a separation begins with seven snappy close-ups between the three men. Devlin is on the defense, trying to protect Alicia from what appears to be a rather odious assignment: her job is to penetrate the household of Alex Sebastian to find out about an apparent Nazi conspiracy. From Prescott we learn (and Devlin, to his surprise, also learns) that Sebastian knew Alicia Huberman for some time, was even in love with her at some point. Shot 14: Devlin reaches the window (to form a two-shot with the third man). Devlin: "I did not know that." Surprised, he moves out of frame. Third man: "We have a job to do." Cut to (shot 15) Devlin entering frame, intense (off-screen) voice of third man: "Sebastian's house is a cover-up; let's get inside and find out." Cut to (shot 16) Prescott: "That's right. You better explain to Miss Huberman what she has to do." Cut to (shot 17) Devlin as he starts and stumbles on a word. Cut to (shot 18) Prescott: "What is it, Devlin?" Cut to (shot 19) Devlin: "Nothing, sir." Cut to (shot 20) Prescott: "I thought you had something to say." In his cold and confident way he notices Devlin's discomfort. Cut to (shot 21) Devlin: "How is the meeting to be arranged?" Cut to (shot 22) Prescott who explains that the best place would be the riding academy Sebastian frequents. Note that in the brief shots Prescott is the stable image. Devlin is restless, moving in and out of frame. After three more shots Prescott says: "Ok, Devlin, that's all." Devlin turns and walks away (shot 23); camera follows him for a short while until it passes and centers on the bottle of champagne, evidently left by Devlin. Cut to (shot 24) a close-up of Prescott looking apprehensively at the bottle and toward the door as if he understands the meaning of it. Prescott's look (a slightly longer duration shot) leaves a lingering afterimage thanks to the strength of the close-up, and also because his face by now is a familiar image in this scene (repeated 5 times). It should be noted that such afterimage effects, especially at the end of scenes, are used frequently by Hitchcock as a form of thinking time.

Cut (shot 25) to a close-up of the bottle; dissolve. The wine standing on the table (symmetry from shot 5 to shot 25) is driven hard by Hitchcock and not without irony. The initial connection is the love scene: Alicia asks him to bring back a bottle of wine. As the conference at the embassy goes sour Devlin eventually forgets it there on the table. Yet, and more importantly, the bottle of wine is a plant. Later in the story a bottle becomes the eye of the storm, the clue, the principal center of the spy endeavor, and the significant image par excellence. It is typical of Hitchcock's strategies to attach multiple layers of meaning to inanimate items: the wine bottle here, the tie in *Frenzy*, the diamond in *Family Plot*.

The above scene, played in brisk separation, is an excellent example of the electrifying manner in which Hitchcock maneuvers this element of structure. It also points to the capacity of cinema for sharp expressiveness even in situations without any provocative physical action.

This brings to mind another phenomenon: the performance of the cast is superb, yet one is tempted to ask: is it the virtuosity of the actors or also the virtuosity of cinema? The actors' efforts here are, in fact, severely fragmented. We see on the screen perfectly framed snatches: a glance, a two-word utterance, a salvo of A, B, A, B brief repartees. Such is singularly different from the great acting on the stage so dependent on a continuum. Consequently, although the impression here may be in favor of the actors, in fact the perfectly constructed cinematic chain of shots is responsible, in most cases, and in Hitchcock films especially, for the sparkling expressiveness. However, in cases where the narrative makes extraneous demands, beyond the capacity of cinema, difficulties arise. The upcoming scene (12) is a case in point. Hitchcock allowed himself to be cornered into a dramatic situation that is more of the theater than of cinema. Needless to say, I see a structural weakness in this scene, a stepping out of the parameters of cinema; I also find it convincingly relevant to the phenomenon of actors performing for the screen. The question is: how to reconcile a romantic love affair with an impending spy operation, where the woman, starved for affection, is surely going to be thrown to "the wolves," and the man, both jealous and ambivalent about the relationship, has to abide by the rules of his agency—and all of the above in one scene. The answer touches upon the platonic variance between diegesis (information on a given action) and mimesis (playing out the action via speech and gestures of the actors). Perhaps, in this case, a cinematic structure without intense fragmentation would have afforded the actors a continuum for a more credible and thus more mimetic performance? For, as we shall see, the cinematic "language" here is visibly incompatible with the intended effort and a few directorial decisions were designed to serve and spoonfeed the surface meaning at hand, rather than yield the deep one.

Let us look then at the text:

Scene 12. Dissolve from the bottle of champagne to Alicia's apartment (shot 1): Devlin enters from right to left, the same way he exited the embassy. This uni-direction (for a change) creates a bridge, of a sort, over the crest of the deletion (time between the embassy and the apartment). At this stage, as the plot thickens, the viewer is already informed about the details of the spy job from the previous scene. Cut to (shot 2) Alicia in the kitchen preparing the chicken (brief, medium shot). Cut to (shot 3) Devlin as he continues walking to the balcony. Cut to (shot 4) Alicia entering the frame; camera follows her to the balcony where she joins Devlin. (Note: this long shot on the balcony is to become the master shot for the scene.) Alicia, as she walks: "Marriage must be wonderful . . ."; she kisses Devlin in passing. Cut (shot 5) to the two in profile in a medium shot. She continues kissing him. The dramatic change of camera angle (to profile) radiates energy. Alicia embraces him, forces his arms to take her around, she: "What's the matter? Come on Mr. D., what is darkening your brow, all this secrecy is going to ruin my dinner." Devlin: "After dinner"; Alicia: "I'll make it easy for you. The time has come when you have to tell me that you have a wife and adorable children . . . and this madness between us can't go on any longer." Devlin: "I'll bet you've heard that line often." Cut to (shot 6) Alicia in close-up with parts of Devlin's face in the frame. She: "Right below the belt . . . as always . . . It isn't fair." Cut to (shot 7) a close-up of Devlin (with part of Alicia's face in the frame). He: "Skip it . . . we have other things to talk about; we have a job." The next twelve shots are of the same configuration: close-ups with the partner's face partially in the frame. (This composition is the first weak link in the structure of the scene; it has, somehow, the wrong ring to it.) Devlin explains to her the details of the job: the need to penetrate Sebastian's household to find out what the operation over there is. In shot 11 Devlin cannot help but remark ironically about Sebastian: "He had quite a crush on you"; Alicia, smilingly (shot 12): "I wasn't very responsive." After the exchange of the above close-ups cut to (shot 20) a medium two-shot; Alicia, upon hearing that she is to contact Alex Sebastian, turns away to sit on a couch; camera pulls back, Devlin stands screen right, in profile (beach seen in background). She: "Go on, let's have it all." Devlin: "The rest is up to you; you are to work on him and *land* him" (a phrase he repeated twice before). Note that shot 20 is a return to the master shot from before.

Cut to (shot 21) a medium shot of Alicia, sitting: "Mata Hari, she makes love for the papers." Offscreen Devlin's voice: "There are no papers . . . you land him, find out what's in his house, what the group around him is up to, and report to us." (While talking Devlin is seen walking behind Alicia's couch as camera pulls back to a medium two-shot). Devlin leans on the balcony's balustrade. Alicia, in foreground: "I suppose you knew about this pretty little job all the time." Cut (shot 22) on the same axis to a close-up of Devlin (start of a separation sequence): "No, I just found out about it." Note that Hitchcock very seldom makes a cut on the same axis, for good reason (since this kind of cut was overused in Hollywood and is conventional to boot). Cut to (shot 23) a tight close-up of Alicia: "Did you not say anything? . . . That maybe I am not the girl for such shenanigans. . . ." Cut to (shot 24) a close-up of Devlin (sternly, but with pain on his face): "I figured it was up to you; if you care to back out . . ." Cut to (shot 25) a close-up of Alicia: "I suppose you said: 'Alicia is good at that, she'll have Sebastian in her hands in a couple of weeks, she's good at it, always was.'" Cut to (shot 26) a close-up of Devlin: "I did not say anything." Cut to (shot 27) a close-up of Alicia (with real pain): "Not a word for that lovesick lady you left an hour ago?" Cut to (shot 28) a close-up of Devlin: "I told you that's the assignment" (end of the five-shot separation). Cut to (shot 29) the master shot (medium long shot, both are in the frame), Alicia: "Don't get sore . . . I'm only fishing for a little birdcall from the dream man. . . ." With irony: "One little word. How dare you gentlemen think that Alicia Huberman, the new Miss Huberman, can be submitted to such an ugly effect?" Camera pulls back as she gets up from the couch and walks over to Devlin with a gesture of hope that he'll take her in his arms. Devlin, instead, lights a cigarette and says: "That's not funny." Alicia, swallowing the rejection: "Do you want me to take this job?" Devlin, after taking the cigarette out of his mouth: "You're answering for yourself." Alicia: "I'm asking you." Devlin: "It's up to you." She turns again to him. Cut to (shot 30) an extreme close-up of Alicia, a shockingly sudden but conventional, through a "silk stocking," studio-type close-up: "Oh darling, what you didn't tell them tell me, that you believe that I'm nice, that I love you, that I'll never change back." Cut to (shot 31) a close-up of Devlin: "I'm waiting for your answer." Cut to a two-shot (32) of each facing the other in profile (also a rather aimless change). Alicia gives Devlin a penetrating look and after a pause turns away, talking: "What a little pal you are, never believing me"; camera follows her as she keeps walking and mumbling; she stops behind a curtained french door; we see her pouring a hefty portion of whisky and finally drinking it down in a gulp (still in profile). She turns in his direction: "When do I go to work for Uncle Sam?" Cut to (shot 33) a medium shot of Devlin on the balcony: "Tomorrow morning"; he walks through the french doors and enters Alicia's space; again they face each other in profile. Cut to (shot 34) an insert medium shot of the dining table with the chicken on a platter. Cut back to (shot 35) the previous two-shot; Devlin seems to be searching for something. Alicia: "It must be cold by now . . . What are you looking for?" Devlin: "I had a bottle of champagne, I must have left it somewhere . . ." Dissolve. (Scene lasts 4 min., 50 sec.).

This rather long duration scene consists of three basic units of structure: a master shot on the balcony, a group of close shots of each of the protagonists (with the other protagonist's face partially visible in the frame), back to the master, followed by a short separation, back to master, then two single close-ups (which cannot be classified as separation), again back to the master. Clearly going back to a traditional Hollywood master shot discipline (here simplified and in my opinion over-fragmented) is strangely out of sync with the rest of the film. One is left with the mind boggling question of why? My intuitive guess is that the scene in some longer version did not work and accordingly it was subjected to doctoring and extra shooting, hence the few bad cuts and jarring transitions (shots 22, 29, 30, 32). And as usual in such cases the end result is a slightly botched and eclectic mix. Theoretically it does show what the parameters of cinema are in a scene that in a novel would take pages of elaboration and in the theater three times as much dialogue.

Hitchcock did develop in his later films, notably in *Psycho*, a much bolder and a cinematically brilliant method of dealing with such scenes, using the element of separation with multiple shots (up to 56). At the time *Notorious* was made there was hesitation about separation beyond eighteen shots. Here (in Scene 12), as we have seen, he uses very few. The two inserted close-ups at the end (31 and 32) are unable to reignite the charisma of a strong and continuous separation. And, since this scene is so central to the major conflict that permeates the whole story of *Notorious*, the inadequacy of its construction creates a small detour from the brilliance of the rest of the film.

Scene 13. Starts with the usual series of dissolves: first to a medium

shot of Devlin with Alicia in a car in the middle of a conversation; he explains that his "cover" is that of an employee of Pan Am, and that the two have met on a plane. Dissolve to a trail in a riding club in long shot. Cut to a medium two-shot of Devlin and Alicia riding their horses toward the camera. The scene has a linear continuity with a practical, down to earth, handling of the narrative. Briefly, the two protagonists spot Alex Sebastian (Claude Rains) riding with a woman companion. They pass them twice without Sebastian noticing Alicia (her riding hat is partially covering her face). So far there are several shots of different sizes and angularity. At this point Devlin, by design, kicks Alicia's horse, forcing it to a gallop. Devlin stays in place, watching; Sebastian, upon seeing a woman on a runaway horse, rushes to help; he stops the horse, recognizes Alicia, and they greet. Devlin observes from afar. The scene has a total of sixteen shots, starting with four introductory ones (mainly informational), then moving into twelve action shots, most with multiangularity. Hitchcock delivers his touch of genius at the end with a triad of shots: Devlin watching from his horse in shots 12, 14, and 16, each closer and closer on Devlin, ending in a close-up; he sees Alicia meeting Sebastian; Devlin looks away, worrying about her. Triads of this sort, three shots progressively closer, become one of his characteristic modes of expression, and of Hitchcock's contributions to cinema language (used later in *The Birds* and in *North by Northwest*).

In the manner characteristic to this film, of ending scenes on a closer shot of a person in the middle of a thought, this one also ends on the close-up of Devlin. Dissolve to a medium long shot of Devlin sitting at the table of an outdoor restaurant; fade out.

Scene 14. Fade-in to an interior of an elegant restaurant: in a long shot Alicia Huberman, in a startlingly luxurious, black shiny dress and head piece to match, is sitting at a table; the transition is contrapuntal to the previous scene at the riding academy. Cut to a medium shot of the doorway as Alex Sebastian enters; camera follows as he notices and walks over to greet Alicia (in long shot); he kisses her hand. Cut to a medium shot as he sits down. Notice how Hitchcock discloses in one brief shot (the entry of Sebastian) the deleted information (namely that Alicia is so far successful at "landing" Sebastian). The viewer intuitively assumes that a flirting scene will follow. Sebastian settles down; the camera adjusts to a high two-shot in profile as they talk. The cut to a high shot (in the middle of Sebastian's kissing her hand) is an important plant, introducing a progressively increasing number of high shots into the iconography of the film, especially connected with Sebastian. The scene continues with nine over-the-shoulder (A, B, A, B) shots as the two exchange compliments. The rhythm of this series is interrupted by Sebastian ordering drinks, at which point there begins a six-shot separation; after two singles they notice something at the back of their table. A long shot discloses Captain Prescott and his party sitting down to dinner. Cut back to the separation as Sebastian explains to her who Prescott is and how the American Embassy is full of agents. The close shots in the separation give the viewer an opportunity to observe Alicia's behavior when challenged to play her secret role; she's cool and controlled and passes her test with gusto. Cut back to two over-the-shoulder shots as Alicia says: "I'm allergic to American agents"; Sebastian: "Did they bother you since you came down?" Cut to a close-up of Alicia: "No, not yet." Cut to an over-the-shoulder medium close shot of Sebastian: "Were they troublesome in Miami?" Cut to a close-up of Alicia: "Yes, that's why I tried to get away from their snooping." Cut to an over-the-shoulder shot of Sebastian: "I wondered why you left your father?" Cut to a close shot of Alicia: "He insisted, he kept insisting"; this shot starts a series of nine close-ups in partial separation: whenever Sebastian speaks Hitchcock reverts to a two-shot; when Alicia answers it is always in a close-up single, a rare shot arrangement, rhythmically repeated. We watch in close-up how she handles direct questions about Devlin with diplomacy, and also how she reacts to Sebastian's profession of his revived interest in her as a woman. Alicia is convincingly charming; she certainly is "landing" him. Sebastian informs her that his mother is giving a dinner party at his home and asks her if she would please come. Cut to close shot of Alicia: "She wouldn't mind an extra guest?" Sebastian in a two-shot: "An old friend is never an extra guest . . . Shall we order? What shall we have today?" He looks around for the waiter. Cut to the last close-up of Alicia, in silence; she looks thoughtful, as if thinking of the future.

As we have seen, the above scene is heavily dependent on dialogue, hence the over-the-shoulder and separation shots. The two important innovations here are the repeated use of high shots reserved mainly for Sebastian, and two-shots alternating with the close-ups reserved for Alicia Huberman, a form I shall call semi-separation. The major symmetry of scenes ending on a close-up of a "thinking" protagonist cumulatively adds a deeper and at times tragic dimension to the drama (as if the characters are clairvoyant about the complications and tribulations waiting for them).

Scene 15. Fade-in to a close shot of Alex's invitation card; fast pan up (disclosure) to medium close-up of Devlin with Prescott in the background. Devlin looks at the card and quickly looks away; they both turn. Cut to a long shot (full disclosure) of Alicia Huberman entering royally in a white fur-trimmed evening dress; as she comes closer to the camera she greets the gentlemen with: "Good evening." Cut to a medium shot of Prescott and Devlin looking admiringly: "Very good." Cut (90° change of angle) to the two men, this time in a profile medium shot (a strong accent in multiangularity) as Alicia enters their frame; Prescott hands her a diamond tiara: "Rented for the occasion." She asks Prescott (since Devlin has moved away with his back to the camera) to help her put it on; Prescott adjusts the tiara; he instructs her to memorize the names of the Germans at the dinner party, not to ask any questions, just to observe. Alicia, who is at the right side of the frame, walks over to the left, stays with her back to the camera, then continues to the window. Prescott's last instruction to her is not to see Devlin unless in an emergency since Alex's people may be checking on her. Alicia exits (the previous was a long duration shot). Devlin settles on a couch. Cut to the door as Alicia leaves; Prescott closes the door, fade-out.

Scene 16. Fade-in to a long shot of a limousine driving toward a huge mansion; cut to a medium shot; the limousine comes to a stop. Alicia gets up to leave; camera lifts above the car to reveal an elegant doorway of the mansion as Alicia is seen mounting the steps toward it. This doorway becomes a familiar image in the film. Short dissolve to a reverse medium shot as the door opens (from dark to light); we see a man (Joseph) letting her in; Alicia asks to be announced. Door closes to dark. Cut to a medium shot of Alicia and Joseph, the servant, moving toward camera; she looks around. Cut to her view: a balcony, and a double door. Cut back to Alicia walking; camera follows her. Cut to a double door; from behind we hear German voices (coming from Alex's office). Cut to Alicia walking and looking around. Cut to Joseph letting Alicia into yet another large room. Cut to a panning shot over vases and stuffed furniture. Cut to a medium moving shot of Alicia looking up as she moves closer to the camera. Cut to a long shot of a balcony and an expansive stairway (eventually to become a familiar and significant image), used afterward in the climactic scenes of the film. We see in this long shot the figure of an older woman coming down the steps (Madame Constantine). Cut back to the medium close shot of Alicia, looking slightly frightened; she makes a minute gesture as if wanting to escape. Cut back to the same long shot of the stairway; the woman comes down and starts walking toward us (the camera moves in closer, thus shortening her walk). The woman stops in a close shot (start of separation), looking forbidding and strong; with a heavy German accent she says: "Miss Huberman, please forgive me for keeping you waiting." Cut to a tight close shot of Alicia: "Not at all." In a voice-over the woman says: "You resemble your father very much . . . I'm Alex's mother." Alicia (still in the close shot): "I knew the moment I saw you." Cut to a medium two-shot of the two women in profile (a 90° change of camera angle). The mother continues about Alex always adoring Alicia. Cut to a close shot of Alicia: "You're very kind." Cut to the mother: "You did not testify at your father's trial?" Cut to a close-up of Alicia: "He did not want me to." Cut to a tight close-up of the mother: "I wonder why?" We hear the voice of Alex Sebastian: "Hello." Cut to a medium long shot; Alex enters the room with extended hands, greeting Alicia, as the camera pans with him to form a medium three-shot: "You met my mother . . ." Cut to a long shot as they pass through the hall to a double door; camera moves with them as the doors open; we see people inside. Cut to a tight close shot of Alicia as she is introduced to five gentlemen, who one by one approach and kiss her hand, in extreme close-ups.

The appearance of Alex's mother, her descent down the giant stairway, as well as her meeting Alicia, make up the strongest scene in the film so far. The introductory shots of Alicia's arrival at the mansion prepared us, of course, but the main impact of the mother's appearance, almost bringing a chill down the spine, is a result of Hitchcock's strategy of properly distributing only five key shots: two medium close-ups of Alicia looking frightened, two long shots of the mother's descent (the second one ending in her close-up), plus a much tighter close shot of Alicia Huberman. Precision is the paramount guide: a few frames longer or shorter, a small change in picture size would make all the difference. The cinesthetic impact here rests on the accurate and in this case terse mix of a chain of shots perfectly concatenated in a given space.

Hitchcock's secret lies in his admirable arranging of shots, as we have seen above. Consider the two medium close shots of Alicia Huberman, the onlooker, intercut with the two long shots of the mother coming down the steps. Why two and not three shots of Alicia Huberman? The logic of the latter would have been to delay the mother's descent, thus adding suspense. Hitchcock apparently discovered, however, that cinema language has its own logic. The two shots of Alicia Huberman are medium close-ups, shots of singular intensity; placing more of these would weaken their penetrating quality by sheer overkill; furthermore, Hitchcock did reserve a place for an additional tight close-up of Alicia Huberman to follow the close-up of the mother greeting her. In this case we witness still another triad of close shots (of Miss Huberman), with the last one closer and of longer duration. The above short separation (five shots) is resolved with the profile two-shot of the two women, a startling and effective change of key, to be followed again by a short (four shot) separation between Alicia and the mother, resolved, in turn, by the entrance of Alex Sebastian—all in all an extremely elegant phrasing, reminiscent of a musical arrangement.

The scene continues, demonstrating intense vigor and originality with five staccato cuts of the five Nazi types taking turns kissing the hand of Alicia Huberman. Two close-ups of Alicia, one at the beginning of the introductions and one toward the end, bracket the above series. The first of these close-ups remind the viewer that Alicia is at work, memorizing the names of the Germans as they are introduced to her (by Alex Sebastian, from offscreen): Eric Matisse, with penetrating blue eyes, a perfect Gestapo officer, smiles and approaches to kiss her hand (from medium shot to extreme close-up); Alicia's hand is seen in the foreground. Cut to the next one: William Rothman, cool and smooth, clicks his heels, says: "Honored," and kisses her hand. Cut to the next, Emile Hubka, fat and awkward, the same type of shot as the one before. Cut to Luster Neer; tall and tight, he kisses her hand the same way as the others. Cut to Dr. Anderson, who for a change smiles sympathetically. Cut to a close shot of Alicia Huberman smiling back (the symmetrical shot to the one at the beginning of the introductions). Cut back to Dr. Anderson: "It gives me pleasure," and he kisses her hand. (Dr. Anderson is singled out with an extra shot, important for their future relationship.)

Cut to a long shot of the whole company entering the dining room with the table elaborately set. Alex's mother starts directing guests to their seats. Cut to a medium shot of Alicia Huberman as she slides into her chair, helped from behind by Alex Sebastian. She is in the center of the frame observing all that is going on. Cut to a medium shot of Emile Hubka; he is nervously showing Sebastian a bottle of wine on the mantle piece. Cut to a close-up of Hubka's finger pointing to a label on the bottle. Cut back to the previous medium shot as Sebastian tries to hush Hubka down and move him out of the way; Hubka is visibly embarrassed and overly apologetic. Cut to a close-up of Alicia Huberman who notices the incident (a plant for future use). She follows with her gaze as the two men walk away. Cut to a long shot of Hubka sitting down at the edge of the table. Cut back to the same close-up of Alicia observing. Cut to a medium shot of Sebastian talking about a movie. Cut to a close shot of Eric Matisse answering that the movie was a disappointment. Cut to a medium shot of Sebastian walking over. Cut to the same close-up of Alicia smiling as Alex Sebastian tells her about Eric's love for movies and how sentimental he is, often crying. Cut to a medium shot of Sebastian as he sits down in his chair. Cut back to the close-up of Alicia Huberman as she directs her gaze toward (what seems to be) the mantle piece. Cut to a slow zoom in, to the bottle of wine. Fade-out.

The dining room part of the scene is centered around the five close shots of Alicia Huberman as an onlooker, without much attention given to the realistic details of a dinner situation. Yet the viewer is left, nevertheless, with a fairly comfortable feeling of having witnessed a dinner party. The terseness with which Hitchcock is driving the narrative to the essential points is achieved here with the repeated use of the familiar image (the close shots of Alicia) around whom things are happening. The zoom shot is also a plant for many other zooms to come, a form that Hitchcock is able to use with a delicate touch, without the arrogance usually associated with such camera moves.

From the arrival of Alicia Huberman at Sebastian's mansion, then, the cinema language has manifestly entered a higher pitch, with a quick succession of brief cuts that keeps up with a realistic linearity of the events, but that at the same time hides many deletions. This ability to condense, at a seemingly leisurely pace, while selectively showing only important details, and meticulously attending to the highlights, is without question one of Hitchcock's greatest contributions to cinema.

Scene 17. A counterpoint to the fast chain of shots in the last scene, this one, about the doom of Emile Hubka, is played in virtually real time with only four cuts. After a fade-in (following the close-up of the wine bottle that ended the previous scene), we see in long shot Emile Hubka pacing nervously in front of a double door. Dissolve to the interior (high long shot) of a smoke-filled room with the group of Germans apparently in conference. Eric Matisse is on the left, Sebastian in the center, Dr. Anderson on the right. They talk about Emile Hubka and his unfortunate behavior before dinner. Eric Matisse is tough: he considers Hubka's slip dangerous and inexcusable. Cut to a closer medium shot, eye level, the three men fill the frame; Eric Matisse proposes to "eliminate" Hubka, as they apparently had other members of their team, for security reasons. He outlines a rather gruesome scheme of an arranged car accident on a mountain road. Sebastian and Dr. Anderson listen, visibly horrified. Cut to a close shot of Eric continuing his monologue about how he perfected the technique of jumping clear at the last moment, leaving the victim to his fate. A noise of the door opening interrupts the talk; Eric Matisse turns his head, flashing an impressive profile. In the gallery of Hitchcock's profiles this one is probably the most frightening. Cut to a medium shot of Hubka nervously entering the room; the camera follows him to the table close to the others; he apologizes awkwardly for the incident with the wine bottle. Dr. Anderson quiets him, blaming it on overwork: "All of us have nerves . . ." Hubka regains his poise momentarily and proposes to leave for a rest. Eric jumps up, insisting on driving him home; despite Hubka's protests Eric keeps pressing; the camera follows them to the door (in reverse symmetry with Hubka's entry). Sebastian and Dr. Anderson shrink in their seats. In a burst of black humor, Eric, just before leaving, asks them to thank the elder Mrs. Sebastian for the excellent dessert; the door closes. Fade out.

The morbid information in the above scene is conveyed in a rather gross manner, yet its pinpointing directness is useful to the story: for one, the viewer becomes aware of the kind of snake pit Alicia Huberman is going to operate in (a sure suspense builder); also, Eric Matisse's character gets the final touching up, sharp enough to last until the end of the film, when Alex Sebastian will be in troubles similar to Hubka's and Eric will have the final word at the close of the film.

Scene 18. At the race track: Alicia Huberman gives her first spy report to Devlin. The structure is contrapuntal to the previous scene. We notice again a sandwich-like arrangement: the dinner scene (16)—intense fragmentation; Hubka's doom scene (17)—minimal fragmentation; the race track (18)—intense fragmentation. This push-pull continuity is one of Hitchcock's modes.

Scene 18 starts with a fade-in followed by several dissolves to a long shot of a crowded race track. Dissolve to a medium long shot of Alex Sebastian and his mother looking through field glasses; they have a conversation about Alicia Huberman; the mother clearly disapproves of her. Dissolve to a medium shot of Devlin coming into frame, looking around (in the middle of a crowd), then leaving. Cut to a medium shot of Alicia standing by the barrier; the viewer has a feeling that she's watched. Devlin enters her frame with a loud hello. Cut to a tighter medium shot of Alicia pretending, with casual smiles, to have a light conversation, while actually reporting on the dinner at Sebastian's, on her impressions of Dr. Anderson, and on the Hubka incident with the wine bottle. Finally she adds: "You can add Sebastian to my list of playmates. . . ." The shots that follow are good examples of skilled one, two, three cinematic punches: (1) a tight close-up of Devlin with a two-second hold on him as he swallows this information, then says: "Pretty fast work"; (2) cut to an extreme close-up of Alicia as she rapidly turns toward him, and says with a hiss: "That's what you wanted wasn't it?"; (3) cut to a close-up in *profile* of Devlin, who says: "Skip it." (Note that the previous close shot of Devlin was face on.)

This amazing triad of close-ups becomes a teaser for the upcoming sixteen-shot separation. Such teasers, a brief series of close-ups, A, B, A, B, too few to be a separation, are standard in Hitchcock's future films; there is an excellent one in *Psycho*, for example, in the confrontation scene between the policeman and Marion (Janet Leigh). The important innovation in the teaser under discussion is the sudden introduction of a profile shot (repeated again shortly after, in the actual separation scene.)

There are certain details here that are worth turning to in spite of their technical nature: in the teaser we saw a frontal close shot of Devlin (longer duration), a close-up of Alicia Huberman who turns to him (on camera), thus presenting her profile, and a cut to Devlin in close shot and in profile (not looking at her, and saying "Skip it"). Devlin does not turn; he remains in exactly the same position as he was when we saw him just before (face on). It is the camera that changes position. Yet there is a possibility of a misreading, and Hitchcock wisely opts for inserting the profile in the teaser before repeating it again in the next separation. Generally, it had been a matter of usage not to change camera positions during separation scenes and to keep the images stable except when a character moves on camera. Hitchcock's dramatic innovation here is, I believe, extending the "language" of cinema. (The only ones who used it shortly after were Kurosawa and Ozu; still, it is hard to say if they were influenced by Hitchcock or if they did it on their own.) The result is a strong, dramatically visual attack upon our senses (as long as we learn how to read it by adjusting to the slight tampering with reality—just as we had to adjust, at first, to close-ups and other elements of cinema), and a striking example of a camera position that injects its own energy into the actor's performance, lifting it to heights unknown in the theater. For Hitchcock it is also an exploration of profiles and, consequently, he films them in a variety of forms and contexts, and thus discovers new dramatic potential in facial geography (just as Voltaire did when he first saw his own profile on a medal).

To return to the triad of close-ups, it is resolved by the familiar two-shot of Alicia Huberman and Devlin in front of the barrier, both presumably facing the race track. Alicia starts covering up again, just in case they are observed by Alex Sebastian, with jokes about betting on a horse on a tip from Sebastian. The separation begins here and continues for sixteen brief, intense shots. It starts with a tight close-up of Devlin, face on, bitterly recalling how Alicia promised to be a new woman. Cut to a close-up of Alicia Huberman as she turns to him (a symmetry with a similar movement of hers in the teaser), saying: "You knew very well what I was doing." Cut to a close-up of Devlin *in profile* (another symmetry with the teaser), presumably looking at the race track, muttering: "Did I?" Close-up of Alicia's profile looking at him: "You could have stopped me with one word . . . but you didn't . . . You threw me at him." The voice of Devlin from offscreen: "I threw you at nobody." Alicia: "Didn't you tell me to go ahead?" Close-up of Devlin, again *in profile*: "A man doesn't tell a woman what to do . . ." Close-up of Alicia furiously turning to frontal position; she picks up her field glasses as Devlin continues (voice over) with the same accusations of what kind of woman she turned out to be, and that he almost believed that she would change. Alicia, looking through her field glasses, retorts, "Oh, you rotten . . ." Close frontal shot of Devlin: "That's why I didn't try to stop you, the answer had to come from you." Close-up of Alicia Huberman still looking through her glasses; a reflection of running horses is seen in the lenses; she says, with resignation: "You never believed in me anyway, what's the difference." Cut to a frontal close-up of Devlin: "It wouldn't have been pretty if I had believed in you." Cut to a much tighter close shot of Alicia as she lowers her glasses slowly and listens intensely to Devlin's ironical muttering offscreen: "And I thought she'd never be able to go through with it. That she'd been made over by love. . . ." She finally puts away her glasses, saying: "You only once told me that you loved me. Oh, Devlin . . ." Cut to a frontal close-up of Devlin: "Listen, you chalked up another boy friend, no harm done." Cut to a tight close-up of Alicia with tears in her eyes: "I hate you." Cut to a frontal close-up of Devlin, who says in turn: "There's no occasion . . . You're doing good work."

Cut to a close shot of Alicia: "Is that all you have to tell me?" (a few tears drop from her eyes). Cut to a close-up of Devlin who turns to her (a natural profile): "Dry your eyes, baby, it's out of character . . . keep on your toes, there's a tough job to do . . ." (the above is shot 16, the last single in the separation).

Cut to a medium long shot of the crowd as Sebastian pushes through. Cut to the original two-shot of Alicia and Devlin (separation is resolved); Alex Sebastian enters their frame; the shot becomes a three-shot. (Note that shot 16 also resolves the Devlin profile since here he turns on camera, thus showing the difference between the previous ones created by camera angularity and this one that is the result of turning his head.) Alicia Huberman, regaining her poise, addresses Alex: "Do you remember Mr. Devlin?" They exchange some small talk about the race; Devlin excuses himself and leaves. Quite unconventionally Hitchcock decided, after this short interlude, to start another separation, this time a shorter one (ten shots) between Alex Sebastian and Alicia Huberman. The change here is in the positioning of Alicia: in the previous separation Devlin and Alicia are in front of the barrier with Alicia in her close-ups more toward the right of her frame, while Devlin is in the center of his. Here, by contrast, Alicia is positioned unexpectedly on the left of her frame and Alex Sebastian is in the center, a small change but characteristically important: it gives Alicia a certain amount of privacy, room to turn away from Sebastian, as if to run away from him. Interestingly enough, when Alicia does turn away to screen right to hide her penned-up emotions from him, her hat almost covers her face (this is her other profile). The separation starts with a close shot of Alicia Huberman (frame left) while Alex speaks offscreen: "I wasn't watching the race, I was watching you . . . and your friend." Cut to a close-up of Alex Sebastian, who continues hinting that Alicia had an arranged secret date with Mr. Devlin. Cut to a close shot of Alicia as she turns away to frame right (as if away from Sebastian), her hat practically covering the frame. Cut to the close-up of Alex (as before): "I watched you . . . I thought that maybe you are in love with him." Cut to a close-up of Alicia as she turns to a frontal position with a smile: "Don't talk like that. I detest it." Cut to a close-up of Alex: "Really? . . . He's very good looking . . . You make a nice couple." Cut to the same as before close-up of Alicia: "Alex, I told you before, Mr. Devlin doesn't mean a thing to me." Cut to a close shot of Alex: "I would like to be convinced." Cut to a brief close shot of Alicia listening. Cut back to a close shot of Alex Sebastian, who continues: "Would you like to convince me, Alicia, that Mr. Devlin means nothing to you?" Sebastian keeps looking penetratingly as the picture dissolves to an exterior long shot of the U.S. Embassy. The above separation, as we see, remains unresolved in the conventional sense, since it ends on only one of the participants (Alex).

The reflection of the racing horses in Alicia's field glasses prompts me to comment on Hitchcock's niggardly attention to physical settings, the surrounding geography and the like. What is remarkable about it is his determined avoidance of such mood builders, as if they would interfere with his focus on the essentials and his freedom from the verité. In any other film a scene taking place at a race track would have the obligatory horses, grand stands, and other details. So far in the film the only more or less explicit exterior was the flying airplane bringing Miss Huberman to Brazil. We did not see or have a sense of Miami in the opening chapter, nor were we given much of a courtroom atmosphere, or any sites of Rio de Janeiro. The most we have seen is a distant beach from the high-rise balcony in Alicia's apartment. Hitchcock refuses to use what is most naturally available to cinema; instead the magic of his language creates its own reality for the screen, engaging our imagination as well as our creative participation. It is similar to a Japanese drawing in which the mere outline of the eyes lets us imagine, nevertheless, the totality of the face; or in which one stroke of charcoal along the line of the spine generates a sense of the whole figure.

The unresolved separation in the race track scene (18) has as a last shot a close-up (of Alex Sebastian), adding to the collection of close shots as endings of scenes. At this point in *Notorious* the viewer is aware that Alicia Huberman feels miserably rejected by Devlin. The next scene puts the viewer in the privileged position of learning that Devlin, in fact, truly loves her (something Alicia will find out only at the end of the film). Such a shrewd narrative strategy, of making the viewer know more than one of the protagonists, makes additional demands on the language, as it has to accommodate the underlying sympathies and worries of the audience. The dramatic on-rush of events, including the upcoming marriage of Alicia with Alex Sebasatian, is constructed in the next scene by means of a most sophisticated separation. Basically it is a three-way separation, A B C, A B C, with an ingenious use of a familiar image that keeps the shots together. I shall revert to numbering the shots, as tedious as it might be, in order to trace down properly the scene's formidable complexities.

Scene 19. Begins with a dissolve from Alex Sebastian in a close-up at the race track to a long shot of the U.S. Embassy (familiar image). The separation starts with a dissolve to (shot 1) an interior, medium shot, of a conference room: Prescott, standing, reports on Alicia Huberman's discovery that Dr. Rensler, a famous German scientist under the present pseudonym of Dr. Anderson, is working at Alex's house on some research. Cut to (shot 2) a medium shot of the door; we hear knocking; a clerk enters to announce that Alicia Huberman is here and wishes to see Captain Prescott. Cut to (shot 3) a medium close-up of Devlin with his back to the camera, as we hear Prescott's voice offscreen: "I don't like her coming here . . . she has me worried lately"; third voice offscreen: "A woman of that kind . . ." At that Devlin, who is still with his back to the camera, suddenly turns around, and looks straight at the undisclosed speaker. Devlin: "What kind is that, Mr. Beardsley?" Cut (shot 4) to a medium two-shot of Prescott and a seated man, who continues: "I don't think any one of us has any illusion about her character." Cut (shot 5) to a medium close-up of Devlin, retorting with irony: "Oh, not at all, not the slightest, she's a woman, but not a lady." Cut (shot 6) back to the medium two-shot (as in shot 4) while Devlin (offscreen) continues with bitter irony about the man's wife, who "most likely, with other wives in Washington, D.C. . . ." Cut to (shot 7) a medium close-up of Devlin, continuing on camera: ". . . are having cocktails while this woman is risking her life . . ." Cut (shot 8) back to the same medium two-shot; Captain Prescott tries to stop Devlin's outbursts and Mr. Beardsley adds: "The remark about my wife is totally uncalled for." Cut to (shot 9) the same medium close-up of Devlin who says with bitterness: "Withdrawn and apologized . . ." and turns away again. So far the separation is an arrangement of one (Devlin) to two (Captain Prescott and Mr. Beardsley), with a wild crescendo in rhythm and intensity, as Devlin takes a strong stand in defence of Alicia Huberman.

The separation continues with a tour de force: (shot 10) medium long shot of the door; Alicia Huberman enters, greets the men present, shakes hands with Prescott, and sits down; the camera, slowly moving

closer to her, ends up in a medium close-up. The fast pace of the previous shots is broken by this longer duration shot, elongated even farther by the camera moving in. The situation is set for some startling
news. Alicia informs the men that she needs to make an important
decision, before noon! The voice of Captain Prescott (offscreen) is heard
complaining about the danger of her coming so openly to the Embassy.
Alicia interrupts him, explaining that something has happened and she
needs advice immediately: Alex Sebastian has asked her to marry him.
Cut to (shot 11) a medium shot of Devlin as he turns around upon
hearing the last word (note symmetry in Devlin's turn, the second time
in this scene). Cut to (shot 12) the same medium close-up of Alicia
Huberman: "I need to give my answer by lunch time." Cut to (shot
13) the same medium shot of Devlin (brief) as he listens intently. Cut
(shot 14) back to the medium close-up of Alicia who looks up toward
where (presumably) Captain Prescott is standing. We hear his voice:
"Are you willing to go so far for us, Miss Huberman?" He leans into
Alicia's frame. His sudden appearance in her frame makes a startling
impression. Hitchcock frames Alicia Huberman in a medium shot rather
than a close-up in order to make room (in the larger frame) for Captain
Prescott's sudden intrusion. By doing so, the director begins a two-to-
one shot separation, Devlin remaining again the one with a single frame.
At the same time, Hitchcock overturns the simplistic conventions that
would have required Alicia, with her startling news, to be framed in a
single, emphatic close shot. This arrangement places the more important character in a medium two-shot and the, at this moment, less
important figure in the single frame.

In the upcoming single shots Prescott, in the center, connects the
Devlin and Alicia Huberman shots just with eye contact. Still in shot
14 Alicia answers Prescott's question ("Are you willing to go so far?")
hesitantly: "Yes, if you wish." Cut to a low close-up (shot 15) of Captain Prescott, who straightens up and turns to where Devlin most likely
stands, and addresses him: "What do you think of it, Devlin?" Cut to
(shot 16) a high medium shot of Devlin who turns and takes two steps
toward the camera, saying, with an edge: "I think it's a useful idea."
While turning to where Alicia presumably is, he adds: "May I ask what
inspired Sebastian to go this far?" Cut (shot 17) to tight high close-up
of Alicia Huberman who looks up and, after a pause, says: "He is in
love with me." Cut (shot 18) to the same medium close-up of Devlin:

"He thinks that you are in love with him?" Cut to (shot 19) a tight close-up of Prescott shifting his look from where Devlin is to (down) where Alicia sits (eye gaze connector). Cut to (shot 20) the same close-up of Alicia answering with hestiation: "Yes, that's what he thinks." Cut to (shot 21) the same medium close-up of Devlin scrutinizing Alicia, while we hear, offscreen, the voice of Prescott: "Gentlemen, this is the cream of the chest." Cut to the same close-up of Alicia (shot 22). She looks up and, half in a void, asks: "Then, it's all right?" Quick cut (shot 23) to the same close-up of Prescott: "Yes, I'd say so." Quick cut (shot 24) to the same medium close-up of Devlin as Prescott continues offscreen: "It's a perfect marriage for us." Cut to the same close-up of Alicia (shot 25). We see, behind her, Prescott's midsection pass by. Note that since the above separation has not been introduced with a larger shot showing the geography of the place or the participants' location, Prescott's walk in shot 25 (behind Alicia) confirms the physical positioning and relationship which was until now indicated by eye contact only.

Cut to (shot 26) the same medium close-up of Devlin addressing Prescott: "There's only one thing: won't it delay us a bit?" We hear from offscreen Prescott's voice: "What do you mean?" Devlin continues: "Well, Mr. Sebastian is a very romantic fellow, isn't he, Alicia?" Cut to (shot 27) the same close-up of Alicia Huberman, whispering "Yes." Cut back to the same medium close-up of Devlin (shot 28) continuing about Sebastian's possible plans to take his bride for an extended honeymoon. Cut to the same close-up of Alicia (shot 29) who suffers, listening to Devlin's mocking tone. Prescott is seen walking behind her (left to right). Prescott voices his hope that Alicia will manage to come back soon. Her voice offscreen: "I think I can manage that." Cut to (shot 30) a low medium close-up (new position) of Devlin, three-quarters turned, who talks while walking. The camera follows him: "Things are going pretty well here. I don't think you need me any more, Captain Prescott." He walks out the door. The camera just then lines up with Alicia Huberman in a medium close-up (she is in line with the door). Prescott's voice offscreen is heard thanking Alicia for her efforts. She turns her face down, broken hearted. Dissolve. In symmetry with the other scenes this one again ends on a close-up of one person.

In evaluating the strength of the above scene one is forced to repeat that the secret of Hitchcock's structures lies in their subtle complexity built with simple materials. Again we have a separation, this time with a greater number of shots (30); again it starts with a teaser of sorts, up to the point of Alicia's arrival. In the teaser, Prescott is placed in a two-shot and only in the second (and principal) part of the scene does he take on the function of a familiar image connector. The unique nature of this separation is, as I already mentioned, the lack of an expository introduction with a clear geography. Eye contact is the only indication of the actors' positions: Prescott's gaze from one side to the other (presumably from Alicia to Devlin) is necessary to indicate where they are in relation to him. Later in the scene Hitchcock twice has Prescott pass, out of focus, behind Alicia Huberman, which is especially gratifying since it confirms beyond any doubt the actual positioning.

To reiterate, at the end of the scene Hitchcock produces a most ingenious resolution through camera placement: when Devlin is leaving the room the camera follows him to the door and, on the way, unexpectedly comes upon Alicia Huberman in close-up (she was "placed" to be in the line of vision). Devlin's exit forms an ideal symmetry with Alicia's entry (also with camera movement). Symmetries abound in this scene: the entry of Alicia with the camera moving in to a tighter shot is similar to the shot of the elder Mrs. Sebastian after her descent on the stairway. It is also similar to Devlin's few steps toward the camera, to a tighter shot. Such changes of picture size without a cut (by either camera movement or by a character's moving on camera) are a needed relief from the bursts of energy coming from multiple cuts.

Dramatically, this scene puts the relationship between Alicia Huberman and Devlin at an impasse. The film now shifts more forcefully to the spy plot, for a while at least.

Scene 20. Dissolve to an interior long shot, in the mother's bedroom: Alex Sebastian is standing in the background; his mother, in a prominent foreground profile, is knitting. She is talking about the impending marriage. The mother suspects that Alicia Huberman came to Brazil to "capture the rich Alex Sebastian for a husband." Alex protests, stating that Alicia didn't even know that he was in Rio. He turns and walks to the door. Presently the camera executes an elaborate half circle dolly movement behind the mother's chair, keeping her all the time in the center, in three-quarter profile. She dominates the frame in this baroque-like setting, augmented by the stark black-and-white photography. Alex, standing by the door, accuses her of jealousy and spite and announces that the marriage will take place next week. They both hope that she will attend; he walks out in fury. Fade-out.

Note that the above scene has no cuts; its indisputable centerpiece is the camera movement in which the imperial mother in her heavily ornamented chair seems to be floating in space. Yet this extravagant camera movement is not merely there to support the mother's dominant position in the household. It is also an example of Hitchcockian cinematic rhetoric, in the best sense of the word. From the start of *Notorious* Hitchcock is checkerboarding heavily fragmented scenes with those containing camera movement (with few or no cuts). As the film progresses, he especially cultivates the latter, upgrading it in elegance and originality. The camera movement in the above scene is a precursor to those more elaborate ones soon to come.

Scene 21. Fade-in (after a deletion, presumably coming back from the honeymoon trip): long shot, night, a car is approaching the Sebastian mansion. Dissolve to a medium long shot of Alicia and Alex walking up the steps (familiar image). Cut to a medium long shot, interior, of Joseph hurriedly walking to open the door (still putting on his jacket). Cut to a medium shot of Alex and Alicia entering the hall and coming closer to the camera. Alex apologizes: "I'm sorry it doesn't look very cheerful here." Cut to a medium shot of all three; Alex asks about his mother; Joseph informs him that she retired early; Alex asks if Alicia would like a bite of food? "No," she says, "I'm tired." They start going up the stairs. Fade-out. Note that Hitchcock does not as yet let people go more than a few steps up the stairway, saving a full ascent for later.

Scene 22. Fade-in, long shot, interior: Alicia, with the help of two servants, is unpacking valises. She calls Joseph to open a closet. They both walk; camera dollies with them. Joseph opens one closet door; Alicia remarks that it is too small for her. She adds: "I need more space." They walk briskly to the right. Cut from their backs as they continue walking to another door. Joseph is in the foreground, his back to the camera; he says: "I have no key for this closet. It is Mrs. Sebastian who is in charge of keys." Alicia thoughtfully says "Oh" and walks toward the camera to a close-up. As she passes Joseph she asks him where Mr. Sebastian is. Joseph informs her that Mr. Sebastian is now at a business meeting downstairs in his office. A short hold on Alicia's face; her mind is working. Cut to the familiar double door. Dissolve to the inside of the office: in medium long shot we see several people standing, grouped around Dr. Anderson, who addresses Alex Sebastian: "I miss Emil Hubka. He was a first class metalurgist." Then after a short exchange he continues: "Well, gentlemen, my work is done." Alex says: "You've been successful?" Dr. Anderson: "Yes." Cut to a medium long shot of Alicia walking briskly toward the double door (camera follows). She knocks and resolutely opens the door. Alex quickly appears with: "Darling . . ."; they talk in the doorway. Alicia excuses herself for interrupting; she tells him about the keys. Alex apologizes and walks with Alicia; camera follows; they start mounting the stairs. Dissolve as they continue walking on the upper level. Alex stops at his mother's door; he knocks: "Mother." Alicia continues walking. The camera follows her (we lose Alex). She is in a medium close-up as she stops at the door to her room. She turns and looks back to where Alex is, and cautiously eavesdrops. We hear (offscreen) a door open and close. Alex presumably enters his mother's bedroom. Cut to a medium shot of the door. We hear faintly, from inside, an ensuing argument. Cut back to the same medium close shot of Alicia listening. Cut back to Alex's mother's closed door. We hear more of the argument about keys. Cut back to Alicia in three-quarter profile, listening. Cut back to the door as Alex emerges, intense. The camera follows as he approaches Alicia's door. We see that she has managed, by now, to slip inside her room. Cut to a medium shot of Alex as he enters and gives her a bunch of keys, adding with a smile: "Darling, you're going to be busy all morning. See you at lunch." He kisses her and leaves. Alicia alone, in a medium close shot, with the keys in her hand, flashes a half smile of success. Dissolve to a two-shot of Joseph and Alicia opening a closet door. Dissolve to a second closet door opening. Dissolve to a third. Dissolve to a fourth. Dissolve to an extreme close-up of a lock: "UNICA." Cut to a medium two-shot of Joseph with Alicia in front of the door with the above lock. He explains: "Mr. Sebastian has a key for this. It's the wine cellar." Alicia looks at him, thinking; she makes the mental connection and walks past him. Joseph follows her. As they walk away (from camera) Alicia looks once more back to the door. Cut to the same extreme close-up of the lock: UNICA. Fade-out.

   Scene 23. Fade-in: medium two-shot of Alicia and Devlin sitting on shoulder close shot (from his to her face) as he says: "Darling, it isn't that I don't trust you, but when you're in love at my age every man that looks at you is a menace, forgive me . . ." Cut back to the two profiles, then a zoom to her right hand which he leans down to kiss. She unclenches her hand; he kisses it (there is no key there). He is about to kiss her other hand when she throws herself upon him in an embrace, with both arms around his neck (camera adjusts to a wider frame). Cut to a close-up of Alicia's hands, now on his back, the UNICA key between two fingers. She transfers it to her other hand and lets it fall. The camera follows it down to the carpet. She pushes the key out of the way with her foot. Dissolve.

Unlike scene 20 (the mother's bedroom), where the star point of construction is the elegant camera movement without any cuts, the above scene is a perfect example of a combination of quick cuts and several camera movements. One of them is an extremely elaborate one, the second in a series of important rhetorical phrasings. The possible shortcoming there could have been the undue attention to the mechanical operation of the camera per se. As in many cases, Hitchcock walks the tightrope, on the edge of overstepping; yet, inevitably, he manages to achieve a maximum of gratification.

Scene 25. A similar design will dominate this scene, probably the most climactic one in the film. Dissolve to a very high long shot from the upper level of the stairway, looking down through the rich candelabra, to the big entrance hall. Guests are milling around (there obviously was a brief deletion from the previous scene); the party has started. We see from far Alex and Alicia close to the door, greeting guests, talking, smiling. The camera zooms very slowly down to her, ending on a close-up of her hand holding the UNICA key. (Note that the above bold camera movement is in the risky category of zooms I mentioned before, and again is successfully executed.) Thus the viewer's attention is glued to the key, while the party itself is only a backdrop to the unfolding drama. Cut to a medium close-up of Alicia's face; she looks toward the door. Cut to a medium long shot of the main doorway (she evidently is expecting Devlin who has not arrived yet). Cut back to the same shot of her face. Cut to a medium shot of Alex who turns around and walks briskly toward her (in profile); the camera follows him until he reaches her. Cut to a medium close shot (over-the-shoulder) from her to him; Alex suggests that it's time to join the at a business meeting downstairs in his office. A short hold on Alicia's face; her mind is working. Cut to the familiar double door. Dissolve to the inside of the office: in medium long shot we see several people standing, grouped around Dr. Anderson, who addresses Alex Sebastian: "I miss Emil Hubka. He was a first class metalurgist." Then after a short exchange he continues: "Well, gentlemen, my work is done." Alex says: "You've been successful?" Dr. Anderson: "Yes." Cut to a medium long shot of Alicia walking briskly toward the double door (camera follows). She knocks and resolutely opens the door. Alex quickly appears with: "Darling . . ."; they talk in the doorway. Alicia excuses herself for interrupting; she tells him about the keys. Alex apologizes and walks with Alicia; camera follows; they start mounting the stairs. Dissolve as they continue walking on the upper level. Alex stops at his mother's door; he knocks: "Mother." Alicia continues walking. The camera follows her (we lose Alex). She is in a medium close-up as she stops at the door to her room. She turns and looks back to where Alex is, and cautiously eavesdrops. We hear (offscreen) a door open and close. Alex presumably enters his mother's bedroom. Cut to a medium shot of the door. We hear faintly, from inside, an ensuing argument. Cut back to the same medium close shot of Alicia listening. Cut back to Alex's mother's closed door. We hear more of the argument about keys. Cut back to Alicia in three-quarter profile, listening. Cut back to the door as Alex emerges, intense. The camera follows as he approaches Alicia's door. We see that she has managed, by now, to slip inside her room. Cut to a medium shot of Alex as he enters and gives her a bunch of keys, adding with a smile: "Darling, you're going to be busy all morning. See you at lunch." He kisses her and leaves. Alicia alone, in a medium close shot, with the keys in her hand, flashes a half smile of success. Dissolve to a two-shot of Joseph and Alicia opening a closet door. Dissolve to a second closet door opening. Dissolve to a third. Dissolve to a fourth. Dissolve to an extreme close-up of a lock: "UNICA." Cut to a medium two-shot of Joseph with Alicia in front of the door with the above lock. He explains: "Mr. Sebastian has a key for this. It's the wine cellar." Alicia looks at him, thinking; she makes the mental connection and walks past him. Joseph follows her. As they walk away (from camera) Alicia looks once more back to the door. Cut to the same extreme close-up of the lock: UNICA. Fade-out.

Scene 23. Fade-in: medium two-shot of Alicia and Devlin sitting on a bench in a small park in Rio. In the background we see the traffic of pedestrians and some cars (evidently on a rear projection screen, in soft focus). During the scene a small boy crosses the screen in front of them (the only realistic rendering). Devlin, leaning forward, talks about the keys: "Get them from him." Alicia: "Get them, how?" Devlin: "Don't you live near him?" Cut to a tighter two-shot. Alicia: "What do I do when I get them?" Devlin: "You look for a bottle of wine like the one that rattled the fellow at dinner that night" (he refers to Emil Hubka). Alicia: "All bottles look alike to me; I'm not a master mind." Devlin: "You're doing well enough." (So far they haven't looked at each other.) Alicia turns to him: "It's not fun, there." Devlin: "It's too late for that, isn't it? . . . Look, why don't you convince your husband to throw a large shindig to introduce his bride [ironically] to Rio society; say, sometime next week." Alicia, with a touch of salt: "Why?" Devlin, still not looking at her: "Consider me invited. I'll try to find out about that wine cellar business." After a pause, Alicia: "I don't think my husband is interested in entertaining, just yet." Devlin, with irony: "The honeymoon isn't yet over, eh?" He looks at her for the first time, just for a moment, with bitterness. He adds: "I trust you, Mrs. Sebastian. You can handle it." Alicia: "I don't think it will be so easy about inviting you. He thinks you're in love with me." Devlin: "You have me invited to the house and I see how happily married you are so the horrid passion for you may be torn out of me." Alicia: "All right, I'll try." Devlin: "Good, next week then." Alicia: "I'll be looking forward to seeing you." Cut back to the larger master medium two-shot. She gets up. Devlin, standing in profile, takes off his hat, saying: "Good afternoon, madame." She leaves frame. Devlin remains, hat in hand. Fade-out.

This simple construction, master, to tighter shot, back to master (again one person ending the scene), is a needed quiet before the storm. The next scene is not only pivotal and turbulent, with intense fragmentation, but is also full of suspense.

Scene 24. Fade-in: long shot of the Sebastian mansion at night, all windows alight. Dissolve to a luxurious grandfather's clock. Dissolve to a long shot of Alicia putting her earrings on as she walks closer to the camera in a medium close shot. She looks around. Cut to a long shot of an open door with a moving shadow on it. We hear Sebastian's voice: "I'll be with you in a moment." Cut to the same medium close

shot of Alicia looking for something. Cut to the same shot of the door
with the shadow of Alex on it. Cut with a most extraordinary movement of camera so far, craning up through the air and down to a close-
up of a set of keys on the dresser. This is another rhetorical elaboration
of Hitchcock's (the keys are to be important in the drama from now
on). Cut to a medium long shot of Alicia still in her doorway (too far
away to justify the previous camera movement as a point-of-view shot).
She starts walking toward the dresser. Cut to Alex's door. We hear him
say how surprised he is that Devlin is coming to the party. Cut to a
close-up of Alicia looking down. Cut to a close shot of the keys in her
hands. Offscreen we hear Alex's voice. She is taking off the UNICA key.
Cut to a close-up of Alicia looking down, then toward Alex's door. Cut
to his door. His shadow is moving back and forth. Cut to Alicia as she
turns around and walks back toward her room. Just then: cut to a medium shot of Alex as he exits his room and enters the hallway. The
camera follows him. Coming closer to the camera his hands are stretched
out, ready to embrace her. Her hands, with clenched fists (the key is
in one of them), meet his in close-up. The camera moves quickly up
to a two-shot of Alicia and Alex in close profiles. Cut to an over-the-

shoulder close shot (from his to her face) as he says: "Darling, it isn't that I don't trust you, but when you're in love at my age every man that looks at you is a menace, forgive me . . ." Cut back to the two profiles, then a zoom to her right hand which he leans down to kiss. She unclenches her hand; he kisses it (there is no key there). He is about to kiss her other hand when she throws herself upon him in an embrace, with both arms around his neck (camera adjusts to a wider frame). Cut to a close-up of Alicia's hands, now on his back, the UNICA key between two fingers. She transfers it to her other hand and lets it fall. The camera follows it down to the carpet. She pushes the key out of the way with her foot. Dissolve.

Unlike scene 20 (the mother's bedroom), where the star point of construction is the elegant camera movement without any cuts, the above scene is a perfect example of a combination of quick cuts and several camera movements. One of them is an extremely elaborate one, the second in a series of important rhetorical phrasings. The possible shortcoming there could have been the undue attention to the mechanical operation of the camera per se. As in many cases, Hitchcock walks the tightrope, on the edge of overstepping; yet, inevitably, he manages to achieve a maximum of gratification.

Scene 25. A similar design will dominate this scene, probably the most climactic one in the film. Dissolve to a very high long shot from the upper level of the stairway, looking down through the rich candelabra, to the big entrance hall. Guests are milling around (there obviously was a brief deletion from the previous scene); the party has started. We see from far Alex and Alicia close to the door, greeting guests, talking, smiling. The camera zooms very slowly down to her, ending on a close-up of her hand holding the UNICA key. (Note that the above bold camera movement is in the risky category of zooms I mentioned before, and again is successfully executed.) Thus the viewer's attention is glued to the key, while the party itself is only a backdrop to the unfolding drama. Cut to a medium close-up of Alicia's face; she looks toward the door. Cut to a medium long shot of the main doorway (she evidently is expecting Devlin who has not arrived yet). Cut back to the same shot of her face. Cut to a medium shot of Alex who turns around and walks briskly toward her (in profile); the camera follows him until he reaches her. Cut to a medium close shot (over-the-shoulder) from her to him; Alex suggests that it's time to join the guests. Cut to the same size shot from him to her; they turn around and walk to where the guests are.

Cut to the main doorway. Devlin enters, gives his coat to the doorman, and walks to the right; the camera moves with him. Note that most of the walks are in medium shot range and because of their proximity to the camera they give the impression of extremely active transits. Devlin stops in medium close shot and looks searchingly around. Cut to a long shot of Alicia with the guests. She notices him, leaves her company, and starts toward him. Cut to a medium shot of Alex Sebastian looking intensely at Devlin (from far away). Cut to what Alex sees: in long shot Devlin is kissing Alicia's hand. Cut to the same in close-up. We see the transfer of the key from Alicia's hand to Devlin's. Cut back to the same medium shot of Alex looking—an interesting twist on the simulated point-of-view shots. While the long shot of Devlin greeting Alicia and kissing her hand could be seen by Alex Sebastian, the next shot (the close-up of the key transfer) could not be and, even though the medium shots of Alex looking brackets the above two shots of Devlin and Alicia, the first is a possible point-of-view, while the second is not. It is noticeable in Hitchcock films that he defies slavish adherence to the naturalistic point-of-view orthodoxy, preferring instead freedom for arrangements that suit him. Cut to a medium two-shot of Alicia and Devlin who pretend to socialize while actually exchanging some remarks à propos the key. Cut to a medium shot of Alex walking briskly (camera follows); he reaches Alicia and Devlin. Devlin thanks him for the invitation. Alex: "We both invited you, Mr. Devlin." Cut to a close-up of Alicia. Cut to a three-shot of them. Sebastian excuses himself and walks away to join the other guests. Alicia and Devlin start walking in the other direction; the camera follows them. Devlin: "He's going to watch us like a hawk." Alicia: "He's rather jealous anyway." Devlin: "Did you get the key off his chain?" Cut to Alicia in a close shot, as they walk: "Yes." They come close to the table where champagne is served. Devlin: "I hope they don't run out of that stuff. They'll be going down to the cellar for more." Alicia, fanning herself with a Spanish fan: "I didn't think about that." Cut to a close-up of Alicia. Cut to a close-up of Devlin. Cut back to the two-shot. They come closer to where the champagne bottles are dispensed by Joseph. A Spanish woman approaches Devlin and takes him away. Alicia, left alone, looks down at the bottles. Cut to a high medium

shot of champagne bottles in a case of ice. This is to become a familiar image, a sort of "clock" that measures the time while our protagonists are searching the wine cellar. The fewer the bottles, the more danger-ous for them, since at any moment someone might come down to the cellar for more champagne. Hitchcock will return with determined reg-ularity to this imaginative "clock" as an ingenious device in his strat-egy for creating suspense.

Offscreen is the voice of Alicia addressing Joseph, while we still see the bottles: "Joseph, do you think we will have enough champagne to last the rest of the evening?" The last part of her sentence is in a me-dium two-shot of Joseph and her. Cut to a very low close shot of Joseph who answers: "I hope so." Cut to a close shot of Alicia, worried, look-ing around. Cut to a long shot of Devlin with the Spanish woman. Cut to a long shot of Alex with a group of people. Cut back to the same close shot of Alicia worried; she walks away from the camera toward Devlin, still with the Spanish woman. Alicia finds an excuse to extri-cate Devlin; they walk away. In a long shot Alex waves his hand to her. Cut to Devlin and Alicia in a medium two-shot settling down on a couch. They talk about the wine that is running out faster than they thought.

As we approach the apex of the spying operation, three distinct actions are already in full swing: 1) our two protagonists are planning their ultimate mission in the wine cellar, 2) Alex Sebastian is jealously watching his wife as well as Devlin, and 3) the supply of champagne is running out. These three actions are distributed by Hitchcock with meticulous precision both in frequency and timing, a necessary condition for properly building tension via parallelism. To catch the components of this precision, probably the most elusive of Hitchcock's schemes, I shall use a more detailed analysis for the upcoming shots (with the risk of augmenting the tediousness of my verbal description of what otherwise is a purely visual experience). Devlin and Alicia are still sitting on a couch in a two-shot, talking; Alex Sebastian has just gestured hello to Alicia from far away, and Alicia has smiled back. She says to Devlin: "You better go out to the garden alone. I'll come soon and show you the wine cellar door." Cut to a medium shot of Alex walking toward them. (Note that most of the movements in this scene are built contrapuntally, left vs. right, front vs. back, etc.). Cut to Devlin and Alicia getting up from the couch; Devlin leaves frame to the right; Alicia takes a step to the left. Cut to a close shot as Alicia and Alex, whom we see walking toward her, enter frame from opposite sides and finally meet each other. Cut to a high medium close shot of Devlin looking down. He walks past Joseph (still dispensing drinks). We see many bottles already missing. The camera follows Devlin who walks through two rooms full of guests. (All three parallel actions are presently at work.) Cut to Alex and Alicia; camera moves in gently to a close-up of Alicia. Cut to an opposite movement of a servant approaching the camera with a large tray full of champagne glasses. Cut back to the same close-up of Alicia who refuses to take a glass. The camera dollies back to a two-shot of Alex with Alicia; she excuses herself and moves out of the frame.

Scene 26. Cut to long shot exterior (shot 1): Devlin pacing in front of the outside door leading to the cellar corridor. After five seconds of pacing he stops, the camera slowly dollies to the little window in the door through which we see Alicia coming down the interior steps to the cellar. She comes closer to a medium shot and turns on the cellar

lights. In the foreground Devlin pushes in the door leading to the corridor. Alicia opens the door from the inside and they meet. The above
shot, lasting about nineteen seconds, is of longer duration than the previous fast cuts with opposite movement; in that sense it is a release
of sorts. Opposite movements are kept alive, nevertheless, with Devlin
moving left to right, and again to the left. Cut to (shot 2) a reverse
angle, from inside of corridor; Devlin enters, passes Alicia, and they
both move right to left (another opposite movement). The camera follows them to the cellar door. Devlin unlocks it; Alicia says that she'll
keep watch at the garden door. Camera pans and dollies with her (in
symmetry with the beginning of the scene); length: 17 seconds. The
above shots (1 and 2), with their camera movements, carry information
about the geography of the place.

Cut to (shot 3) a low medium shot of Devlin inside the wine cellar
examining bottles (7 sec.). Cut to (shot 4) a medium close-up of Alicia
stepping to the right (camera dollies with her); she opens the door to
the garden and stands in it, guarding nervously. The camera dollies
closer to a close-up of her face; she turns her head to the left (7 sec.).
Cut to (shot 5) a parallel action upstairs at the bartender's counter; in
a very low angle medium shot of Joseph dispensing wine glasses in the
foreground; he looks left and down (2 1/2 sec.). Cut to (shot 6) what
Joseph sees: from a very high angle a medium shot of bottles on ice,
only five left (2 1/2 sec.). Cut to (shot 7) medium shot of Devlin in
the cellar. He walks to the right; the camera follows him to a medium
close-up as he examines the bottles and labels (5 1/2 sec.). Cut to (shot
8) a close-up of a wine chart (2 sec.). Cut to (shot 9) a medium close-
up as Devlin moves bottles and reaches into the shelf for another one;
he examines the labels (7 1/2 sec.). The next fourteen shots will be
composed only of brief cuts. Cut to (shot 10) a close-up of the wine
chart; Devlin's hand turns the pages (2 1/2 sec.). Cut to (shot 11) a
close-up of a bottle moving toward the camera, apparently displaced
by Devlin's hand (1 1/2 sec.). Cut to (shot 12) a close-up of Devlin's
face looking intently (at the labels) (1 1/2 sec.). Cut to (shot 13) a close-
up of the same wine chart with Devlin's hand (1 1/2 sec.). Cut to (shot
14) a close-up of the same bottle (as in shot 11) still moving foward (1
sec.). Cut to (shot 15) a tight close-up of Devlin's face looking (1 sec.).
Cut to (shot 16) a close-up of the wine chart; Devlin's hand turns the
pages (1 1/2 sec.). Cut to (shot 17) a low angle close-up of a bottle

toppling over from right to left (*1 sec.*). (Note the change of angularity to a low angle while the previous shots were all eye level.) Cut to (shot 18) a low angle close-up of Devlin as a shadow of the bottle crosses over his face; he quickly looks down (*less than a sec.*). Cut to (shot 19) a high angle close-up of a falling bottle. The camera follows in a swish down to the floor; we see and hear it smash on the floor (*less than a sec.*). Cut to (shot 20) a low angle close-up of Alicia who is startled by the noise (half a sec.). Cut to (shot 21) the same close-up of Devlin looking down (one sec.). Cut to (shot 22) a high angle tight close-up of the broken bottle on the cement floor (*one sec.*). Cut to (shot 23) a low angle close-up of Alicia looking to the right. The camera starts pulling back and follows her in medium shot as she walks left to the wine cellar (6 sec.). The length of this shot releases somewhat the tension built up by the series of very brief cuts but does not lessen the suspense. Cut to (shot 24) a low angle medium shot of Alicia entering the cellar space (in reverse screen position to the one in shot 23). She snaps to Devlin: "What happened?" (Note: this is the first dialogue spoken since shot 2—the previous twenty-one shots are, for all practical purposes, silent.) Devlin's voice: "Vintage sand." After a pause: "We've got to leave things as we found them; help me find a bottle of wine with the same label as these others." Alicia: "But it isn't really sand, is it?" (2 sec.). Cut to (shot 25) a high angle close-up of the broken bottle. Devlin's voice-over: "No, it's some kind of metal ore" (one sec.). Cut to (shot 26) a long duration medium shot, with occasional close-ups. Alicia comes closer to Devlin; she kneels down next to him in a two-shot; they both look down, surveying the disaster. Alicia gets up; the camera dollies to a medium close-up of Devlin; he reaches for an envelope in his jacket; the camera pans fast down to the broken bottle; we see Devlin gathering the spilled black sand into the envelope (total duration: 21 sec.). The length of the shot represents a second release after the previous action; it also runs counter to the wishes of the viewer, who, as always in similar situations, wishes for the action to go faster, so the protagonists can escape the imminent danger of being discovered.

Cut to (shot 27) the upstairs (parallel action); medium shot of Joseph serving wine. Cut to (shot 28) a high shot of the ice container, only three bottles left. Cut (shot 29) back to the medium shot of Joseph looking around (for Mr. Sebastian) (4 sec.). Cut to the cellar (shot 30).

In a medium shot (facing screen right—opposite to the direction of Joseph), Alicia is cleaning up the counter; she hands Devlin a bottle; the camera follows, showing Devlin putting the envelope in his pocket and then starting to fill the empty bottle with the rest of the sand. Cut (shot 31) to a medium close shot of Alicia saying: "I'm terrified." Cut to (shot 32) a medium shot of Devlin still filling the bottle through a paper funnel: "Let's pretend we're janitors; janitors are never terrified"; camera pans up to Alicia who retorts, disregarding his cool: "I have a feeling we're too slow." She leaves the frame toward the door, to check. Cut back (shot 33) to Devlin finishing filling the bottle with sand. Cut (shot 34) to a medium shot of Alicia coming back to the cellar, saying: "I'm afraid Joseph might be coming." Cut to (shot 35) the same shot of Devlin, his nerves under control: "How unfortunate." Cut back to Alicia (shot 36); she again leaves the cellar to check. Total length of shots 30 through 36 is fourteen seconds. Cut to the upstairs (shot 37), Joseph walking briskly toward the camera (opposite to the movement of Alicia in the previous shot), looking for Mr. Sebastian; the camera follows him until we see Sebastian. Cut to (shot 38) a high long shot as Joseph respectfully approaches Mr. Sebastian and talks to him (8 sec.).

Cut back to the cellar (shot 39). High medium close-up of Devlin cleaning up the floor, pushing some of the glass debris under the wine shelves. Camera moves up to include Alicia in a tight two-shot. Cut to (shot 40) an extreme close-up of the neck of the sand-filled bottle being fitted out with a jury-rigged cover (one sec.). Cut back to Devlin (shot 41) finishing up; they both leave the cellar in a hurry as camera follows (10 sec.).

As we arrive at the pinnacle of the climax, note the strategy of Hitchcock's rhythmic pulsations (in the duration of shots) and also his distribution of parallel action (upstairs vs. wine cellar), so ideally priming the pump of suspense. The above scene (26) starts with shots 1 and 2 of longer duration (total 36 sec.) as our protagonists are about to enter the wine cellar; shots 3 and 4 in the cellar are shorter (14 sec.). The parallel action in shots 5 and 6 totals 5 seconds. Back in the cellar, shots 7, 8, and 9, examining the bottles, total 14 seconds. The next sixteen shots (9 to 25) are in rapid staccato (from 2 1/2 sec. to 1/2 sec. in length). Then follows a slow-down (shot 26, 21 sec.). After this, the parallel action upstairs, the "prime pump" of the imminent danger, contains three shots in 4 seconds. Back to the cellar for a medium-length succession of six shots lasting 14 seconds. Again the upstairs "clock" (shots 37 and 38 — 8 sec.), and the final 3 shots in the cellar, as our protagonists leave and are spotted — a painstaking 10 seconds, under the circumstances.

Unlike similar strategies in many films of suspense, Hitchcock does not build his crescendo to the very climax; he rather slows down. His quick cuts (sixteen shots in succession) generate a pile of energy that keeps ticking like a bomb during the slower shots that follow. The viewer has been trained to expect the "explosion" at any moment during those slow downs (rather than during the speed ups). The countdown (of the champagne bottles) in the parallel actions keeps us on the edge of our seats.

There is nothing strikingly new in this schemata except the precision (again, the difference between genius and mediocrity) of Hitchcock's decisions, of where he places the camera, and for how long, and in what succession. His generosity in the amount of shots and repetitions is often on the border of overstatement; but, each time, he instead hits the bull's eye. On top of it Hitchcock persistently continues to chisel in his symmetries, subsymmetries, and opposite movements that cumulatively create a strong cinesthetic impact.

Shot 41 starts with a reverse angle of Alicia and Devlin locking the cellar door; he gives her the key; we hear someone coming (2 sec.). Cut to (shot 42) a long shot of a moving shadow next to the stairway (1/2 sec.). Cut back to (shot 43) a two-shot of Alicia and Devlin reaching the garden door. Alicia: "They have seen us" (one sec.). Cut to (shot 44) a closer two-shot as Devlin says: "Come here, I'm going to kiss you." He grabs Alicia in an embrace and starts kissing her (8 sec.). Cut to (shot 45) a medium shot of Alex Sebastian and Joseph looking (1 1/2 sec). Cut to (shot 46) a long shot, through a little window pane in the doorway, of the kissing (1/2 sec.). Cut to (shot 47) a closer medium shot of Alex Sebastian looking intensely while Joseph sheepishly lowers his eyes. Alex asks Joseph to go back upstairs where he may be needed. Alex starts descending, Joseph goes up (7 sec.). Cut to (shot 48) a close-up of the kiss (2 1/2 sec.). Cut to (shot 49) a closer shot of the kiss (with a change in camera angle) (3 sec.). Cut to (shot 50) a reverse angle of the kissing (3 sec.). It is quite obvious from the last triad of shots that our protagonists are not just kissing for show, that the spark of love is reignited (for a moment at least). This narrative shift releases the tension, momentarily, of their being caught as spies. Cut to (shot 51) a medium long shot of Alex Sebastian walking toward camera (1 1/2 sec.). Cut to (shot 52) the kiss in close-up. Devlin to Alicia: "Push me away" (1 1/2 sec.). Cut to (shot 53) Alex going through door into a close-up: "I'm sorry to intrude on this tender scene" (8 sec.). Cut to (shot 54) a two-shot of Alicia and Devlin as he moves to the right. Alicia to Alex Sebastian: "I couldn't help it, he was drinking" (2 sec.). Cut back (shot 55) to the same close-up of Alex Sebastian: "So he carried you down to the cellar?" (4 sec.). Cut to the two-shot of Devlin and Alicia (shot 56). She says: "Please, Alex" (1 1/2 sec.). Cut to (shot 57) the same close-up of Alex Sebastian: "You love him" (1 1/2 sec.). Cut to (shot 58) the same two-shot of Alicia and Devlin. Devlin speaks to Alex with a sort of apology: "I knew her before you and loved her before you, but I wasn't as lucky as you. Sorry Alicia." Alicia to Devlin: "Please go." Devlin leaves, passing in front of her (5 sec.). (A shadow of reverse symmetry to an earlier scene, where Alicia leaves passing in front of Devlin.) Cut to (shot 59) a medium two-shot of Alex on the right, Alicia in profile on the left. After a long pause Alicia says: "I came down because he wanted to make a scene . . ." (10 sec.). Cut to (shot 60) a frontal close-up of Alex: "He kissed you" (2 sec.). Cut to (shot 61) a close-up of Alicia: "I tried to stop him . . ." (1 1/2 sec.). Cut back (shot 62) to the same close-up of Alex: "We'll talk about it later. Your guests are upstairs. Would you please go to them" (5 sec.). Cut to (shot 63) a close-up of Alicia as she turns and leaves frame (1 1/2 sec.). Cut to (shot 64) the same close-up of Alex looking after her, tense, with fury (5 sec.). Again an important part of the scene ends on a single close-up of relatively long duration, after a flair-up of quick shots.

Cut to (shot 65) the upstairs, a long shot of Sebastian's mother coming down the steps as Devlin puts on his coat. Camera moves in closer as the mother addresses Devlin: "Mr. Devlin, leaving so soon?" Devlin excuses himself with some obligation in town, thanks her, and leaves. The mother is alone in the frame in a medium close-up (8 sec.). Cut to (shot 66) Alex Sebastian in a long shot with his back to the camera (opposite to the position of his mother); he approaches Joseph, suggesting they go down to the cellar to fetch some more champagne. They both turn and walk toward the camera (5 sec.). Cut to (shot 67) a long

shot of the stairway leading to the cellar; the two walk down; camera
follows Alex as he passes close to the door, then dollies in to his hand
with keys, in close-up; he fingers the keys looking for the (missing)
UNICA (10 sec.). Cut to (shot 68) a close-up of Alex looking down
(1 1/2 sec.). Cut to (shot 69) a medium shot of the closed cellar door
(1 sec.). Cut to (shot 70) the same close-up of Alex thinking, realizing
the key is gone; camera slowly pulls back to a two-shot. Alex tells
Joseph that perhaps they don't need any wine, they may get by with
what they still have upstairs. They both go back to the stairway. Dissolve (after a long deletion) to (shot 71) a very high long shot looking
down to the grand entrance hall. (Note that this is the third such shot,
so far, making it a familiar image whose ultimate dramatic peak will
take place in the next scene). We see from far Alex's mother with Alex;
Alicia stands nearby. The mother walks away, Alex steps toward Alicia
(8 sec.). (This shot releases the tension from the previous shots.) Cut
on action (shot 72) to a medium close two-shot as Alex enters Alicia's
frame; both start walking. Alicia: "I'm really sorry . . ." Alex: "Oh
my dear, I shall never forgive myself for behaving like a stupid school-
boy"; as they continue walking in profile camera dollies with them.
Alicia: "Then, you believe me?" Alex: "Of course, it's not worth mentioning again." Alicia thanks him. She wonders if Alex is coming up
with her; "No, not right now," he has a conference with Anderson in
his study. Camera moves back as Alicia starts climbing the big stairway. Alex adds: "It was a very successful party"; he watches her go
(19 sec.). Cut to (shot 73) a frontal close-up of Alex looking after her
with utmost severity (2 1/2 sec.). This shot seems to take ages; by now,
Alex suspects something. . . . Again a single, thought provoking close-
up ends the scene.

   Scene 27. Music starts: dissolve to a medium shot of Alex walking
away from the camera (opposite to his previous close-up), taking off
his dinner jacket; he approaches his dresser (the same one from which
Alicia took the key); he stops, hesitates, and finally reaches into his
pocket for his key chain. Cut to a long shot (1 1/2 sec.) insert of Alicia
in her bed. Cut back to medium shot of Alex with keys in his hand
(14 sec.). Cut to an extreme close-up of the keys, as Alex after a pause
throws them down on his dresser (2 sec.). Cut to a medium shot of a
big grandfather's clock showing midnight (familiar from before the party).
Dissolve to a closer shot of the same clock just striking six a.m. (4

sec.). Dissolve to a medium shot of Alex in bed, not sleeping, he turns on his side. Quick insert of the other bed with Alicia. Cut back to Alex getting up, he puts on his robe and walks away from the camera, which starts dollying after him as he approaches the dresser (22 sec.). Cut to an extreme close-up of the keys, with the UNICA key back on the chain (3 sec.). Dissolve to Alex walking through the wine cellar door toward the camera (opposite movement); the camera dollies back as Alex comes to the rack of bottles in a medium shot. He looks at them and walks away while still looking around. All seems to be in order (18 sec.).

Cut to a medium high shot of the sink with remains of water (half a sec.). Cut back to Alex looking intrigued. Getting tense he walks back to the rack with the bottles (6 sec.). Cut to a close shot of the labels on the bottles as the camera pans from one to the other; Alex's finger checks each label: 1934, 1934, 1940, camera stops here (6 sec.). Cut to a reverse close-up of Alex's face seen from inside the rack and in between the bottles (1 1/2 sec.), a rather unusual angle that, in turn, starts an unusual triad of shots. Cut to a reverse tight close-up of the neck of the bottle kept in Alex's hands horizontally with sand seen inside (2 sec.); the bottle faces to the *left* of the frame. Cut to another reverse shot of Alex and the same bottle in a medium close shot; the bottle now faces to the *right* of the frame. Something is disturbing him; he moves the bottle around (5 sec.). Cut to an extreme close-up of the top of the neck of the bottle (this time facing center), Alex fingers the makeshift cover (1 sec). The above triad with graphics pointing in opposite directions is a classical example of achieving a strong cinematic effect via counterpoints. I shall return to this at the final evaluation. Cut to a medium shot of Alex with the bottle in his hands. He removes the fake cork cover and looks down to the floor; camera also moves down (music peaks and stops). Alex's hands reach under the rack where he finds the grains of metal ore, debris of glass, and finally the broken part of a bottle with the label 1934. Camera moves into a tight close-up, the number 1934 filling the whole frame (14 sec.). Again, as in previous scenes, the climax is at the same time a slight release of tension because of the longer duration shot (after a crescendo of brief fragmentation).

As is often in Hitchcock's films, we observe here, in detail, the resolution of a puzzle that is well known to the viewer, yet which had been, till this moment, a puzzle to the main character. Only now does Alex know with painful finality that his wife is a spy. What is more, Hitchcock is able to shift, if only briefly, the viewer's sympathy toward Alex—a negative character in the film, after all. Presently, to illustrate more vividly Alex's pain, Hitchcock assigns to it the most powerful and original shot in the film: a shot without cuts, a complex crane camera movement that lasts seventeen seconds, starting with an already familiar high long shot from the balcony looking down to the big hall (music starts again). Alex, seen from above, enters the doorway (after coming up from the cellar), walks to the big stairway (so far never scaled in toto by anyone in the film), and walks resolutely up all the stairs, his shadow prominent on the wall; the camera lifts with him and at the same time moves in closer, until Alex reaches the top landing, in close-up.

This extravagant structure is not in any way a gratuitous or grandiloquent statement, nor a show of cinematic gymnastics. Neither is it calling attention to the camera per se, despite the rather elaborate technique employed in its execution. In a smooth and modest way Hitchcock eases in here a most elegant and eloquent cinematic structure that speaks volumes (without the help of dialogue) about the condition of the betrayed Alex Sebastian. A great part of the success lies in the fact that several elements of this shot were deliberately introduced before: the high long shot looking down to the big hallway was seen on at least four occasions; the stairway was seen half a dozen times, each time briefly, as people walked up or down (for a few steps only); craning shots were used to some extent in several scenes; and, finally, the technique of enlarging image size through mise-en-scène, as actors approach the camera, was used in many scenes. In this shot all of it comes together, resounding as if with cinematic trumpets. The shot is self-contained and powerful; in a sense, the impact defies words since it is a purely visual experience. To paraphrase it, without any pretence of rendering full justice to the intensity of that impact: we observe from high above a small, crushed man, ascending in desperation the elegant stairway, and, upon reaching the upper landing, showing his tortured face as he comes closer and closer.

This Hitchcockian oratory is an exercise in counterpoint for, in the next scene (28), Alex Sebastian shows his real colors, as a weakling, a mother's boy, and eventually a conspirator in a crime to kill his wife. The short-lived sympathy for him turns into a quickly dissipating memory.

Scene 28. Dramatically powerful, it keeps up the momentum of the previous scene. In addition, the film noticeably picks up speed. The scene starts with a dissolve to (shot 1) a long shot of a bedroom. Alex is seated in a stuffed chair in the background; his mother is sleeping in a bed in the foreground. We hear him address her meekly: "Mother" (4 sec.). This shot is an introduction to a complex separation sequence. Cut to (shot 2) a medium shot of Alex in a devastating double profile (his reflected profile visible in a mirror) (3 1/2 sec.). Cut to (shot 3) a reverse long shot of the mother in bed; she stirs and, upon seeing her son, asks why he is up so early. She projects an exceptionally frightening image. Cut to (shot 4) a slightly low medium shot of Alex, closer and three-quarters to the front. He asks his mother for help (3 sec.). Cut to (shot 5) a medium shot of the mother sitting up in bed; she is, as always, ready to help: "Is there something wrong?" she asks in her heavy German accent (2 sec.). Cut to (shot 6) a medium close shot of Alex, from a bit of a higher angle. He mumbles: "Alicia." Cut to (shot 7) a closer medium shot, from a lower angle of the mother, deviously smiling: "I knew it, I knew it. . . . Is it Mr. Devlin?" (11 1/2 sec.). Cut to (shot 8) a very high close-up of Alex looking down; at the start we see only the top of his head; finally he lifts his head and delivers his tragic line: "I'm married to an American spy" (10 sec.). Cut to (shot 9) a closer medium shot of the mother. She digests this devastating news, taking her time. In this painfully long-lasting shot we see her reaching for her cigarette (without looking for it), then for a lighter, and finally she lights it (25 sec.). Dissolve to (shot 10) a brief long shot insert of Alicia sleeping in her bedroom (5 sec.). Note that the ongoing separation is thus interrupted, evidently in order to allow for the deletion, during which Alex and his mother made progress in discussing the present dilemma. Dissolve back to the separation (shot 11), a low angle medium shot of the mother sitting on her bed; she is actively in charge: "They must have picked her because of her father." Cut to (shot 12) a slight high angle long shot of Alex sitting in the corner of a couch: "I must have been insane. . . . What do I do now. . . . I'm finished, they'll find out . . ." (6 sec.). (Notice how the shots are swinging from high angle to low). Cut to (shot 13) a medium shot, slightly low angle, of the mother sitting on the bed, leaning forward: "They won't find out" (2 sec.—an exceptionally short duration shot; the mother was assigned until now much longer duration shots than Alex). Cut to (shot 14) a medium long shot of Alex still on the couch (slightly low angle and farther away than shot 12). He keeps on the same track: "There is no excuse." Alex gets up from the couch and walks forward. He sits down on the edge of the bed; camera retreats, keeping him in medium shot (9 sec.). Cut to (shot 15) a low medium close shot of his mother listening (1 sec.). Cut to (shot 16) a high angle close-up of Alex in left profile: "I'd do it myself, kill the fool" (12 sec.). Cut to (shot 17) a medium close shot of the mother saying resolutely: "They'll never think that you're married to an agent" (2 sec.). Cut to (shot 18) the same close shot of Alex who keeps bemoaning in the same defeatist tune (3 sec.). Cut (shot 19) back to the same medium close shot of the mother, who retorts: "You're protected by the enormity of your stupidity" (10 sec.). Cut to (shot 20) the same profile medium shot of Alex, who says that he'll take care of Alicia (2 sec.). Cut (shot 21) back to same low angle shot of Alex's mother, cigarette in her mouth, who continues to put on her robe (1 1/2 sec.). Cut (shot 22) back to the same profile of Alex; he holds his head in his hand in distress; he doesn't know what to do (7 sec.). Cut to (shot 23) a long duration shot that represents the resolution to the separation. The mother, in medium shot profile, cigarette still in her mouth, is getting out of bed; she walks over to where Alex is sitting, passes in front of him (notice Hitchcock's repeated use of this kind of passing of one character in front of another one), and eventually sits down on the other side of him. During her walk over she states with determination: ". . . Let me arrange this one . . ." The camera finally pulls back to accommodate the two in one shot (the resolution of the separation). The mother presents her scheme: "Listen to me. There must be no suspicion of her or you. She must be allowed to move freely, but she'll be on a leash. She could become ill and remain ill for a time . . . until . . ."; her voice is hung up in mid-sentence, music stops (27 sec.). Cut to (shot 24) a close-up of Alex totally hypnotized by his mother; he seems to agree with the plan (10 sec.). Dissolve. (Again a scene ends with a close-up of one character.) The sense of an ending is felt, an ominous realization that in one way or another the drama is coming to a *finis*. The hung-up voice of the mother, a rather strange sublimation in a realistic scene, and the final close-up of Alex is, perhaps, the trigger for such a feeling; but, most likely, the cumulative effect of the last three scenes is what adds up to this almost visceral sense of an impending closure.

Scene 29. Fade-in, long shot: Alicia is sitting between Alex on her right and Alex's mother on the left. Not without a slight touch of perverse irony Hitchcock is showing us a peaceful family tableau. They are gathered around a table in the garden for coffee and small talk. Without a cut the camera moves closer to Alex, then quickly pans along the table to a high close-up of one cup of coffee as Alicia's hand picks it up and brings it to her lips (camera moves up) and drinks it. After a short hold the camera moves to the left toward the mother who is attentively knitting. This brief scene, as we see, comes directly to the point and in accordance with what we learnt previously of the mother's scheme to make Alicia ill. The fast camera movement seeks out angrily the source of the illness. The terseness of this revelation takes away the edge of its potential grossness.

Scene 30. Dissolve to a close-up of Alicia (after a deletion) dressed differently. Cut to a wide two-shot of Captain Prescott and Alicia, both sitting on a large couch. The unexpected appearance of Prescott is an unusual form of slow disclosure in that it is executed via a cut, not through the usual camera pull-back. The reason Hitchcock chose the unusual form in this case can be traced to his orchestration: this scene must have cuts since the previous one did not. Indeed, the scene has the classical structure of a separation bracketed with two-shots at each end. The introductory close-up of Alicia shows her suffering from a severe headache. Prescott in the two-shot: "I think you should be proud of yourself Mrs. [he hesitates] . . . Sebastian. That sand that Devlin brought in shows uranium ore. So now we know what we are driving at. Your job from now on would be to find out where it comes from, the location of the uranium deposit. But that isn't the main reason I asked you to come up. I wanted to tell you I'm going to change your contact in a week. Mr. Devlin has been transferred to Spain." Cut to a close-up of Alicia: "Spain? Does Mr. Devlin know that?" Close-up of Prescott: "Oh, yes, he asked for the transfer." Close-up of Alicia: "Why?" Cut to a medium close shot of Prescott: "I guess he. . . ." Cut to a close-up of Alicia, listening. Cut to the same medium close shot of Prescott: "I guess he finds Spain more interesting." Cut to the same close-up of Alicia: "I guess there isn't very much for a brainy

fellow like Mr. Devlin to do in Rio any more." Cut to a close-up of Prescott: "Oh he's . . . it is more . . ." Cut to the same close-up of Alicia: "In the meantime, I'm to report to Mr. Devlin as usual?" Cut to the same close shot of Prescott: "Oh, yes, he'll be here until the new man arrives." Cut to a two-shot (the separation is thus resolved); they both get up. Alicia: "I'll keep my two eyes wide open. Good-bye." Prescott follows her to the door with his "Good-bye." Dissolve. (Total length of scene—65 sec.) Inasmuch as we just learned that Devlin is to leave soon, we feel even more that closure is at hand.

Scene 31. Dissolve to a close shot of an almost empty cup of coffee, an ominous reminder; the camera lifts from the cup of coffee to a long shot of the backs of Alicia and Alex walking down some steps in the garden. Alicia suddenly has a spell of dizziness and seems to be collapsing. Cut on action to a medium shot that also includes Dr. Anderson, who walks over to help her. To his question as to what happened, Alex mutters something about her being "just striken," and Alicia says, "I don't know," and after a pause, "I'll be all right"; music starts. Dr. Anderson is visibly concerned. Dissolve. This brief scene telegraphs instantly that the poison has started working, but this information is for the benefit of the viewers only, since Alicia and her American friends are, so far, ignorant of it. Nevertheless, it also contributes to the mounting feeling of closure. Hitchcock will continue playing on the delayed status of who knows what for the next few scenes until the final one, when full disclosure takes place.

Scene 32. Dissolve to a street scene (the dramatic music from the previous scene continues). Dissolve to a medium long shot of Alicia walking shakily; she approaches Devlin who is sitting on a bench. She sits down at the end of the bench with ample space between them and starts small talk. Separation starts with a more open frame for Devlin and tighter close-ups of Alicia, whose beautifully lit and photographed image is contrasted with occasional rear projection activities of passersby. The construction is that of a classical separation (as in Scene 30 with Prescott), a series of singles bracketed by a long shot introduction and a two-shot conclusion. From her appearance we gather that Alicia is on a downhill slide. Although she feels sick, she still doesn't know or does not suspect the poison. At present she plays the old tease game with Devlin. Provoked by his statement that she doesn't look too hot, ". . . sick?" she answers "No . . . hangover." Devlin: "Back to the bottle again?" Alicia: "Sort of . . . lightens my chores." Alicia tries desperately, knowing that he is to be transferred from Rio, hoping he will confess . . . but to no avail. Devlin keeps harping at her for having fun, drinking. Finally Alicia, hardly in control of her malaise, hands back to Devlin the scarf he gave her in Miami (before their car ride). Devlin retorts: "Cleaning house, eh?" Alicia, after a long pause: "Good-bye now." This is the last of the close-ups (22 in toto). She gets up into a medium two-shot. Devlin, who remains seated, asks: "What do you mean, good-bye?" Alicia, standing: "Just good-bye. Fresh air isn't good for hangovers." Devlin: "Sit down. You're still tight." This is the resolution of the separation. Now come the extra four close-ups to end the scene. Alicia in close shot: "I don't want to." Devlin in close-up: "Where are you going?" Alicia, close-up: "Back . . . home." Cut to a close-up of Devlin in profile as she passes in front of him (in low close-up); Devlin is looking with concern (3 sec.). The scene ends in double symmetry: a single shot of character and a pass in front of a character. (The length of the whole scene is 98 sec.)

Scene 33. Fade-in, medium long shot in the parlor room: Alicia, Alex, Alex's mother, and Dr. Anderson (standing) around a coffee table (this is the third coffee-drinking scene since the poisoning was initiated). An elaborate camera movement, curving and moving in, is in progress:

camera at first approaches the mother, who pours coffee into a cup as
we hear offscreen Dr. Anderson inquiring about Alicia's health. It worries him; she looks sick; she should see a doctor. Alicia, offscreen: "I
never go near doctors. They always want to cart you away to a hospital." Dr. Anderson, offscreen: "Maybe you belong in a hospital" (a
significant expression that will reverberate at the end of the film). While
we hear this exchange Alex's mother has finished pouring the coffee;
she picks up the cup; camera follows in to a close-up; as the cup is
placed on the table, the mother's hand withdraws. Dr. Anderson's offscreen voice continues: "Tell me, when did you first feel sick?" Camera tilts up from cup of coffee to Alicia's face in close-up (it is a bit of
a surprise to realize that the coffee *was* indeed intended for Alicia).
Alicia answers weakly: "Oh, I don't remember. Maybe the party, I
think." This long duration shot that lasts forty seconds is followed by
a no less elaborate multiangular construction with an extremely dis-
ciplined pattern of repetitions in triads.

Cut to (shot 2) a medium shot of Alex in his chair with a bunch of
travel leaflets in his hands. He quickly interrupts with a suggestion
that perhaps the best for Alicia would be a trip by boat, maybe to Spain
(by curious coincidence, Devlin is to be transferred to Spain) (10 sec.).
Cut to (shot 3) a low medium two-shot of Alicia and Dr. Anderson who
is leaning over. We see the foreboding cup of coffee in front of her.
Alicia answers Alex's suggestion: "I don't think so. I don't care much
for boats" (3 sec.). Cut to (shot 4) a medium shot of the mother sitting
behind two pots of coffee (one presumably has the poisoned brew). She
addresses Alicia: "We could go together, my dear . . . if you could bear
to leave Alex behind for a few weeks" (6 sec.). Cut back to (shot 5) the
two-shot of Alicia and Dr. Anderson. After a remark by Alicia about
her tendency to seasickness Dr. Anderson proposes that she go to the
mountains where he's going in a week. Alicia: "Oh, you're leaving?
I'm sorry. I'll miss you" (22 sec.). Cut back (shot 6) to the same medium shot of Alex who worriedly listens to Dr. Anderson, lest he tell
too much to Alicia. Dr. Anderson's voice offscreen: "I'm delaying my
work too long. If you'll come with me . . ." (5 sec.). Cut to (shot 7)
the third and final repeat of the two-shot (triad) of Alicia and Dr.
Anderson as he continues: "The mountains won't make you seasick
and the Amarest Mountains are beautiful . . ." (8 sec.). Cut to (shot

8) a third repeat of the medium shot of Alex (triad) who cuts into Anderson's sentence: "What Alicia needs is rest, not mountain climbing" (4 sec.).

Cut to (shot 9) a low medium shot of Alicia and Dr. Anderson (from a more frontal angle). Alicia: "I've heard of the Amarest." Dr. Anderson: "Did you, really?" Alicia picks up her cup of coffee and starts sipping (5 sec.). Cut to a (shot 10) close shot (first in this scene) of Alex watching Alicia (1 1/2 sec.).Cut to (shot 11) a close-up of Alicia drinking coffee; she lowers her cup and says: "Yes." Cut to (shot 12) a third repeat of the medium shot of the mother also looking at Alicia (the conspirators are on the watch) (1 3/4 sec.). Cut to (shot 13) a repeat of the frontal two-shot of Dr. Anderson and Alicia (as in shot 9) who puts her cup on the table and continues: ". . . little native towns. Tell me, are you going to Leopodonna?" Dr. Anderson: "No, I'm going to Santa Ma . . ." (7 sec.)—he is cut off by Alex. Cut to (shot 14) repeat of the close-up of Alex: "Care for some brandy, Otto?" (2 sec.). (The conspirators are on guard, making sure that Alicia does not get any new information.) Cut to (shot 15) a repeat of Alicia's close-up. She notices Alex's maneuver. She looks at Anderson and then to Alex (3 1/2 sec.). Anderson's voice offscreen: "No, no, thank you" (a reply to Alex).

Cut to (shot 16) a third and final repeat of the frontal two-shot of Alicia and Dr. Anderson who, without intending it, is just about to reach for Alicia's cup of coffee while continuing: "I never drink more than one brandy and even this is sometimes too much. I'll just finish my coffee" (5 sec.). Cut to (shot 17) a close-up of the two cups of coffee; Anderson's hand lifts one cup out of frame (1 sec.). Cut to (shot 18) a medium long shot of Alex and his mother practically jumping out of their seats to caution Dr. Anderson (an unavoidable allusion to a scene in *Hamlet*). Mother: "No, that is . . ." Alex: "Oh, but that's Al . . ." (1 1/2 sec.). Cut to (shot 19) a close-up of Alicia. She notices the panic; she looks down at the coffee, then at the mother and Alex (2 1/2 sec.). Cut to (shot 20) a high medium long shot of Alicia and Dr. Anderson, who replaces the cup and says: "Oh, I'm sorry" (1 1/2 sec.). Cut to (shot 21) a repeat of Alicia's close-up. She is now digesting her discovery, looking penetratingly at the two conspirators and again at the cup of coffee. Dr. Anderson's voice offscreen: "Perhaps Alex is right, my dear child. When you are young, rest is the best doctor" (7 sec.). Cut to (shot 22) a close-up of the cup and saucer. Dr. Anderson offscreen: "and if you . . ." (2 sec.).

Cut to (shot 23) a repeat of Alicia's close shot; she turns her gaze to where the mother sits. Dr. Anderson continues offscreen: ". . . lie still for a few days, reading, relaxing . . ." (6 sec.). Cut to (shot 24) a medium shot of the mother; camera dollies in to a close shot of her. Dr. Anderson continues (offscreen) ". . . forgetting all your troubles . . ." (2 sec.). Cut back to (shot 25) the close-up of Alicia's face more intense. Dr. Anderson continues offscreen: ". . . it might be as good as medicine or . . ." (3 sec.). Cut to a medium shot of Alex, camera dollies in to a close-up of him. Dr. Anderson's voice: ". . . sea air . . ." (1 1/2 sec.). Cut to (shot 27) the fourth repeat of Alicia's close-up; she closes her eyes and, as if in a trance, starts trembling. Dr. Anderson's voice continues: "And when I come back you will be all well, making us very happy once more" (5 sec.). Cut to a higher angle two-shot of Dr. Anderson and Alicia, who struggles to get up; she leans on a chair; Dr. Anderson helps her; camera dollies to a close-up of her, as she mutters: "Excuse me, I want to go to bed. I feel . . ." (9 sec.). Cut to (shot 29) a brief shot of Alex as his mother enters his frame (in long shot); both watch Alicia. Alex (as if from a distance): "Pain again, darling?" (1 1/2 sec.). Cut back to Alicia's close-up as she looks toward where Alex stands (3 sec.). Cut to (shot 31) a long shot of Alex and his mother standing as before; the background light begins to brighten until the two figures become silhouetted, slowly go out of focus, and stretch, as in a distorting mirror. Alex: "Shall I take you up to your room?" (echo-like sound) (4 sec.). Cut to (shot 32) the same close-up of Alicia looking as if in a daze (1 1/2 sec.). Cut to (shot 33) the third repeat of the silhouetted figures of Alex and his mother; the shadow-like images keep twisting in distortion as they seem to walk toward the camera. Echo of the mother's voice: "May I help you, my dear? Some hot water, maybe?" (5 sec.). Cut back to Alicia's close-up (shot 34). She looks, then covers her face with her hands; she slowly lowers her hands one at a time, turns to camera and starts advancing, as camera dollies back at her pace. Alicia, with echoing voice: "No, no, please . . . don't bother . . . I'll be all right" (9 sec.). Cut back to (shot 35) the shadow figures superimposed over doors as the camera keeps moving toward them (in simulation of Alicia's walk) (2 1/2 sec.). Cut back to (shot 36) a repeat

of Alicia in close-up still walking forward as camera dollies back
(1 1/2 sec.). Cut back to (shot 37) camera dollying to the door with the
shadow figures twisting and growing larger. The doorway is hardly rec-
ognizable as the camera crowds in closer. Dr. Anderson's voice in a
distant echo: "If you don't feel better in the morning, I insist you call
a doctor. I don't like the way she looks, Alex. I'm worried . . ." (The
music that starts in shot 21 when Alicia realizes that she is being poisoned increases in volume covering Dr. Anderson's voice) (3 1/2 sec.).
Cut to (shot 38) a reverse shot of the other side of the door as Alicia
opens it and walks in; camera moves slightly back, keeping her in a
medium close-up. She keeps on looking, ever so intensely (8 sec.). Cut
to (shot 39) a long shot of double doors, out of focus and twisting
(1 1/2 sec.). Cut back to (shot 40) a repeat of Alicia's close-up; she turns
her look from left (where the doors are) to screen right. She is unsteady
on her feet (3 1/2 sec.). Cut to (shot 41) a long shot of the familiar big
stairway across the hall, in and out of focus and twisting (2 1/2 sec.).
Cut to (shot 42) another repeat of Alicia's close-up; her eyes closed,
she tries to keep her balance while walking forward; camera dollies
backward (5 1/2 sec.). Cut to (shot 43) medium shot of the bottom of
the stairway as camera dollies in; focus changes and stairs are "twisting" (2 1/2 sec.). Cut to (shot 44) a repeat of Alicia's close-up; she
stops; unable to stand, she starts falling back (5 sec.). Cut to (shot 45)
a high long shot looking down to the hallway as Alicia collapses at the
bottom of the stairway. Alex and the mother come into view from screen
right; Dr. Anderson and Joseph come quickly to Alicia's aid, putting
her on her feet and helping her to climb the stairs. Camera cranes down,
keeping them in view. Alex and his mother look on (25 sec.). Cut on
action to (shot 46) a medium close-up of Alicia supported by Dr.
Anderson (on the right) and Joseph (on the left); camera moves back
with them (1 1/2 sec.). Cut to (shot 47) a brief close-up of Alex looking
(at Alicia); he also seems to be climbing the stairs (1 1/2 sec.). Cut to
(shot 48) a repeat of the medium close-up of Alicia with a glimpse of
Dr. Anderson at her side. She anxiously glances to where Alex is;
frightened, she exclaims (already at the top of the stairs): "No, no, go
. . . go away! No-no." She passes camera (5 sec.). Cut to (shot 49) a
close shot of the mother who crosses the camera's view; camera starts
panning; we see the mother joining the rest of the group around a pil-

lar; eventually we see her approach the door to Alicia's bedroom as Alex begins to open it (6 sec.).

Cut to (shot 50) a reverse medium long shot inside the bedroom (on action of the opening of the door). Dr. Anderson and Joseph help Alicia to her bed; camera pans with their movement. The frame is busy. Alex is by the door; the mother twice crosses the camera's view in both directions, bossing as usual; the camera in the meantime follows Alicia as she is lowered onto her pillow. Dr. Anderson: "We must get a doctor. The poor child is suffering too much." Alex and his mother enter the frame. They place themselves on each side of Alicia in prominent profiles. Dr. Anderson (offscreen): "I'll call the hospital and get a doc . . ." The mother cuts in: "Don't worry, dear Otto. We'll get a doctor. A good one who can take the very best care of her." Camera continues to move in on Alicia and stops on a tight close-up. She shifts her eyes from Alex to the mother in total surrender. Alex's voice offscreen: "Joseph, disconnect the telephone. Madame must have absolute quiet. Take it out of the room, Joseph." This is the second longest duration shot in the scene (32 sec.) in symmetry with the starting shot (1—39 sec.). Both beginning and ending shots are built with camera movements only. The symmetry goes even farther if one considers that a single shot of Devlin brackets this scene on both ends: his is the last shot of the previous scene, sitting on a bench, and the present scene dissolves into a shot of Devlin waiting fruitlessly for Alicia, also on a bench. The whole scene is built with apparent simplicity but vigorously constructed with designated repetitions, mostly within the element of multiangularity, similar to the drunken driving scene. The narrative contains only one new bit of information: the location of the mountain where, presumably, Dr. Anderson mines his uranium. Remarkably, Alicia, who is already consumed by poison, still has the presence of mind to do her spying. All the rest is an elaboration on information already known to the viewer. Hitchcock excells in such elaborations (of the already known).

The lengths of shots shows a typical Hitchcockian rhythmic pattern: long duration shots punctuate the beginning and the end of the scene, while in between are crowded quick fragmentations in a multiangular checkerboard. The most numerous are the seventeen shots of three seconds or less in length; next are the shots of six seconds or

less (13); then shots of ten seconds or less (9); finally the four shots of longer duration (20 sec. or more). The center of attention in the first shot (39 sec.) is the ominous cup of coffee, the final destination of the camera dolly; the consequence of that threat, Alicia helplessly in bed, is seen in a dolly-in to the victim, in the last shot of the scene (32 sec.). The distorted imagery seen by Alicia is reminiscent of the distortions in the beginning of the film after the drunken driving (Devlin upside-down). The sense of an ending is being felt more strongly; however, Hitchcock is taking a slightly delaying tack (total length of the scene is 3 minutes).

The next two shots do not represent scenes even though they take place in different locations (which was my method of determining divisions into scenes). They are, in fact, transitions leading eventually to the final scene of the film; they also reaffirm the strict linearity of the narrative. From Alicia's tortured close-up in bed (Scene 33), dissolve to a long shot of Devlin sitting on the same bench as before, next to a small park in Rio; he presumably is waiting for Alicia. Cut to a long shot of Alicia in her bed; camera pans to the right where Alex's mother is knitting in her chair and, as we see, keeping watch on Alicia. Dissolve to an exterior at night; Devlin is pacing back and forth in front of the bench, still waiting. (The music is loud during these two transitional shots. The length of the transitions totals 13 sec.).

Scene 34. Cut to an interior: in a medium two-shot we see Prescott lying on a couch and manicuring his nails; Devlin is standing next to him; they talk about Alicia. Cut to a close shot of Devlin (start of separation) who continues: "That drinking of hers, I don't believe it." Cut to a medium shot of Prescott: "Why should she lie to you?" Devlin's voice offscreen: "She wasn't drunk, she was sick." Cut to the same close shot of Devlin: "Maybe that's why she hasn't shown up." Prescott offscreen: ". . . It sounds like a hangover to me." Cut to the same close shot of Devlin: "I'm going to pay her a call." Cut to the medium shot of Prescott: "I don't want you to mess things up. We ought to close this case in a few days." Cut to Devlin's close shot: "I won't mess things up. Just a social call. I'm a friend of the family." Cut to Prescott's medium shot: "Ah, well, go ahead if you want to. Don't take any chances . . .", he continues his manicuring. Cut to a medium two-shot (separation is resolved), Prescott continues: "Oh, call me up when you're back." Devlin: "I'll do that;" as he leaves Prescott looks after. Fade-out (33 sec.).

Scene 35. Fade-in to long shot: taxi arriving at the familiar mansion of Alex Sebastian. Devlin leaves the taxi and starts up the stairs toward the entrance door. Cut to interior hallway; Joseph opens the door. Devlin enters in medium shot. They both stand at the still open entrance door. Camera moves in on Devlin to a close shot. Devlin: "I'm sorry to hear that. How long has she been ill?" Joseph offscreen: "About a week." Devlin: "Has she had a doctor?" Joseph offscreen: "I think so. We're all concerned about her. If you will wait here, Mr. Devlin, I'll tell Mr. Sebastian . . ." Devlin: "Right." Joseph crosses in front of (sic) Devlin and leaves the frame; Devlin takes two steps forward to a tighter close-up. Cut to a medium reverse shot of large doors opening; in steps Joseph (a typical slow disclosure; we assume it is Alex Sebastian's office). Alex offscreen: "What is it Joseph?" Cut to a long shot of the office; the group of familiar Germans, with Alex at the desk, are in conference. Offscreen voice of Joseph: "Mr. Devlin to see you." Cut to a medium close-up of Alex: "Oh . . . tell him I'll be with him in a minute." Cut back to the same medium shot of Joseph at the door: "Yes, sir." He exits. Cut back to the previous long shot of the conference. Alex: "Go on, Professor, this sounds serious to me." Eric Matisse, the good-looking Nazi (whom we remember from the first part of the film), standing in three-quarter profile in the foreground interrupts: "Serious to me too. Tell us what happened Monday." Dr. Anderson, standing next to the desk: "When I left the bank a man was following me. The next day I saw the same man beside me." Cut to a close shot of Alex attentively listening. Cut to a low close shot of Eric Matisse in prominent and threatening profile walking slowly and looking at Alex. Cut to a high three-quarter profile of Alex, worried. (Note that the succession of the last two shots is the only indication that Eric Matisse was looking at Alex!) Cut to a medium shot of Devlin sitting in the hallway; he looks up. (Again the succession of those two shots suggests that Alex may be worried about the role of Devlin in the spy affair.) Cut to what Devlin sees (a rare true POV shot): a long shot of the stairway and the upper landing. We see the mother walking from one set of doors and entering another room (presumably her own bedroom).

Cut back to the same medium shot of Devlin still looking up; he gets up (like a man who has made a decision). Music starts; Devlin walks to the stairway; camera follows; he starts running up the stairs by twos. Cut to a reverse medium long shot: Devlin takes the last three steps, reaching the upper landing; he goes around the pillar (familiar from previous scenes). Camera stops following him; he hesitates for a moment, then moves to a door and starts to open it. Cut to a reverse angle medium shot inside the room as Devlin enters through the door (in darkish light). Cut to a long shot; someone is moving in the bed. Cut to the medium shot of Devlin as he rushes forward. Cut to an extreme close-up of Alicia on her pillow, looking ill (she is lit by the side lamp). Cut to a long shot of Devlin approaching toward camera. Cut back to the same extreme close-up of Alicia looking up. Cut to a medium shot of Devlin in profile. He lowers his face to Alicia's; camera follows until they form a tight two-shot. Alicia tries to touch his hand with hers. Devlin whispers: "Alicia, Alicia, what's wrong with you?" Alicia in a weak voice: "I'm glad you came." Devlin (his cheek touches hers, partially covering her face): "I had to. I couldn't stand it anymore." (Alicia's other hand touches Devlin's head.) He continues: "It wasn't a hangover the other day. You were sick then?" She mumbles something. Devlin: "What's wrong with you, Alicia?" She: "They are poisoning me. I couldn't get away." Devlin suddenly lifts his face: "Sure, when?" Alicia, on her white pillow, clearly lit by the side lamp: "Since the party, Alex and his mother . . . they found out. . . ." Devlin puts his hand under her head. He lifts her up to a sitting po-

sition. Camera follows them both in close-up profile. Devlin: "Sit up. I'll try to get you out of here" (so far the scene lasts 2 1/2 min.). Alicia: "I thought you had gone." Devlin keeps lifting her to her feet. He: "No, I had to see you again. I was to leave Rio because I love you. I couldn't stand seeing you with him." Cut to a tight two-shot close-up. She kisses him and whispers: "You love me? Why didn't you tell me before?" He: "I know. I couldn't see straight. I was thick headed." Camera executes a circular movement around their locked faces as they kiss each others' cheeks. Alicia: "You love me; you love me." He: "Long ago, all the time, since the beginning." Cut to a medium two-shot. He helps her put on a robe. Alicia: "I'm afraid I can't make it. They gave me pills to sleep." He: "Keep awake; keep talking." He helps her dress; he kisses her. Devlin leaves frame to get her coat from a closet. Camera stays on her, moving back a little; she looks pathetic. Devlin comes back to the two-shot with her coat. She tells him some details of Alex's discovery: "The rest of the crew don't know about it or they would kill him, like Emil." They start walking toward the door. She tells him about the mountains where the uranium is mined. He: "Good girl. We'll hear about that later." They reach the door. Alicia: "But I'm afraid they're all in the house." Cut to a wider angle: with the sweep of the door opening, the light of the upper landing rushes in.

Cut back to Devlin and Alicia in medium close-up, walking; camera follows. Alicia: "Don't ever leave me." Devlin: "You'll never get rid

of me again, Alicia." Cut to a medium shot of Alex walking up the
steps, seen through the balustrade. Cut back to the medium two-shot
of Alicia and Devlin, walking, camera follows. Devlin, who must have
noticed him, says: "Brace up, here he comes." Cut back to the medium
shot of Alex walking up the stairs. Cut to a closer two-shot of Alicia
helped by Devlin as they pass behind a column (familiar). The column
obscures a cut to a tighter shot of the two as they emerge (very brief).
Cut back to a close shot of Alex who has not reached the upper landing: "What is it? What are you doing, Mr. Devlin?" Cut to a tighter
low two-shot of Alicia and Devlin: "I'm taking her to the hospital to
take the poison out of her." Cut back to the close-up of Alex: "Poison?" Cut back to the low two-shot, Devlin: "How would you like
your friends downstairs to know?" As Devlin talks, cut to a medium
long shot of the mother coming out of her bedroom door, still fastening
her robe; Devlin offscreen: "Maybe they should be told." Cut to a wider
medium shot of Alex entering the frame, crossing over in front of Devlin
and Alicia. He stands close to Alicia, reaching for her as he says: "I'm
taking her back to her room." Devlin, who stands on the left side of
the frame, responds with cool determination: "I'll raise a rumpus if you
try." He reaches with his right hand to the side pocket of his jacket
(presumably for his gun). The mother suddenly enters frame from the
background; her head is between Alex's and Alicia's as Alex looks at
Devlin's hand; the mother cuts in: "He knows?" Alex: "Yes" (so far

the scene has lasted 4 1/2 minutes). Offscreen voice from below: "What's happening Alex?"

Cut to a high long shot looking down to the entrance hall. We see Dr. Anderson and the other Germans looking up. Dr. Anderson is taking a few steps forward. Cut to a close two-shot of Devlin holding Alicia; offscreen Dr. Anderson's voice: "Is she worse?" The mother answers "Yes." Cut to a brief close-up of Alex exchanging a glance with Devlin (presumably). Cut to the same close two-shot of Alicia and Devlin. Cut to a close-up of Alex looking precariously at the two; he takes his first step down the stairs. (Note that during the descent of the group, the camera will follow them down in *all* the shots, until they come to the hall.) Cut back to the high long shot of the Germans below. Cut to the close-up of Alex going down a few more steps; he shifts his look from Devlin down to the Germans. Cut to a tight close-up of the mother as she also descends the steps and says, whispering: "Help her, Alex." Cut to the same close-up of Alex as he turns to where Alicia and Devlin are. Cut back to the familiar close two-shot of Alicia and Devlin, who says: "I'm glad you have a head on you, Madame." Cut back to the same close-up of Alex still walking down the steps;

he turns and says: "I'm not afraid to die." Cut back to the close shot of the mother, with desperation in her eyes (1/2 sec.). Cut back to the close two-shot of Alicia and Devlin, who ironically says: "Now you have your chance. Tell them what she did." Cut to the same close-up of Alex looking briefly down the stairs.

Cut to the high long shot of the Germans. Dr. Anderson inquires: "You need any help, Alex?" The camera moves a little closer to the Germans as our group descends. Cut to a medium shot of the four descending. (Note that this is the first variant in the fragmentation; till now it was rhymed with close shots and two-shots only.) Devlin answers Dr. Anderson's question: "No. We'll handle her." Cut to the Germans; camera comes closer but still is in long shot. Dr. Anderson: "Where are you taking her?" Cut back to the same medium shot of the four descending (1 1/2 sec.). Cut to the familiar close-up of Alex in a state of horror (1 sec.). Cut to the familiar close two-shot of Alicia and Devlin slowly descending the steps. Devlin: "You answer that, Sebastian" (1 1/2 sec.). Cut to the medium shot of the four; the mother quickly fills in: "To the hospital." Cut to the close-up of Alex walking in silence. Cut to the close two-shot of Alicia and Devlin looking down (to the Germans). Cut to the same close-up of Alex just about leaving the frame as he descends. Cut to the high long shot of the group of Germans; camera comes closer to them. (Note that the size of the image of the group of Germans is, in a sense, a measure of our protagonists' progress in their descent, since we see them only in close shots; the larger the Germans, the closer our four are to reaching the hallway.) Dr. Anderson: "I'm glad. You should have not waited so long, Alex." Cut to the close two-shot of Alicia and Devlin going down (1/2 sec.). Cut to the close-up of Alex walking down. Cut to Alicia and Devlin, close two-shot: Devlin: "What am I going to do . . . start shooting?" Cut to Alex's profile, tight-lipped (1/2 sec.). (Note that Alex is seen in most of the shots of descending in profile.) Cut to the mother with a look of despair on her face (1/2 sec.). Cut to Alex; close-up, descending. Cut to a low medium four-shot of the group. Cut to a close two-shot of Alicia and Devlin. He whispers to her: "Hold on, darling, we have only about twenty yards to go." Cut to an eye-level medium long shot of the Germans. Camera moves in closer. Eric Matisse asks: "What happened, Alex?" Cut back to the low medium four-shot of the group as Alex, startled by the question, mumbles: "Umm . . ." Cut to a three-quarter profile close shot of Eric waiting for an answer. Cut back to a close shot of Alex standing as if in a trance. He turns to Eric, manages an "Oh." Cut back to the close shot of Eric. Cut to the close shot of Alex who finally mumbles: "She collapsed . . ." Cut to the familiar close two-shot of Alicia and Devlin as Alex continues (offscreen) "Mr. Devlin heard her scream . . ." Cut to the close shot of Alex who continues: ". . . while he was waiting for me." Turning to Alicia: "Come, darling." Cut to the familiar four-shot. Devlin: "Yes, I telephoned the hospital, as soon as I saw how she was." Cut to a frontal close-up of Eric; he is tense; he walks two steps toward camera.

Cut to the four-shot (same as before) as Devlin and the group reach the bottom of the stairs; the mother asks: "Do you have a car, Mr. Devlin?" Devlin: "Yes, right in front." Mother: "Go ahead, Alex." Cut to a medium close shot of Eric walking over to the mother (forming a two-shot). He addresses her: "You're going with them, mother?" She: "No . . . Alex will call me up." Cut to a reverse angle long shot of Devlin with Alicia and Alex walking (seen from the back) toward the main door, already ajar, and a group of a few Germans around them. Cut to another reverse medium long shot seen from outside the house looking in as they exit (start of long duration shot). The camera retreats, keeping them in a three-shot, Alex on the right helping somehow, Devlin on the left with Alicia on his arm. They descend the front steps; the group of Germans stay in soft focus by the door. Devlin and Alicia approach the car; Alex opens the door; camera backs up (over the roof of the car) to the other side window (a reverse symmetry to a familiar maneuver from a previous scene with the car).

Cut to a medium shot of Eric Matisse and two other men looking down (to where the car is); they step forward. Cut to a medium long shot through the window of the car. The camera pans from the profile of Devlin by the window to Alex on the other side of the car imploring to be let in. Swish pan to a close-up of the door's safety lock as Devlin's hand pushes it down: "No room." Cut to a close-up of Alex banging on the window: "You must take me. They're watching me." Cut to a close-up profile of Devlin: "That's your headache." Cut to a close-up of Alicia with a weak smile on her face. The car moves away, out of frame; Alex stays in. Cut to a medium two-shot of Eric and one of the henchmen who tells him: "There's no telephone in her room to call the hospital." Cut to the same medium shot of Alex in a state of shock;

Eric's voice offscreen: "Alex, would you come up, please, I want to talk to you." Alex turns and slowly walks up the stairs. Camera adjusts to include the view of the Germans and the doorway in medium long shot. Alex reaches and crosses the door; they all enter inside; door closes; it's dark; music intensifies; even a sliver of light under the threshhold goes out; a natural fade-out. After a pause, an old fashioned title—The End—is superimposed over the dark door.

The length of the section of this scene covering the descent of the stairs is approximately sixty seconds. The whole scene (Scene 35) lasts almost six minutes. Seven set-ups are repeated. The most numerous in the repeats are close shots of Alex, seventeen in all—a rather unexpected statistical discovery. The next most frequent, quite predictably, is that of the close two-shot of Alicia and Devlin, totalling eleven. The shot of the whole group descending is repeated seven times; the Germans, who, as I already mentioned, are acting as some sort of clock for the progression of the group's descent, are repeated six times, to which we may add the seventh time when we see Eric Matisse in close up. The mother has only three shots. The whole scene contains fifty-three shots in toto. The most amazing factor is the use of the salvo of brief fragmentations during their descent that does not create, what would have been expected from it, a crescendo speed-up of action. The opposite happens, the descent remains slow.

What is remarkable about this scene is that it carries a powerful after-image of the protagonist's miraculous and daring liberation; and, even though the last shot of the film is of Alex walking to his certain doom, the central focus remains with the two lovers. By and large, in *Notorious* Hitchcock orchestrated an extensive network of such after-images, an invisible yet penetrating thread running through the film. The last scene is the strongest in the network, in addition to being an uplifting closure to this fascinating work of cinema art.

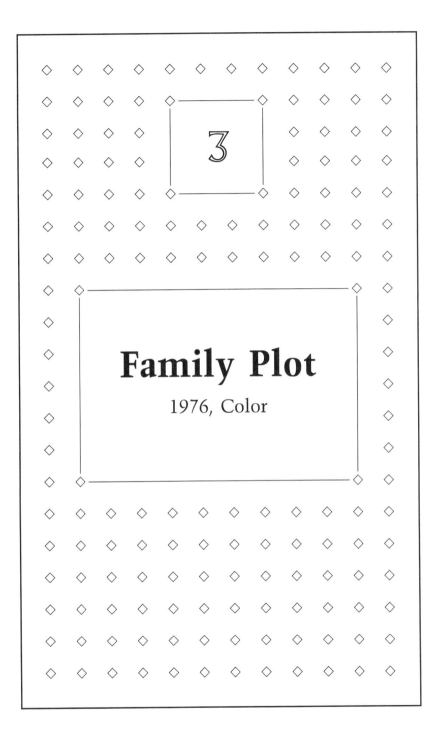

3

Family Plot

1976, Color

◇————————————◇

F_{AMILY PLOT} was the last film of the master before he died. As in *Frenzy*, here too Hitchcock was free to use the actors he wanted rather than the obligatory famous stars (Hollywood's hedge). The questions of reality, as a consequence of the above, are formidable.

I shall return to those later, but at the moment it's enough to state that *Family Plot* contains more believable situations, less accent on watching performances as such; there is a sense of life that exists outside the screen, even though Hitchcock persists in his strict fictionality and sublimates reality with a sense of humor seldom seen in suspense drama. *Family Plot* is a high vernacular exercise in parallelism built around the framework of a search. As a structural task it poses an overpowering challenge to Hitchcock, and is solved brilliantly.

The plot, in brief, involves a spiritualist, Mme Blanche (Barbara Harris), who is not only a charming charlatan but also a talented practitioner of her trade. She is engaged by a wealthy old lady, Mrs. Rainbird (Cathleen Nesbitt), to search for a man of around forty, an illegitimate son of her sister Harriett, who was given away as a baby to cover up a potential scandal and to protect the family name. After forty years, Mrs. Rainbird, at seventy-eight, has pangs of guilt and wants to make up for old mistakes and reinstate the lost nephew to her family and inheritance. The offer of ten thousand dollars in this service, if successful, stuns Mme Blanche, who apparently never dreamed of such a sum. Her boyfriend, George Lumley (Bruce Dern), a would-be actor working as a part-time taxi driver, is also her partner for research and other services. After her lengthy séance he picks her up with his taxi. They have their usual lover's squabble, until he learns about the big prize from Mrs. Rainbird. He will have to do a lot of investigative work. As happens quite seldom in life, but rather often in the movies, the taxi comes to a screeching halt for a woman in black who is crossing that very street in front of the taxi, and who, it turns out, introduces the first segment of the parallel action (however, this will become clear later). We follow the woman and leave our two protagonists in the taxi. The blond woman in black (Karen Black) enters a building guarded by police, is announced, and let in. She carries a gun. She is to pick up the ransom, a giant gem, for a kidnapped millionaire, a Mr. Constantine. Without a word she guides her police escort in a helicopter to the site where the still unconscious Mr. Constantine is to be liberated. Then we see the two kidnappers, Eddy (William Devane), also known as Arthur Adamson, and Fran, the woman in black, examining the diamond on their drive home. Their house is ingeniously equipped with a room hidden behind a brick wall for their kidnapping enterprise. Ed secretly hangs the diamond, using Scotch tape, on the big chandelier by the stairway.

In the meantime George, impersonating a lawyer, starts the investigation in search of the Rainbird nephew. He gets some information from a daughter of the former chauffeur of the Rainbirds. It turns out that the people to whom the baby was given forty years ago, the Shoebridges, died tragically in a fire, presumably also with their adopted son; the circumstances of their death are foggy and an unresolved mystery surrounds it. George goes to the cemetery where the Shoebridges are buried. He finds two gravestones, one for the son. The gravedigger, in a scene shadowing the one in Hamlet, confirms that not all is clear about the son's grave. George follows the lead to the monument maker who in turn finds evidence that the gravestone for the son was purchased five years after the fatal fire. At the county register of deeds George finds out that a certificate of death for the son, Edward Shoebridge, was denied to a certain Joe Maloney, who was the petitioner. George gets his address and proceeds to find that Maloney is a gas station owner, a shady character and not at all cooperative. Maloney manages to get George's license plate number. Maloney arrives at Ed's jewelry store with the news of George's snooping. It turns out that Ed and Maloney were old conspirators in the fire that killed the Shoebridges. Maloney is scared; he offers to kill George. Ed, who has a devilish rabbit smile, says to cool it; he will look into it. He gets George's license and address.

Blanche, in the meantime, at the dead end of her search, finds out during the next séance with Mrs. Rainbird that the parson who baptized the illegitimate baby may know his whereabouts. George follows up by going to St. Ann's Cathedral to see Bishop Wood, the former parson in question. By sheer coincidence, at the end of the mass George witnesses an operetta-like kidnapping of the bishop, in full view of the congregation, by a pair of fast operatives dressed as church attendants and whom we recognize as our duo: Ed and Fran (the plot of the film is interwoven with humor of every kind, from black to purely comedic, making the above scene more digestable than would otherwise be the case).

During lunch in her kitchen, Blanche receives a call from Maloney who offers, for pay, to give them information on Eddy Shoebridge. They make a date at a diner on the highway. They excitedly drive to the meeting. While they wait in the diner, Maloney surreptitiously cuts the brake lines in their parked car and goes away. Disappointed about the no-show, George and Blanche start driving home. A most hilarious and suspenseful scene ensues. They survive the drive down the serpentine road without brakes; Maloney meets them again on the road, wants to ram them with his car, but he miscalculates a turn and perishes in a ball of fire down a ravine. At Maloney's funeral George finally finds out from Joe's widow that Eddy, since the murder of his foster parents, lives under the name Adamson. With this information Blanche finds her way, after a funny search, to Adamson's jewelry shop and eventually his home just at the time when Eddy and Fran are ready to make a pickup for new ransom (another diamond) and to return Bishop Wood. After several complications Ed subdues Blanche, gives her the rest of the drug injection (left from the bishop), and puts her to sleep in the mystery room behind the brick wall. (Blanche, as we find later, must not have been totally drugged, since she hears Ed tell Fran, "Let's then go get the diamond for our chandelier"). They drive away to return the bishop. George, in the meantime, while looking for Blanche, finds himself in front of Ed's house where her car is parked with the keys inside; he forces open a basement window and enters the house. Ed and Fran have just returned with their new diamond; George hides inside. He finds out about the lot of Blanche. While Ed prepares for the disposal of Blanche, George enters the secret room she is in and, by clever conspiring with her, they arrange to trap Ed and Fran in the very room they have devised for their kidnap victims. The film comes to a most happy (and comedic) ending as Blanche finds the diamond on the chandelier and even fools George into believing that she is truly a psychic.

The first scene of *Family Plot* is a long one by Hitchcockian standards, almost 9 1/2 minutes in duration. It is a truly slow overture (supported by the central musical themes of the film). Characteristically for Hitchcock, though, the scene spells out the kind of iconography the film will embody: a singular mix of comedy and suspense. The scene is heavily loaded with dialogue, and for good reason, since it introduces the rather involved plot.

Scene 1: The traditional length credits for principal actors are dispensed with, and, after a brief main title and the names of the screenwriter, Ernst Lehman, and director, Alfred Hitchcock, there appears, superimposed over a crystal ball, the face of Mme Blanche in close-up (shot 1). She speaks with a strange voice, as if in a trance. The structure starts with a slow disclosure; after 30 seconds we realize that she must be a medium; the camera pulls back to a medium close shot of her, then starts a slow pan to the left, passing by lamps and stuffed furniture indicating a rich Victorian interior, finally coming upon a close-up of the distinguished-looking, wealthy old lady involved in the séance. We learn that Blanche "works" through an intermedium, Henry, and is able to "contact" a deceased relative of the rich lady, who speaks animatedly to Mme Blanche: "I think I know who it is, Mme Blanche" (the first time we hear her name); "I think I know what's bothering her." (Total length of the first shot is 49 sec.). Cut to a medium close shot of Mme Blanche, then cut to a wider medium shot of the old lady as they continue talking; again a repeat of the same medium shot of Mme Blanche and finally a repeat of the shot of the old lady, a total of four single shots lasting 27 seconds. The above is not a full-fledged separation but rather a "teaser" for an upcoming multishot separation. Mme Blanche, by now, has presumably called in the "spirit." In addition, she has won total credibility by supposedly divining that the spirit does not let the old lady sleep nights, keeping her tortuously awake. (We learn in the next scene that Blanche picked up her information from her sleuth boyfriend.) It should be noted that the above is performed by Mme Blanche in quite a comedic manner.

After the teaser comes a cut to (shot 7) a high long shot of the two women sitting in their soft chairs. (We see them for the first time to-

gether in one frame). The old lady continues increduously: "How could you know about my nightmares? I never told a soul about them . . ." A full separation follows containing 27 single shots in A, B, A, B. The average length of the single shots is about 7 seconds, a few longer ones last 12–15 seconds. Both the A and the B are medium shots, with the frame for the old lady a bit larger. Mme Blanche is performing with virtuosity, howling and gesturing, using several voices, but the bulk of information is coming from the old lady, Julia Rainbird. She repeats that she knows who the spirit is: It's her sister Harriet, since deceased, who fills her with guilt and nightmares. She has had enough of her ". . . I don't need her to goad me on, I know what to do" (shot 11). She gets up, animated, camera follows. In shot 12 the size of the image of Mme Blanche changes to a close-up. She listens intently as she intuits that a confession is forthcoming. She covers her face with her oddly bejewelled hand, but between her fingers keeps an eye on her client—this is funny, and also points to her subtle deception. In the next shot (13) Mrs. Rainbird remains in her previous medium shot, still standing. She says: "Tell her to go away . . . Let her stop it." She sits down. After a pause: "Don't let her go, don't let her go away . . ." Cut

(shot 14) to the same close-up of Mrs. Rainbird listening. The next four shots (16 through 19) are very short in duration, from one to two seconds, a real speed-up of the rhythm, as we see Mme Blanche in a new high medium shot in three-quarter profile howling like a dog and generously gesticulating while the shots of Mrs. Rainbird remain constant (medium close shots). Frightened by the howling, she asks: "What is it? What's wrong, Mme Blanche?" Mme Blanche keeps impersonating Harriet. Mrs. Rainbird listens and occasionally adds bits of new information. The rhythm stabilizes to shots of between 5 and 8 seconds. Each time Mrs. Rainbird speaks, Mme Blanche opens her eyes, absorbing new parts of the puzzle, and then again howling. The most important information comes through in the A and B shots 22 to 29; Mrs. Rainbird addressing the spirit of her sister: "I'll do what I can to make up for it. I'll find your son and take him into my arms . . . as if he's my own. I'll make him one of us and give him everything, *everything* [with enthusiasm]." Turning to Mme Blanche: "But I need her help, her memory. It's over forty years ago. I don't know where the child was taken to, or was given to, I don't know where he is now or who he is . . ." (While this dialogue is heard the same A and B shots continue). By now Mme Blanche knows enough, and during a long duration shot (shot 30, 13 1/2 sec.) she starts winding down the séance in her guttural voice saying her goodbyes to the spirits. By shot 34 Mme Blanche collapses on a coffee table to her right. Cut on action (shot 35) to a high medium two-shot, a resolution to the separation (which lasted 3 minutes) (symmetrical with the introduction in shot 6). We see Blanche still passed out and Mrs. Rainbird: "Are you all right? Do you remember what happened?" Blanche, after a short while, comes to, acting as if from a dream; in a most hilarious manner she asks for a drink. She's offered some sherry; after drinking, she innocently says that she remembers only the gist of what was said. (The two-shot, 35, lasts almost one minute.) Again a cut on action (shot 36) to a medium close-up of Mme Blanche sipping some sherry. Cut (shot 37) to same medium shot of Mrs. Rainbird: "Tell me what you remember of the séance" (both 36 and 37 are brief shots).

Cut to (shot 38) the same medium close-up of Mme Blanche who is just then disposing of a passing hiccup and, while absent-mindedly putting away her small accessories in a jewelry bag, in a most innocent voice summarizes what she has just learned from Mrs. Rainbird: "About forty years ago you arranged to have your sister Harriet's baby given away without a trace" (10 sec). Cut to (shot 39) the same medium shot of Mrs. Rainbird listening: (offscreen voice) ". . . and now you find your bad dreams and troubled conscience tell you to find the grown-up person and take him into the family and bestow your wealth on him." Mrs. Rainbird: "Excellent . . . and why did I force my sister to give the child away?" (17 sec.). Cut to (shot 40) same medium close-up of Mme Blanche: "Illegitimate" (2 1/2 sec.). Cut to (shot 41) Mrs. Rainbird (same shot as before); in a long duration shot (18 1/2 sec.), she explains that an illegitimate child would have been a scandal in those days and had to be covered up at all costs. The next six shots continue in a similar A and B fashion. Mme Blanche is listening with great interest, and while Mrs. Rainbird elaborates on how she must protect the name Rainbird and therefore must seek the missing person in a secret fashion, Mme Blanche swallows another sip of sherry and comments, "It's a wise decision." Finally Mrs. Rainbird comes to the reason she called for Mme Blanche. Note that the above ten shots (lasting one min., 25 sec.) represent a most unusual reprise of a new separation after the previous one was already resolved. I shall return to this shortly.

Presently another unusual form follows: namely, ten shots in a variant of the over-the-shoulder mode, in this case from the back of the head of Mrs. Rainbird (screen left), to the face of Mme Blanche (screen right) and vice versa in an A and B fashion. During the next ten over-the-shoulder AB shots, Mrs. Rainbird explains that she is seventy-eight years old and wants to go to her grave with a quiet conscience . . . , she wants to make up for her past mistakes, would Mme Blanche help her? Mme Blanche is ready to try. Mrs. Rainbird: "I'm too old for trying. I have time only for results. Find him for me, Mme Blanche, whoever he is, wherever he is." She offers to pay ten thousand dollars for the service. Mme Blanche, upon hearing the amount, mutters: "Ten . . ."; stops, gives a singsong sign and finally mumbles: "Let's not consider this a payment for me. There are many charities dear to my heart." Mrs. Rainbird is delighted. She regards the arrangement as completed. She gets up; it's her bedtime; Mme Blanche is up too; they both walk through the Victorian setting; Mme Blanche drags behind her her white silk scarf. She: "This has been a most memorable evening, Mrs. Rainbird . . ." Camera pans with them. Mrs. Rainbird: "I hope you can make it a rewarding one. And at the risk of repeating myself, I hope you'll not forget that nobody, absolutely no one. . . ." Cut to shot 58, a 90° side angle long shot as they approach the door: ". . . should know of our search, the Rainbird name must be protected." Mme Blanche replies eagerly: "My jaw is locked." They exchange goodbyes; the door opens. (The ten over-the-shoulder shots including shot 58 last 2 minutes.)

Cut to (shot 59) exterior, Rainbird mansion, high long shot, night, the theme music gets stronger (a rather playful melody); a red taxi is waiting in the driveway. Mme Blanche is seen exiting the main door; Mrs. Rainbird closes it from the inside. Mme Blanche, in her nonchalant manner, white scarf still trailing behind her, approaches the taxi. The driver opens the door of the back seat, ready to go.

The taxi rolls out of the driveway and between the pillars of the entrance. The shot moves higher as the taxi comes closer and drives by. The camera pans with the taxi until it disappears, obscured by nearby trees. The taxi drive is a transition to the next scene; the high shot here is significant since, again in a Hitchcockian manner, it prepares us for an upcoming, extremely original high shot (at the end of Scene 2), which in turn is a transition to Scene 3.

Scene 1 is lengthy (9 1/2 minutes), and for good reason. Not only does it lay out the map of the plot, the humor and the texture of the syntax used by Hitchcock, but, as we have learned from this dialogue, it promises to be a search for someone—someone who may or may not exist. That in turn predicts some sort of parallelism between the searchers and the searched, which indeed will take place. Scene 1, then, puts a solid foundation under the principal part of that parallelism, namely the searchers. All this is done through painstaking slow disclosures; and even the taxi driver who appears casually only at the tail end of the scene will soon be disclosed as one of the principal searchers. Second, the plot so outlined requires lengthy dialogue; and the introduction of a character like Mme Blanche, who balances between seriousness and zestful fun, requires more screen time. Finally, elements of subtle symmetry between Mme Blanche in this scene and Mme Blanche in the very last scene of the film needs the kind of stamping-in so it will carry her after-image for the whole length of *Family Plot*. The scene is otherwise rather simple: a camera movement begins and ends the scene. A teaser four-shot separation is followed by an introductory two-shot and a 27-shot separation. Another separation soon after is in turn followed by a series of over-the-shoulder A, B shots, a novel strategy here, partially justified by the nature of the relationship between the two participating characters (to a certain degree formal and professional) and by the fact that the principal thrust here is information via dialogue for which over-the-shoulder shots are convenient conveyors. During the separation Mrs. Rainbird is the most constant image (medium shot), while Mme Blanche has three small variants, two in size (medium shot, close shot) and one three-quarter profile (side shot). The succession of shots with the variants is far from simple; upon careful scrutiny, one sees the wisdom for each change of image size or camera position.

There is one minor matter I would like to comment on, namely the few cuts on action in this scene. They occur whenever there is a cut from an introduction (two-shot) to a separation or from a separation to a resolution (two-shot again); for example, when Mme Blanche passes out in medium shot, her collapse is picked up on action in the next long shot; or, when at the end of the above two-shot, Mme Blanche starts drinking her sherry, the cut to her medium close-up is perfectly on action as she continues drinking. (There are a few more such cuts in the scene.) Such phrasing is helpful in maintaining the leisurely pace of the scene and preserving the sense of unity of (real) time even though small deletions occur. The most unusual phenomenon in this scene is the use of one separation after another. Normally such an arrangement does not work; a separation defies rewarming. Ozu, the Japanese master, tried it without success. Hitchcock makes it work only thanks to the addition of the over-the-shoulder series. Finally, it is worth repeating that the transition from this scene to the next one is a high shot of the taxi leaving the Rainbird mansion and that this is a typical Hitchcockian plant; the transition to the scene after this will be an even more spectacular high shot, and throughout the film high shots will be used as strong accents, in most cases as endings of scenes or transitions. In the above case of the taxi the high shot is not really needed except as a symmetry and a plant for the future; as a structural plan it is brilliant.

Scene 2. A remarkable example of the element of separation confined to an extremely simple format, without camera movement, without an active mise-en-scène (unlike in *Frenzy*) and in a rigidly restricted space (inside a moving car), and for that it can be called masterly. The cinesthetic impact is total, despite some challenging odds like the already mentioned restricted space and, even more importantly, the lack of eye contact between the participants: Blanche is sitting in the rear seat and George is in front, driving. In separate frames of their own (A B A B), as is well known, characters need to have eye contact to sustain the "connection," a connection that is eventually completed in the perception of the viewer. Hitchcock could have eliminated this difficulty in some way by seating them both in front (as in *Notorious,* for example), but he deliberately did not do it. He also avoids the crutches often used in films to embellish car scenes, like occasional shots of the road, the car, the mirror, or a variety of rear projection views. In this scene we see the outside of the car only in the beginning shot (as part of the introduction to the separation) and at the end (as the resolution to the separation). Incidentally, both are very high shots, not only for reasons of symmetry but for the benefit of the repeated iconography of such high shots (in this film).

Hitchcock was apparently determined here, as always, to experiment with new possibilities for separation. This separation (in Scene 2), a long one by normal standards, lasts only $3\frac{1}{2}$ minutes, but contains

53 shots; the pace is rapid. In fact 31 of these shots are below 5 seconds in duration.

To repeat, the transition from Scene 1 to Scene 2 is the high shot of the taxi leaving the Rainbird mansion. Shot 2 is a medium two-shot (frontal) of Blanche in the back seat (screen left) and George, whose face we see for the first time, at the wheel (screen right). George, with pipe in mouth: "So, how did it go?" Blanche: "Doing Henry is murder on my throat" (8 sec.). After this introductory shot we will see fifty-one single A, B, A, B shots, both medium close-ups, Blanche slightly larger, and stable in picture size; George in his frontal shots occasionally looks back (toward Blanche) showing his left profile, but four of his shots are from behind him (crossing the axis of view), during which he also looks back toward Blanche (showing his right profile). Those looks to the back are significant parts of the structure because they are taken from the front and back, and in crossing the axis they add energy and the sense of three-dimensionality and also simulate eye contact between the protagonists. This simple device electrifies the exchanges from A to B. I should add that the rear projection we see through the windows is flat and neutral. Hitchcock's pacing between the single shots is of paramount importance; for by its rhythm he controls the performances, giving screen time only for the amount of time he wants it to last, cutting off when he wants to. But one has to mention that all of the above is enhanced by snappy, humorous, and intimately vulgar dialogue and excellent acting. At first Blanche teases George about her success with Mrs. Rainbird. George (shot 11) happily injects that he is glad to have helped her with his research: "I came through for you again, didn't I, darling?" He looks back toward Blanche. Blanche (shot 12): "What are you talking about, George?" George (shot 13): "What do you mean what am I talking about? You know damn well what I'm talking about—all that information I dug up gabbing to the local pharmacist about how she was driving him crazy trying to get sleeping pills without a prescription!" Blanche (shot 14): "That could have been very, very useful to me. Why didn't you tell me about that?" George's reverse angle from his back as he is turning to camera (shot 15): "What do you mean, why didn't I tell you? I told you, you know damn well I told you, Blanche." Blanche naively (shot 16): "No, you always think you tell me things and you forget to. I have to go through heaven and hell and the great beyond with Henry." George (*frontal*) turning again to her (shot 17): "Henry my ass! It was me, it's always me. By my research you're as psychic as a dry salami." Blanche (shot 18): "Nasty, nasty, nasty" (the above information undermines in the mind of the viewer Blanche's supposed psychic powers). George, upset (shot 19): "I'm sick and tired of having you have me by my crystal balls." Blanche (shot 20): "Leave your crystal balls out of this, George." George, turning to her for a moment (shot 21): "No, let's leave Henry out of this and keep the bullshit for your customers." During the ensuing exchange we learn that George is an actor and a temporary cabdriver. Blanche assures him that if she collects what Mrs. Rainbird offered her he will not have to drive a cab any longer. She tells him about "the ten big ones." He is incredulous. In shot 36 Blanche adds: "We can even get married." George (shot 37): "Why are you always a wet blanket?" Blanche (offscreen): "Oh, you always flatter me." During the next ten shots Blanche teases him with the repetitive response "nobody knows" to George's questions about the man they are to search for. Finally she tells him about the lead to the Rainbird chauffeur, ". . . but he too has been dead for twenty-five years." George (shot 49): "For Christ's sake, Blanche." Blanche (shot 50): "No, no, don't fret, our water bed will be no fun at all tonight. As an actor you should know that fretting will ruin a performance." George, after listening (shot 51): "You're not going to have . . ." (Cut to—shot 52—long shot of highway, 3 sec.) ". . . to worry about my performance tonight, honey." Cut to (shot 53), George as he continues and looks back: "As a matter of fact, on this very evening you're going to see a standing ovation." He slams on the brakes and comes to a screeching halt. Cut to (shot 54) a medium long shot of a woman with a big black hat crossing the street in front of the taxi, from right to left (2 sec.). Cut to (shot 55) a very high long shot from above the taxi as the woman in black continues crossing. Then our taxi, at the changing of the light, moves forward and out of frame. This is the resolution of the separation. The camera (shot 55 continues) cranes down and dollies behind the woman; a strong and lively variant of the film's theme music signals the beginning of another scene.

The separation in Scene 2 is contrapuntal to the one in the previous scene in more than one way. The former is longer in duration, more formal, with implicit and subtle humor. The latter (in the taxi) has a snappy succession of A, B shots, with brief cuts, explicit humor, a sprinkling of lovers' vulgarities in the dialogue, sexual overtones, and a more earthy tone.

One cannot stop admiring the austerity and the terseness in the shots inside the taxi. Hitchcock avoids using even a single shot of the rear view mirror, a most natural way to confirm the existence of Blanche in the rear seat. In fact, the framing of the frontal shot of George is sufficiently wide to be able to incorporate a "piece" of Blanche behind him, which it does not. The vitality and vividness of this scene is proof again that a totally realistic bearing, including deep focus, is not a condition to effective cinema.

The resolution to the separation is audaciously original (the high shot of the taxi), since it connects at the same time two scenes (the taxi is seen departing as the woman in black is passing by). Unexpectedly, it is also, with its craning down shot, more than a hint that the woman in black is not just a casual pedestrian; it suggests that there might be or will be a connection between these people, although at the moment one is taken by the camera on a ride to follow the mystery woman, and one temporarily sets aside Blanche and George.

Scene 3. Continues with a very high long shot: the woman in black continues crossing the street. There is an overlap from the previous scene that should be taken into consideration; namely, the already talked about shot 54, a two-second medium eye level long shot of the woman whom we see for the first time as she starts crossing the street. She hears the screeching brakes (of George's taxi), hesitates in her gait, and throws a fleeting glance to her left (where, we assume, the taxi is), and continues walking. Her look, a perhaps momentary eye contact, is the only connection between her and the taxi, since they are in separate frames. The next shot cuts to the very high angle, already mentioned above, at the start of which we see the taxi leaving the frame. From this point the actual Scene 3 starts. The almost absurd coincidence of joining here what eventually will become the major parallel action in the film is again, in the Hitchcockian manner, a calculated plant; for there will be other incredible coincidences in this drama and they will all play well, with Hitchcock controlling the thin line between realism and fictionality, making them almost interchangeable.

From the high shot the camera cranes down to eye level (as described before) and dollies behind the woman in black (in medium shot) until she reaches a checkpoint with a policeman in it. She forms an intriguing silhouette against the brightly lit booth; it is already night-time. Silently she hands the guard a note; he reads it; she takes it du-tifully back with her gloved hand. The policeman calls on the phone: "The person has arrived. It's a woman, not a man"; then to her: "Please follow me." They leave the frame (50 sec.). Cut to a long shot in a darkish courtyard; the guard and the woman walk away from the cam-era toward an office building; they approach and start opening a door (18 sec). Cut to a reverse angle; the swinging door forms a natural wipe to a close-up of the woman, a severe-looking blond with dark glasses and the formidable black hat; camera swishes quickly down to a pointed pistol she is holding in her right hand (3 sec.); the latter camera move-ment is perfectly synchronized with a loud flourish of the musical tune that accompanies, so far, the action of the scene. This music adds here a dimension of ambivalence through its humorous pomposity. Again, Hitchcock seems to be determined to risk walking the tightrope be-tween the serious and the satirical.

Cut to a medium shot of a group of officials behind a counter. One with glasses addresses the woman: "As long as you have Victor Constantine we cannot touch you, so you may as well put that [he points to the pistol] thing away." Cut to our woman in medium shot profile with gun in hand; camera pans with her walking forward to the counter; camera moves in as she puts the pistol away and picks up a small pouch from the counter. The camera keeps moving in to a close-up of a large sparkling diamond; she holds it in her gloved hand (16 sec.). Cut to a close-up of her face looking down (at the diamond) (1 sec.). Cut back to a close-up of her hands; she puts the diamond on a jeweler's scale. While she weighs it the man says: "I presume we are entitled to some assurance that Mr. Constantine is alive." Again a quick cut to a close shot of her face (3/4 sec). She is emotionless. Cut back to the close-up of her hands removing the diamond from the scale and placing it in a jewelry pouch. Voice of the man: "All radios have been removed from the helicopter as you instructed." Cut to a full long shot from the side; we see for the first time the whole group and the woman in the same frame. Note that such a shot is normally used, in a ma-jority of films, in the beginning as an establishing shot to a scene. Hitchcock consistently avoids such master shots as introductions and instead prefers, as we have seen, slow disclosures; eventually (as in the above) he may give us a full shot.

The mystery woman on the right is in profile. She hands them a
note. The man in glasses reads it aloud: "Mr. Constantine will be unconscious but in perfect condition. Just let him sleep the drug off." She
takes the note back from them, silent all the time (the theme tune is
with us, stronger from the time we see the diamond). The man with
the glasses asks the sergeant to turn on the lights. Cut to the guard as
he steps to a door and turns a switch; through the open doorway we
see in the distance a small helicopter. Cut back to the group shot as
they all move to the right, the woman in the lead. After they file through
the door, cut to a high long shot (exterior); we see the group descending
a few steps and walking toward camera. The music is marchlike, in
step with them. One of the men walks ahead faster; the camera is with
him; the rest of the group is left behind, out of frame. The man approaches the helicopter. Cut to close shot of the helicopter door opening, a uniformed police pilot at the controls. The man speaks to him:
"Don't try to be a hero." The pilot: "Yes, sir." At that moment our
woman appears, gun first, slips into the helicopter, and sits down. We
see her and the pilot in a two-shot profile. The man with glasses, before
he closes the door, addresses her: "Well, we've done our part." He shuts
the plexiglass door. The police pilot asks the woman: "Where are we
going?" Cut to a close-up of a compass on the dashboard; the woman's
gloved finger points to #6 on the compass. Cut to a frontal two-shot
of the two; the pilot leans forward. Cut to the same close shot of the

compass as he adjusts the direction on the automatic pilot. Cut back to the frontal two-shot (briefly) as the rotor noise gets louder. Cut to a long shot of the group of men swept by the wind. Cut to a medium long shot of the helicopter lifting from the pad and up into the air above. Cut (again) to the group of men looking up; the man with the glasses shouts above the noise: "Not a single goddamn mistake." Cut to the helicopter high up in the air, on its way. (So far the length of teh scene is 3 1/2 minutes).

The next 29 shots in this scene are of a steady rhythm, with average cuts every 5 seconds or less, with one exception: in the very middle of that section (shot 14) the helicopter landing lasts 20 seconds, as a break in tempo. The medium frontal two-shot of the woman and the police pilot inside the cockpit becomes the standard repeated shot (10 times); there are also six simple repeated close shots (4 of the pilot, 2 of the woman). Up in the air, inside the cockpit, in a medium two-shot, the pilot asks: "How far are we going?" (5 sec.). Cut to a close-up of the woman, silent (5 sec.). Cut back to two-shot. Pilot: ". . . you still have the victim. I'd like nothing better than to toss you right out of this thing on your head." The woman disregards him; she points to the compass (6 sec.). Cut to a close-up of the compass with the needle moving (3 sec.). Cut to a close shot of the pilot: "You sure have this little trip mapped out, don't you?" (4 sec.). Cut back to the close-up of the compass (3 sec.). Cut to the familiar medium two-shot. The woman looks toward her window, her gun nonchalantly pointing toward the pilot's seat. Pilot: "I bet that thing isn't even loaded." The woman looks at him coldly and shoots the pistol at the opposite wall (6 sec.). Cut to tight close-up of the bullet hole in the wall (1 sec.). Cut to a close-up of the pilot jumping at the firing; he turns to the wall (1 1/2 sec.). Cut back to the bullet hole (1 sec.). Cut back to the same close-up of the pilot who turns to look at the pistol (1 1/2 sec.). Cut to a close-up of the woman who turns to the pilot and orders him with gestures to land (3 sec.). Cut to a close-up of the pilot looking down for a landing; he mutters: "Golf course, uh huh . . ." Cut to a long shot of the helicopter coming down and landing (20 sec.), the longest duration shot in this scene. Cut to a medium shot of the helicopter from the side; the woman is descending; the pilot looks on (5 sec.).

Cut to a long shot of the woods in the distance, a flashing light can be seen signalling. Cut back to the medium two-shot of the helicopter from the side; the woman gestures to the pilot to wait (3 1/2 sec.). Cut to a long shot of the woman walking in the direction of the signal in the woods (8 sec.). Cut to a medium shot of the pilot descending from the helicopter; he looks intensely toward the woods (9 sec.). Cut to a long shot of the woods (6 sec.). (This shot, as well as the previous two, contains deletions of time). Cut to a panning medium long shot as the woman enters the frame inside the woods. She reaches her partner who apparently was waiting for her; camera keeps panning fast down to a close-up of a man's face on the ground; he is just waking up (the victim) (7 1/2 sec.). Cut to a medium two-shot of the woman and her partner, a small dark-haired man with a mustache; both handle the jewelry pouch (2 1/2 sec.). Cut back to the medium shot of the pilot looking, with flashlight in hand (1 1/2 sec.). Cut back to the long shot of the woods where a flash of light is seen in the distance (2 sec.). Cut back to the medium two-shot of the woman (with her flashlight on) and her partner. With the help of a jeweler's loop he starts examining the diamond and says: "Brilliant." Cut to a frontal extreme close-up of the sparkling diamond; his fingers turn it around; we hear the man: "Absolutely perfect . . ." (2 sec.). (Note the fast rhythm.) Cut to same medium shot of the pilot who apparently has seen the woman's light; he exits frame in a run (2 1/2 sec.). Cut to a medium long shot panning with the pilot in the woods as he reaches the victim. We hear a car start and leave (the kidnappers).

The scene, by Hitchcock's coda, has started with camera movements (panning, dolly, crane) and symmetrically ends also with camera movements. In fact, the symmetry is precise since the beginning has a pause between the camera movements and so does the ending (pan with the woman in the woods, pause, pan with the pilot in the woods). But the most noteworthy aspect of this scene's cinema language is the seemingly simple structure of actions with minimal dialogue. Note that Hitchcock repeats the details several times, like the close-up of the diamond, the compass, and the bullet hole. He then intermixes them with repeats of close-ups of people reacting. In most films such details are treated as inserts (magnifications) to be shown once, for the sake of information only. In Hitchcock's case they become a whole network of specific continuity. The repetitions are not there to seal the items in the memory of the viewer but in order to create a linguistic continuum, a phrasing, a satisfactory cinematic sentence!

The helicopter part of the scene lasts 2 minutes, 15 seconds; total length of Scene 3: 5 minutes, 45 seconds.

Scene 4. In this scene we have a closer view of the two kidnappers in their car returning with the loot. Fran, the woman, turns out to be not a blond (she uses a wig) and not tall (6 inch heels, "my feet are killing me"). Arthur Adamson (Eddy), a professional jeweler to boot, is the master of the operation, an arrogant type, cool but ready with a joke for every occasion. The first shot in the car is a frontal medium two-shot (13 sec.), followed by a seven-shot (A, B) separation of average length of 5 seconds each. The exchange between them is light and snappy as Fran slowly divests herself of her paraphernalia (wig, shoes, glasses, hat, coat). In shot 3 Eddy in close-up asks: "Did you see anyone we know?" Cut to a close-up of Fran removing her overcoat: "Two men who looked like police and the third had to be FBI." Cut to a close-up of Eddy: "You mix with the nicest people." Cut to same close-up of Fran removing her wig; Eddy continues offscreen: "Did you say anything to them?" Fran: "Not a syllable." Cut to close-up of Eddy: "Now, you see, honey, I told you that you could learn to keep your mouth shut . . ." Cut to the same close-up of Fran; Eddy continues: ". . . if you tried." Fran finished changing: "Look who's here." Cut to (shot 9) a medium two-shot (resolving the separation): Eddy looks at her; they kiss. Eddy: "Has anyone seen a tall, blond woman around here lately?" Fran: "Gone . . . poof . . . who needs her?" Then, as a special emphasis, Hitchcock adds two more single shots: a close-up of Eddy, who in answer says: "I do . . ." (1 1/2 sec.) and a close-up of Fran, who thoughtfully looks at him while his voice is heard after a pause" . . . at least one more time." Fran is not elated (5 sec.). We assume that Eddy is referring to some future "job." Note that it is the second time in this film that Hitchcock attempts to add single shots after a separation is completed and resolved. Here, again, it seems to be justified since that last exchange between Eddy and Fran was serious and thus not comparable to the light, joking tone that prevailed during the separation. In addition, the two single shots are placed at the very end of the car scene. The next one is a long shot exterior of Eddy's house; the car turns the corner toward a garage door; the camera moves in closer. Cut to a closer shot, from the side, of the automatic garage door closing as the car disappears.

The shots of the garage door (it too will play a role in this drama)

is a natural transition to a series of disclosures in the interior of the house where the viewer is virtually taken on a tour of the kidnapper's lair and the secret details of their trade. The succession of shots in this part of the scene is designed to be pragmatic, down to earth, and informational. Close-ups are reserved for small details; there are no separations; and single shots of Fran and Eddy are only in sets of 3 shots at the most. First we are introduced to the interior of the garage, then to an adjoining half basement where we visit the hub of their operation. Both locations will play prominently in the film. In this half basement, behind a seemingly solid brick wall, is located a specially designed room. The brick wall is partially a hidden doorway with ingenious locks, switches, and intercoms. Those are operated from the outside by taking out thin bricks that cover the respective devices. Fran and Eddy enter the room to clean up after Mr. Constantine, their recent victim. We watch how the system works as they unlock, switch on, uncover, and replace bricks. The above operation is shown in tight close-ups with match cuts on action from medium shots of Fran and Eddy. Fran collects the bedding; Eddy cleans up the dishes (Mr. Constantine left some of the wine); Eddy is to take care of the chemical toilet (it is below his dignity). They joke and move around as if it is a routine.

Back in the living quarters Fran puts her wig away in the refrigerator; Eddy prepares to put the ransom diamond away by first getting out some Scotch tape. They keep up their jovial conversation with its sexual innuendo. Finally they go upstairs to retire (again, a stairway). Fran asks casually: "Where are you putting the diamond, dear?" Camera lifts with them up the stairs; he replies: "Where everyone can see it." She: "You didn't"; he: "I did." At this point the camera pans to the chandelier and zooms slowly to the diamond among the crystals, attached there with Scotch tape; it glitters in close-up with all its twinkles. The voices offscreen; she: "Are you going to tell me?" He: "You'll have to torture me first"; she laughs: "I intend to." The picture of the diamond starts fading out very slowly. The whole scene lasts 3 minutes, 40 seconds, and has 25 cuts. At present we already know both sides of the parallel, the searchers and the searched, even though the latter are not yet clearly pinpointed in the narrative as such.

The elaborate fade-out stands alone, unreciprocated, since Scene 5 that follows does not start with a fade-in. (It was mostly the avant-guardist who used such unorthodox phrasings.) Consequently the fade-out that closes Scene 4 is a half of a "punctuation mark," not a time lapse and not a closure. Hitchcock introduces here a decorative touch of significance, since a similar shot (of the sparkling diamond on the chandelier), in perfect symmetry, will reemerge at the very end of the film. One can state safely that such plants for future shots and symmetries are a major element in Hitchcock's strategies.

Scene 5. Starts with a straight cut to a flash of light following the darkened screen of the fade-out: we see in a long shot the office of Mr. Constantine, the liberated kidnap victim, sitting behind his desk, facing three investigators seated across from him. (We are familiar with them from the ransom pickup scene with Fran.) The scene is a satire on debriefings. Mr. Constantine in a state of annoyance begs the interrogators to let him be: "I've got a lot of work to catch up on, gentlemen" (12 sec.). This is an introduction to a 32-shot separation of complex construction that ends without a resolution (without a full shot.) Note the symmetrical imbalance: the scene starts without a complimentary fade-in and it ends without a resolved separation. Mr. Constantine is the principal image, always in single frames and, what is most interesting, always moving and walking, the camera following him and keeping him in medium close shots. The investigators, in chairs arranged in a semicircle, are framed in two-shots or singles. Mr. Constantine, with his good sense of humor, dominates the scene. At one point asked why he thinks the female kidnapper (whom he had not seen, only heard) is twenty-four years old, he answers emphatically: "Because a man of my age [he's about fifty-five] when kidnapped by a woman wants her to be twenty-four, that's why!" The dialogue pokes fun at the FBI and their methods of investigation. The details of the kidnapping, which Mr. Constantine is made to repeat endlessly, echo what the viewer already knows. It is easy to visualize his ordeal having seen the secret room and the paraphernalia of the kidnapper's routine. The mise-en-scène of Mr. Constantine's movements, his constant walking up to the wall and back, jabbing at the investigators, and, most importantly, his keeping a piercing eye contact with them, is constructed with such skill and perfection as to appear simple and lifelike yet, in fact, is extremely complex. Most of the shots are between 1 and 3 seconds in length; only Mr. Constantine's walks are longer. In spite of such a fast pace the scene manages nevertheless to float, thanks to the camera movements that follow Mr. Constantine and the humor that prevails to the end. In the last shot (shot 32), we see Mr. Constantine devastated on hearing the FBI man's request to start his story over again, for the fourth time; all he says is: "Shit!"

Scene 6. Cut to an exterior long shot of a Rolls Royce parked in front of Blanche's house: we see George approaching the house, looking over the luxurious car (20 sec.). Cut to medium long shot of the courtyard. George crosses it away from the camera; he rubs his back (a repeated gesture of his); he enters the back door to the kitchen cautiously, so as not to disturb a séance in progress (8 sec.). Cut to a medium shot interior, kitchen. George crosses to a doorway draped with Indian material. We hear Blanche's loud performance from the other room (11 sec.). Cut to a reverse shot from the other room looking frontally at George in a close shot as he parts the drapes and looks toward Blanche (2 sec.). Cut to medium two-shot of Blanche with client; Blanche is "in touch" with Henry, her personal medium, accompanied by the appropriate sounds (12 sec.). Cut back to the same close shot of George behind the slit in the drapes; he steps back (1 1/2 sec.). Cut on action to a medium shot from the side as George withdraws and walks over to the cabinet where he picks up a small metal rod and returns to the drapes (10 sec.). Cut on action to a close-up of George's hand poking the rod through the slit in the drape in order to hit gently the hanging glass chimes. Blanche howls again offscreen calling Henry (8 sec.). Cut back to the close-up of George looking in through the slit in the drapes trying to get Blanche's attention (1 1/2 sec.). Cut to a close-up of Blanche in the middle of her trance. She notices George, a fast and almost funny camera zoom to an extreme close-up of her eyes (3 sec.). Cut to a close shot of George making signs to her to come out (3 sec.). Cut back to the extreme close-up of Blanche's eyes (3 sec.). Cut back to the close shot of George by the drapes insisting, with gestures, that she come out (3 sec.). Cut to a new camera position: high medium two-shot of Blanche and her client. Blanche shouts: "I'm ready for you, Henry . . . I'll go wherever you want me. Where are you taking me, Henry . . ." She gets up in a dancelike position and starts pirouetting toward the curtain (40 sec., so far the longest shot in this scene). Cut on action to a reverse shot of Blanche entering through the drapes on the kitchen side in a medium shot from the side, still howling and performing, by voice, for the benefit of her client in the other room. She walks over to George, scolding him for interrupting a séance. George needs her car keys to drive over to the daughter of the Rainbird's chauffeur whom he has unearthed. As she argues with George and looks for her keys, Blanche in a hilarious way continues her shouts at high pitch in the direction of her client. George leaves with the keys; Blanche, howling and sending good-byes to "Henry," goes back to the curtain (32 sec.). Cut to a reverse frontal medium close-up of Blanche opening the curtain (3 sec.). (She's seen from the inside of the room by her client.) Cut to a medium shot of her lady client sighing with delight and asking: "Did you find Walter?" (4 sec.). Cut back to the medium close shot of Blanche who, in a stupor, asks "Where?" (2 sec.). Cut back to the lady: "In the kitchen" (1 1/2 sec.). Cut back to the medium close-up of Blanche who, after a pause, says: "I did," and smiles (7 sec.). Blanche's charmingly absent-minded smile ends the scene, summing up its humor appropriately.

The scene has 19 shots and lasts 3 minutes, 10 seconds. With many of its cuts executed on action, it is a strictly linear construction played almost in real time, not unlike the scenes with Fran and Eddy in their house (Scene 4). The only outrageous move is in the sudden zoom into Blanche's eye that cannot be justified by any logic of the situation but is in line with its humor, perfectly expressing the mood and tone of the scene. In the strict sense it could be called a visual joke. As we can see it now, the parallelism is beginning to come to life. If we consider Blanche and George the principal action and Eddy and Fran the secondary, we have seen so far the former twice, the latter once. George's research is on the move, as we shall see shortly.

Scene 7. Cut to a high long shot of a busy floor of a department store: George is seen making inquiries; a man shows him the way (11 sec.). Cut to a medium close shot of a saleswoman behind a counter. Camera pans to the left to include George on the other side of the counter; they are in a medium two-shot taken from the side. George, who is dressed appropriately, presents himself as Frank MacBride from the law firm of Ferguson, Ferguson, and MacBride, in itself an amusing impersonation. George is inquiring about the saleswoman's background. She is a middle-aged woman with an intelligent but plain face. She answers: "My background, dull as dishwater. What in the world would you be wanting with that?" George (still in the two-shot): "Let's just say that the information I'm interested in would be worth a great deal of money" (40 sec.). The above introductory two-shot, where we see them in profile, is followed by 23 over-the-shoulder medium shots (in A, B, A, B). Note that Hitchcock prefers a tight framing of such shots: from the back of the head of one person to the frontal face of the other and vice versa. The first shot in the series is toward the saleswoman, the last is toward George. As already mentioned, this type of shot lends itself well to longer exchanges of dialogue containing mainly information. Scene 7 is in that category without losing any of its lightness and humor. George surprises the saleswoman with his knowledge of her family background; she is the daughter of the late chauffeur in the Rainbird family. George would like to know if she knows any friend of her father's who might have heard about an adopted child of forty years ago. She tells him about a buddy of her father's who did adopt a child, but unfortuantely he is already dead, the whole family perished in a fire. Quite possibly the child died too. The manager of the department sternly asks the saleswoman to attend to some waiting customers. George manages to sneak in a crucial question: "Where can I look for him?" The saleswoman, as she leaves the frame: "Try the Barlow Creek Cemetery." George turns to camera and leans on the counter.

The scene lasts 3 minutes, 26 seconds. The 23 over-the-shoulder shots, that in a conventional film would spell tedium, are alive here, and sparkle with earthy intelligence and humor. Taking as a given the excellence of the dialogue and the actors' performances, it is the tighter framing, as well as the pacing of the cuts, that is responsible for Hitchcock's success. Even though the information conveyed in this scene is discouraging, the humor that is woven in enlivens the plot. The last shot, of George pondering what to do next, is not only within the Hitchcockian coda of ending scenes on a single meaningful close shot, but it is also a good example of how to slow down a fast-cutting chain of shots and thus give the viewer time to think; in this case, of what George will, after all, do next.

Scene 8. Cut, in perfect linear continuity, to the above mentioned cemetery: in a high long shot (shot 1) Blanche's white car rolls in; camera pans and lowers to eye level as George stops and looks around; the only sound heard is the chirping of birds. In contrast to the fast paced previous scene this one, so far, takes its time. George enters a keeper's hut, comes out, starts slowly walking toward camera (47 sec.). Cut to a (shot 2) medium shot; the camera pans over gravestones (3 1/2 sec.). Cut to (shot 3) George walking in medium shot; he cleans his pipe on a stone (5 sec.). Cut (shot 4) back to a pan over gravestones (2 sec.). Cut back to (shot 5) George walking; he takes out his tobacco pouch (11 sec.). Cut back (shot 6) to the pan along the gravestones (2 sec.). Cut (shot 7) back to George walking while filling his pipe; he comes to a close shot and almost leaves frame left (8 sec.). Cut to (shot 8) medium shot of George walking to the right (change of camera angle); he stumbles over a stone, says "Sorry," and keeps walking to the left (19 sec.). Cut to (shot 9) two gravestones, both with the Shoebridge name (4 sec.). Music starts; George steps into frame in a low medium shot looking down (4 sec.). Cut back (shot 10) to the two gravestones (3 sec.). Cut to (shot 11) a low close shot of George looking apprehensively (4 sec.). Cut (shot 12) to a closer shot of the inscription on the gravestone: Edward Shoebridge 1933–1950 (3 sec.). Cut back (shot 13) to the close-up of George as he says to himself: "Dead end, Blanche, dead and buried" (5 sec.). Cut (shot 14) to George's legs in foreground medium shot; in the far distance someone seems to be digging. Eventually we see the person crawl out and walk toward George. Music becomes stronger. The camera adjusts to a medium low two-shot. The man wears a worn out leather vest and an old hat and has a deeply creased face. The whole set-up, as I mentioned in the synopsis, brings to mind the gravedigger scene in *Hamlet*. The old man addresses George: "I'm the caretaker. Can I do something for you?" The above shot is made significantly more impressive by its framing under a bare tree,

its branches stretched out against the sky (the longest duration shot in the scene: 25 sec.). Cut to (shot 15) a slightly higher medium two-shot from the side; George: "Oh, I'm just a friend of the family . . ." (2 1/2 sec.). Cut to another 90° angle change of the two, and the second of a series of five over-the-shoulder shots. This time the gravedigger faces the camera: "None left, bad, bad . . ." George: "You mean the fire?" The gravedigger, looking down at the stone: "Never liked them multiple funerals . . ." (12 sec.). Cut (shot 16) back to the other angle, this time George facing camera. Gravedigger continues: "too much work." George, pointing down: "They died together, but they're not buried together in the same hole. How come?" (10 sec.). Cut (shot 17) to the gravedigger facing camera. He looks penetratingly at George and says: "Search me." George points to the gravestones, walks over and out of frame (6 sec.). Cut on action (shot 18) to George entering frame in medium shot by the gravestones. (Beginning of an eleven-shot sep-aration.) Edward Shoebridge's stone is clearly the smaller and the newer of the two. George touches the stones, then points to the bigger one (6 sec.). Cut to (shot 19) a new low medium close-up of the gravedigger under the bare tree looking down, an awesome image indeed (2 sec.). Cut back to George (shot 20) examining the two gravestones; he points to the bigger one: "Died in 1950." Then, pointing to the smaller one: "Died in 1950" (6 sec.). Cut to (shot 21) the same medium close-up of the gravedigger under the tree; he looks down unmoved (3 sec.). Cut to (shot 22) the same medium shot of George at the gravestones. He continues: "Both died on the same day." He taps the bigger stone with his pipe: "Old stone." He taps the Edward stone: "This . . . practically new stone" (7 sec.). Cut back (shot 23) to the same medium close-up of the gravedigger; he half smiles, deviously, and finally says: "Smart fellow, aren't you?" (5 sec.). Cut (shot 24) back to George at the stones. He asks with a certain anxiety: "Why? Did I stumble onto something?" (4 sec.). Cut back (shot 25) to the same medium close-up of the grave-digger; he looks, his eyes smiling, and after a long pause: "Well, it was nice meeting you. I better go back to my work. I have a job coming here tomorrow." He walks away (6 sec.). Cut back (shot 26) to George at the stones; he looks after the gravedigger with a worried expression, then starts digging with his pipe behind Edward Shoebridge's stone (5 sec.). The scene, lasting 3 minutes, 53 seconds, is comparatively slow. The last eleven-shot separation, on the heels of a five-shot over-the-shoulder sequence, is impressive because of its significant imagery, es-pecially that of the gravedigger—quite appropriately, since we see for the first time the "family plot" of the film's title. From now on things will begin to unravel at a faster clip.

Scene 9. Cut directly via slow disclosure to a gravestone carving establishment: the music changes from the ominous tune to light rock emanating from a small radio coming into view as the camera moves back. At first we see an extreme close-up of the letters "DIED" on a slab of marble. The camera lifts and keeps moving back to reveal a young woman with long blond hair busy chiseling the marble. The camera continues to move back, ending in a long shot. We recognize George, in front of a large shed, talking to the owner of the establish-ment, who, annoyed by the loud music, asks the girl to turn the radio down. Cut to a medium shot of the two, the owner on the left, George on the right. One assumes that George, who is still impersonating a lawyer, is inquiring about the Shoebridge gravestones. The owner com-plains that he will have to dig into this old files. George insists. The owner: "You know, Mr. McBride, you lawyers are always alike, trou-ble, trouble, trouble." George pats him on the shoulder. Owner: "Let's go, I don't have all day . . ." They enter the shed. Cut to a medium long shot of the interior: a cluttered workshop with file cabinets and a desk. George finds a seat; the owner goes through his files. Cut to a tighter two-shot: we see the side of George and the profile of the owner, who asks for the date of death. George doesn't know. This is the start of a series of nine over-the-shoulder shots. In the A we see the owner's profile through the back of George; in the B, a frontal shot of George through the back of the owner. The content is pure information, as is usual for these types of shots. The length of the shots varies between 4 and 9 seconds. The owner finds the record, including payment for the elder Shoebridges, but nothing for Edward. Then the owner remembers something, someone ordered the stone for Edward years later, in 1965. He keeps looking for another file. During the last 3 shots in this series the owner recalls a rumor he heard that the young Shoebridge set the suspicious fire himself and his body was never found (so far the scene lasts 1 minute, 40 seconds). At this point, and provoked by this startling hypothesis, begins a series of close-up in a 17-shot separation. George starts pressing: "You mean there is no body in the grave?" The owner, also in close-up: "As I recollect that's why the local parson wouldn't say any service for Eddy." George, in close-up: "Wasn't there a death certificate?" Owner, in close-up: "I don't know about it and I don't need to know. I'm just a businessman, Mr. McBride." After 6 shots of separation comes an unusual disruption in the form of a wide two-shot as the owner announces that he has found the document of payment: $395 in cash for the Edward Shoebridge stone on November 12, 1965. George makes a note of this information. The separation resumes here. The owner recalls that cash payment since normal transactions in this business are by check. He also recalls that a dark, balding fellow, around thirty, in a tow truck like those used in garages, picked up the gravestone and took it away. The last shot as the pattern goes is of George in close-up, cooking up the next scheme. The whole scene lasts a total of 3 minutes, 12 seconds. As in Scene 8 (cemetery) an over-the-shoulder series is followed by a longer separation sequence, although here (Scene 9) the separation is interrupted by a two-shot and immediately resumed without a hitch.

Such an interruption is certainly risky, since the two-shot may signal a resolution to the separation, i.e., its end. Hitchcock, the master of this element, still experiments where others failed; for separation, with its intensity of contact, cannot be easily restarted. Hitchcock solves the problem by injecting a familiar image repeated five times in the outgoing sequence of two-shots, and for that reason it is more easily acceptable. This two-shot lasts 12 seconds, much longer than any of the single shots of the separation, while George takes notes of the important information from the file of Edward Shoebridge; hence the two-shot is mainly a carrier of information. It is important nevertheless to note that a new pattern is at work, already present in several scenes, of introducing separation sequences with a few over-the-shoulder shots.

Scene 10. Starts with a medium shot of a glass door with a sign: Registrar of Deeds. Through the opaque glass we see two figures talking to each other in a profile silhouette, one of them Alfred Hitchcock himself (his often used personal signature). Camera pans from them to a long shot of the interior of the office where we see George talking to the woman in charge. She informs him that she has located a death certificate for the elder Shoebridge and an application for one for Edward Shoebridge from November 1965. She reads from the document that the latter was denied inasmuch as the applicant could not furnish any proof of death and the body was never found. George asks who the applicant was. The clerk reads out: "The request was made by a certain Joseph Maloney, 426 Main Road, Barlow Creek . . ." George takes notes, thanks her, and quickly walks toward the camera (presumably to the door, where Hitchcock was seen before). This scene, without a single cut, lasts exactly one minute, a typical pause before a gathering storm. Having picked up the rhythm of linear continuity, the viewer expects George to look for Mr. Maloney. That is what indeed follows, except it is via slow disclosure.

Scene 11. Starts with a medium shot of George sitting at the wheel of the white car (Blanche's): he gazes intensely. Cut to a long shot of an empty gas station. Cut back to George looking. The transition from George walking out of the office of the registrar of deeds to George sitting in a car gazing is remarkably effective: somehow the energy generated by his walk is suddenly arrested, yet at the same time it is continued by the intensity of his gaze. A few details also help to sharpen the transition: George walks out of a darkish office with the blinds drawn; here, he sits in a white car in a sunny exterior. Also he walked out on a diagonal to screen left and here he sits in the car on screen right. Effective transitions from scene to scene (or from one dramatically self-contained unit to another) are essential to generate energy at such junctures. Usually, one can judge the quality of a film by observing the cinesthetic values in the transitions. The transition to the scene at the gas station may not be spectacular; however, the delicate play of opposites results in a visceral jolt unavoidably felt by the viewer.

Scene 11, to repeat, starts with a medium shot of George in profile sitting in the white car looking at something in the distance (2 1/3 sec.). Cut to what he sees: a long shot of a gas station with a prominent sign, J. Maloney. The shot gratifies the viewer's expectation, George is on the right track (5 sec., long enough in duration for the full disclosure). Cut to (shot 3) the same medium shot of George in the car, pipe in mouth. Eventually he starts the motor (12 sec., the second longest duration shot in the scene). This shot is wiped out by a huge trailer passing in front of the camera, an interesting interruption. The trailer, after passing, opens the view into the same long shot of the Maloney gas station as before (2 3/4 sec.). Cut back to the medium shot of George in the car looking (3 sec.). Cut to a medium shot of a man and a woman standing behind the window of the gas station's office looking out (3 1/2 sec.). Cut to a long shot of George in the car (3 sec.). Cut back to George in a profile medium shot in the moving car, as camera follows (5 1/2 sec.). Cut to a high long shot of the white car moving on the road; George is making a wide turn toward (presumably) the gas station. Cut to eye level long shot of George arriving at the Maloney gas station (14 sec.). The last 10 shots show a meticulously fragmented sequence of brief shots, a slow disclosure in preparation for a confrontation (with Joe Maloney). Cut to a medium shot of the man and the woman in the station's office; the man moves to the door; the woman looks out (5 sec.). Cut to a reverse medium shot; the man, most likely Maloney himself, walks out the door (on the outside) and heads toward the car at the pump (camera follows him). He asks: "Fill 'er up?" (12 1/2 sec.). Maloney looks like a shady character, an example of perfect typecasting. Cut to a medium shot of Maloney turning around to attend to the gas pumps (5 sec.).

Presently Hitchcock maneuvers with multiangularity. Maloney is moving around the car performing his duties. We see him at different angles while George is the stabilizing image, taking his time, asking to have his oil checked, windshield cleaned, delaying the crucial inquiry as Maloney paces like a caged animal. Briefly we see them in a medium two-shot when George emerges from the car (11 sec.). Cut to a single medium shot of George trying to strike a match on the metal of the car, reminiscent of a similar situation in Hitchcock's *The Birds* (5 sec.). Cut to a medium shot of Maloney pumping gas: "Be careful with your match" (2 1/2 sec.). Cut back to a medium shot of George, apologetic: "Sorry." He observes Maloney's every move (5 1/2 sec.).

Cut to a medium shot of Maloney's back as he walks to the front of the car to check the oil (4 sec.). Cut to a medium two-shot of Maloney at the hood and George looking up to where the sign is, asking: "Is this your place?" Maloney answers with a rather indifferent "Yes" (3 1/2 sec.).

At this point starts a relatively long (33 shot) separation composed of medium shots between George and Maloney, the latter in constant motion (which makes this separation singular). George starts his inquiry in earnest, although in a stealthy manner intended to entrap Maloney. The pipe, wielded by George like a sword, is humorous, as well as being Sherlock Holmesian. At first he determines Maloney's identity and, little by little, comes around to the subject of Edward Shoebridge. Maloney resists; he never heard of any Shoebridge. George uses a carrot: "You can make yourself some money, Mr. Maloney." Maloney tries to find out, sneakily, what George would do with the information. George: "Well . . . it is confidential." The average length of the shots is from 3 to 5 seconds. The movements and changes of Maloney's position keep the multiangularity active and dramatically fitting. Hitchcock then sneaks in a passing and momentary two-shot from another angle (at shot 19 of the separation), where we see Maloney enter George's frame and exit immediately. In a close shot, he asks: "Why do you want to find him?" Cut to closer medium shot of George: "That's confidential too . . ."

At this point, and for the last 13 shots of the separation, Hitchcock switches to close-ups of George, mostly in profile, and medium close-ups, face on, for Maloney. George presses on: "Tell me, why did you put a headstone on an empty grave, Maloney?" "What headstone?" asks the startled Maloney. George: "The same one you paid 395 dollars in cash for back in 1965." They are locked together in eye contact, no

more movements. Maloney, after a telling pause: "You owe me 2 dollars and 47 cents" (for the gasoline). George persists: "You went to the County House and asked for a death certificate for Edward Shoebridge. You were turned down." Cut to a new shot of Maloney as he turns his back to the camera. This is the last shot of the separation. The next shot is a medium two-shot: Maloney in profile next to George facing camera. Maloney asks if he'll be paid by credit card. George: "No credit card, you always preferred cash, Mr. Maloney." George pays the cash and enters his car. Maloney is left alone, standing. Cut to a medium shot of the woman, Maloney's wife as it turns out later, looking out the office door, worried (later in the film, she will always be in the same state of worry). Cut to a frontal medium shot of the car with George driving (1 1/2 sec.) followed by a cut to a medium long shot of Maloney scribbling on a pad (music is louder, signaling a conclusion of the scene) (2 sec.). Cut to a diagonal shot of the car, showing in the corner of the frame the license plate (2 sec.). Finally, as a concluding shot, a close-up of the pad of paper in Maloney's hand with the license number 885 DJU on it (2 sec.). This jotted note is a plant for future use. The scene lasts 5 minutes, has 65 shots, and, what is remarkable, is played out almost in real time (considering that George did not need any oil or water and hardly any gas). The only modest deletions occur at the beginning (the car driving to the station) and at the end (the car leaving). And, as mentioned before, the skillfully interwoven multiangularity within a separation gives this scene a distinct stylistic look, as opposed to the usual ping-pong rhythm of A, B, A, B, close-ups. However simple and mundane the appearance may be, a careful analysis yields the underlying high vernacular. Dramatically, the suspense is heating up, and the viewer at the same time starts to worry about George.

Scene 12. The linearity of the narrative takes a twist: for the first time in the film Maloney crosses over the boundary of the parallelism; he creates a bridge between the primary action of George, Blanche, and Mrs. Rainbird to the other, secondary action of Eddy and Fran, the kidnappers. The parallelism has not yet merged; for that, the viewer will have to wait a while, but after this scene we will be aware that there is a definite connection between the two plots.

The scene starts in a modestly elegant jewelry shop. Eddy, who for the first time is addressed as Mr. Adamson, is sitting in a medium long shot with a customer to whom he is showing pearls (5 sec.). Adamson is on the left of the display table; the customer is on the right; both are in profile; the glass door to the store is in the center. This positioning, however plain, is of interest because the next shot crosses the axis: we see Adamson in a reverse angle medium shot on screen right, still talking to the (by now) offscreen customer. Upon hearing the door chimes he turns to camera (to where the entrance door is assumed to be). He reacts with a sour face to what he sees. The above crossing of the axis signals something important to come and is compounded here with a slow disclosure as we wait to find out what it is that Adamson sees (10 sec.). Cut to a medium low long shot of the glass door; behind it stands Maloney dressed in a jacket, but without a tie; he cuts a menacing figure (2 sec.). Cut back to the previous medium shot of Adamson, who excuses himself to the customer, then asks the saleswoman to take over. He gets up (camera adjusts), looking toward the door (7 sec.). Cut back to Maloney as he approaches the door, ready to enter. The shot becomes low angle when Maloney is close to the camera (4 sec.). Cut back to Adamson standing, as before; when Maloney enters his frame both start walking to an office door; camera follows as they pass by a large mirror in which we see their profiles, with tense facial expressions. Adamson tells the saleswoman that he'll be busy in his office; we hear her answer: "Yes, Mr. Adamson" (this is the first utterance of his assumed name) (6 1/2 sec.). Note that the above mirror shot permits the viewer to see the two characters from the back and in profile at the same time and is similar to Hitchcock's more often used shadow images.

Cut to a medium shot of the interior of Adamson's office as they enter one at a time in front of the camera. Adamson stands screen left. Maloney passes out of frame. We shall see him in the next cut sitting

on the couch. This starts one of Hitchcock's longest separations, consisting of 51 shots (slightly shorter than the one in *Psycho*). The 6 shots
before, a slow disclosure and a teaser separation (4 shots Adamson-
Maloney), are a typical Hitchcockian introduction to an important scene.
What ensues is like a waterfall of dramatic disclosures and startling
revelations that put the viewer in a privileged position: we learn ahead
of our protagonists, George and Blanche, that the innocent heir to Mrs.
Rainbird's fortune is a criminal. Among other schemes he has apparently killed his adopted parents, having hired Maloney for the job, who
in turn occasionally blackmails Adamson for small handouts.

Maloney hands Adamson the note with the license number and tells
him about the snooping, imposter lawyer McBride who asks uncom-
fortable questions about the past and seems to know a lot about the
Shoebridges. At one point, Maloney pulls out a switchblade knife; he
is ready to take an assignment to kill George. Adamson, with his devilish smile revived (after a period of worry), tells him to cool it, he'll
look into the situation himself and let him know what to do next.
Maloney is extremely nervous, fearing for his skin. They are interrupted by a knock on the door. The saleswoman announces that two
men from the police want to talk to him. Maloney is near panic.
Adamson covers his nervousness with a cool look. At this point the
separation is resolved in a long two-shot.

In the long separation, the fast clip of the single shots varies between 1 1/2 and 7 seconds; the majority average 4 seconds; the only
exceptions are shots 36 and 37, lasting 15 and 11 seconds respectively
(when Maloney spills most of the confessional details of their common
crime). The stabilizing shots are those of Maloney, all of them static,
most in close shots, in a sitting position. The shots with Adamson are
flexible, some in movement, panning, some with his back to the camera, then turning suddenly to face camera, not unlike the mise-en-scène
in similar separations in *Notorious*. There are two incisions into the
A B A B between Adamson and Maloney: in shot 27, a close-up of the
white notepaper with the license number Maloney hands Adamson;
the second one is the close-up of the switch blade flicked open by
Maloney, in shot 41. The only touch of humorr is in shot 12 when
Maloney steals cigarettes (in the only wide medium shot in the separation), taking advantage of Adamson's turning to the wall. The resolution of the separation in the two-shot (shot 58) is the only time the

viewer sees the spatial relationship between the two characters since the separation was never introduced with an expository (establishing) shot. Also, this long separation has an epilogue in the form of the long duration static three-shot with the policemen at the jewelry store. As a result, we are able to unwind from the tension created during the separation.

Adamson, after a pause, goes to meet the police in the main store. Cut to Adamson in the store walking to greet the two plainclothesmen (one of whom we remember from the inquiry of Mr. Constantine). Camera follows Adamson and settles on a three-shot without any cuts. The police are conducting a routine inquiry in the jewelry trade about the big ransom diamond on the loose. Adamson regains his internal calm. He assures the men that he'll keep his eyes open, even gives the police some advice. The conversation brings out touches of humor, which we lost during the Maloney separation. The police thank him and leave. Adamson turns back to his office, camera pans with him. (This interlude, lasting one minute, 45 seconds, is the longest duration shot in the film.) Cut to a reverse angle as Adamson opens the door and enters his office in medium shot (1 1/2 sec.). Cut to reverse view: the office is empty, but the window is open and the drapes are blowing in the wind. Maloney has apparently run for his life (5 sec.). Cut back to the medium shot of Adamson looking, with a smile on his face (4 sec.). Cut to the empty couch on which Maloney was seated (1 1/2 sec.). Cut back to the medium shot of Adamson, who turns to the door and tells the saleswoman to close up the store; he looks around the room, smiling (14 sec.). Cut back to the same shot of the window with the drapes (1 1/2 sec.). Cut to a close-up of the Maloney note with the license number of Blanche's car (2 sec.). Cut to a panning shot as Adamson picks the note up from the floor and reads it in a close shot. Cut to a tight close-up of the note with the number, a symmetry with a similar shot at the end of the previous scene.

The scene lasts almost 7 minutes (the separation alone is 3 3/4 minutes). The piercing of the shield of mystery about the connection between the two parallel plots in the film seems to be, on the surface, only a clever narrative maneuver. The execution in Hitchcock's cinema language, however, is paramount to its success. A careful overview of the details of structure, as in the above analysis, will yield some of the answers to the difficult question of the relationship between cinema form and content. Note how the opposites, the main tool in Hitchcock's arsenal, are kept alive: the separation in Scene 11 (Maloney's gas station) had George as the stable image while Maloney was moving around; here, in Scene 12, Maloney is the stable image while Adamson is in movement. Also, the clever placing of the longest duration shot (with the policemen) is contrapuntal to the fast-paced fragmentation of the 51-shot separation. The ebb and flow of the viewer's feelings and thoughts is, to a great extent, controlled by the small changes in framing, positioning (graphics), and timing. The innocent, as it seems, crossing of the axis at the beginning of the scene (when Maloney appears at the door of the jewelry store) is crucial in building up the tension that slowly creeps up to a crescendo during the separation.

Scene 13. Takes us in perfect linearity (after a time deletion) to a shot that is a consequence of the last shot in the previous scene (the piece of paper with Blanche's license number) to a close-up (shot 1) of a street sign "Castle Rd." The two written signs back to back form the transition. Since this scene has a Hitchcockian classical construction of "complex simplicity" I shall, in order to hammer it in, revert again to shot numbers and timing of shots. Shot 1 (street sign) lasts 2 1/2 seconds. Cut to (shot 2) a medium close-up of Adamson in three-quarter profile sitting in his car looking forward, then quickly glancing at his side view mirror (out of frame). One assumes he looks toward the street sign (3 sec.). Cut to (shot 3) a wide long shot of Blanche's house at night with the familiar archway from which Fran appears walking toward the house, examining the shingle. Two passing cars drive by on the road in front of the house (indicating that Adamson most likely is on the other side of the road). Shot 3 lasts 9 seconds. Cut to (shot 4) the same (as in shot 2) medium close-up of Adamson in the car looking (first repeat) (1 1/2 sec.). Cut back to the long shot of Blanche's house (shot 5). Fran snoops around, then walks to the road, camera pans with her until the side window of the car comes into view, which indicates that she's heading toward the car. Two pedestrians are seen on the sidewalk. Note that the hood of the car is evident in the foreground bottom frame in both shots 3 and 5. The five shots have rounded up a semantic unity; therefore the viewer is now certain that Adamson is watching Fran and that both are spying on Blanche. (Shot 5 lasts 11 1/2 sec.).

Cut to (shot 6) the same medium close-up of Adamson (third repeat) who continues to follow Fran's movements (1 3/4 sec.). Cut to (shot 7) a long shot of Fran framed prominently through the car window. She crosses the street. The spatial relationship between Adamson's car and Blanche's house is definitely established. A passing car (across the frame) forces Fran to speed up (8 sec.). Cut to (shot 8) the same, fourth repeat of Adamson in the car. His eyes follow Fran, thus through him as an onlooker the viewer can judge Fran's progress and the direction of her movements (1 1/3 sec.). Cut to (shot 9) a medium long shot of Fran, by now closer to the car, walking across the frame (2 1/3 sec.). Cut to (shot 10) the same medium close-up of Adamson (fourth repeat); he continues to follow Fran by turning his face to the right, then left, as she fleetingly passes by the rear window. In a sense this shot resolves the separation since we see them both in the same frame (even for a fraction of a second). Yet Hitchcock keeps persisting in the fragmentation for another shot (8 sec.). Cut to (shot 11) a close-up of Fran as she enters the frame at the passenger side window. Theme music stops the moment she says: "Your friend Blanche Tyler is a spiritualist." Adamson's voice (offscreen): "A spiritualist?" Fran, looking in through the car window: "That's what it says on her shingle. Also, there's no one home." Adamson (offscreen): "A spirit is never home. Get in" (7 1/2 sec.). Cut to (shot 12) a frontal medium two-shot as Fran sits down next to Adamson. It is noteworthy to point out that it took Hitchcock 12 shots (fragments) to accomplish both the slow disclosure and the separation as well as the deletions (like the walk of Fran to the car which would last much longer in real time). At this point, shot 12 settles down to an exchange of dialogue. Fran: "What do you think we should do?" Adamson: "We'll wait. We still don't know who the man is." A car's headlights skim the interior of their car (10 3/4 sec.). Cut back to the familiar exterior of Blanche's house (shot 13). Another car passes by (1 1/2 sec.). Cut to (shot 14) the same medium two-shot of Fran and Adamson in their car. Fran is smoking nervously (3 sec.). Cut to (shot 15) the same exterior of Blanche's house. A red car (familiar) drives in from the right and stops in front of the door (3 1/2 sec.). Cut back to the two-shot (shot 16) of Adamson and Fran. Adamson: "That must be her" (3 1/2 sec.). As it turns out, shot 12, the resolution of the first separation, acts now as a beginning of a new one, this time between the two in the car, as the onlookers, and what they see in front of Blanche's house. Cut to (shot 17) the same wide view of the house. George and Blanche leave the car. George comes around the cab and takes the bag of groceries from Blanche, she reaches into the cab and pulls out another bag and gives it to him. They start to go into the house (23 1/2 sec.). Cut to (shot 18) the same two-shot of the on-lookers in the car (2 1/2 sec.). Cut to (shot 19) the same long shot of the house; Blanche is already at the door (deletion); George follows her with the groceries (3 3/4 sec.). The pantomime begins to look comedic. Cut to (shot 20) the same shot of Fran and Adamson looking and talk-ing; Adamson: "That must be the fellow with the pipe who called on Maloney . . . A cab driver" (7 sec.). Cut to (shot 21) a closer medium two-shot, from the side, of Blanche and George arguing. Importantly, this is a first change in angularity, painlessly tampering with the so-called point-of-view (POV) principle (since the onlookers are still in the same position in the car and cannot see things from the side). Hitch-cock likes to play with POVs where most films tend to be meticulous about them.

Blanche and George face each other in profile; he takes two steps down and moves closer to the car.

BLANCHE: "What's this? Where are you going?"
GEORGE: "I'm going home to my own bed where I can get some sleep."
BLANCHE: "No, you're not."
GEORGE: "Blanche, is that all you've got on your mind?"
BLANCHE: "What are you saving it for, a rainy day?"
GEORGE: "Hey honey, you never know when you're gonna need it."
BLANCHE: "You're not being friendly, George."
GEORGE: "Blanche, I'm too pooped to pop. I'd be useless."
BLANCHE: "You're always too useless to me. You're always pooping out when I need you the most."
GEORGE: "What about when I'm out there looking for . . ."

Loud passing car horn obliterates the voices. This is the longest du-ration shot in the scene (27 sec.). Cut back to (shot 22) the same shot of Fran and Adamson, the onlookers. Adamson smiles in his old dev-ilish way. We hear the conversation at the house: Geroge (offscreen) as the car horn fades in the distance: ". . . We can collect a huge amount of money. You call that being useless?" Adamson's smile sours upon hearing the above (3 sec.). Cut to (shot 23) the same new angle of George and Blanche as in 21.

> BLANCHE [continuing]: "You know what I'm talking about. Come on inside and stop being difficult."
> GEORGE: "Not tonight, Josephine. I'm outta here." [He puts a pipe in his mouth.]
> BLANCHE: "You're a fink."
> GEORGE: "If I'm a fink, honey, you're an ungrateful bitch."
> BLANCHE: "What about tomorrow?"
> GEORGE: "What about it?"
> BLANCHE: "We've got important work to do. I want you to be sure about Eddie Shoebridge" (15 sec.).

Cut to (shot 24) the same shot of the onlookers. Adamson bitterly digests what he just heard. Fran looks worried. A passing car noise again covers the rest of the sentence (1 1/3 sec.). Cut to (shot 25) George and Blanche (sharing the frame); George shouting protests; he is busy to-morrow; he must work with his cab. He begins walking away (10 1/2 sec.). Cut (shot 26) back to Adamson and Fran looking and listening (1 1/2 sec.). Cut (shot 27) George and Blanche in a new frontal medium long shot (similar to the one from the beginning of the scene but closer). George walks around the taxi, gets in. Blanche stands by the door of her house. The taxi drives away. Blanche, furious, enters the house (13 1/2 sec.). Cut to (shot 28) the same shot of Adamson and Fran. The ensuing dialogue summarizes the situation.

> FRAN: "You better give me a quick synopsis. I'm confused."
> ARTHUR: "Simple. A cab driver is shacked up with a sex-starved me-dium named Blanche Tyler. And, don't ask me why, but appar-ently they're on the trail of some spook named Eddie Shoebridge. Fortunately not on the trail of your favorite kidnapper and mine."
> FRAN: "How can you be so sure? You did hear them talk about col-lecting a huge hunk of money. Couldn't that be the reward that's on our heads?"
> ARTHUR: "You got yourself a point there, Francis, old girl. But only time will tell if it's any good. One thing's certain: we're not going to change our game plan. Not now."
> FRAN: "Buy me a drink Arthur."

Arthur reaches for the ignition to start the car (43 sec.).

The most important aspect of Scene 13 is the end of the mystery in the parallelism. By now the two sets of adversaries are seen together, although only one side has seen the other. George and Blanche will do so only at the end of the film. The viewer has good reasons to worry about George and Blanche. Hitchcock, instead of spinning the action into high gear, delays the dramatic climaxes. The next two scenes do just that.

Scene 14. Back in the Victorian setting of Madame Blanche's séance with the wealthy Mrs. Rainbird: in the background we hear heavenly singing. The two ladies are together in a medium long shot; Mrs. Rainbird sitting on the left, Blanche already in a trance, on the right, with ample space between them. A separation sequence is just about to start. Cut to a medium frontal shot of Mrs. Rainbird listening while Blanche talks to her medium Henry about hearing a baby crying. Cut to a semi-profile of Blanche, acting out a tortuous scene with the invisible Henry about the chauffeur. Cut back to Mrs. Rainbird (repeat of the previous shot) as she listens intently. Cut to the same shot of Blanche asking Henry to inquire where the baby is being taken . . . then about a graveyard, headstone, repeating in dramatic form the information we know she received previously from George. Cut back to Mrs. Rainbird listening, animated. Cut back to Blanche who speaks about Shoebridge. Cut back to Mrs. Rainbird who in turn prompts Blanche to talk to the chauffeur—while offscreen Blanche screams about the house on fire. Cut back to Blanche begging Henry to go back to the chauffeur. Cut back to Mrs. Rainbird who suddenly remembers something: "Listen to me, Madame." Cut to a new tight close-up of Blanche in profile, strongly backlit—she listens. Cut to a new medium close-up of Mrs. Rainbird: "I remembered something else that could be terribly important." Note that on the eleventh and twelfth shot of the separation, after a gradual increase in tempo, the camera moves closer in. Hitchcock makes us wait through the next nine shots, as Blanche unwinds her séance, to hear what Mrs. Rainbird has to say that is so "terribly important." Cut to the same close-up of Blanche; she asks Henry to wait. Cut back to Mrs. Rainbird (brief). Cut back to Blanche still talking to Henry. Cut back to Mrs. Rainbird (brief). Cut back to Blanche (brief). Cut back to Mrs. Rainbird (brief). Cut to a new (shot 19) medium close-up of Blanche in three-quarter profile as she bids Henry goodbye and turns suddenly to Mrs. Rainbird with naive pretense, as in the previous sessions, asking "What happened?" Cut to the same medium close-up of Mrs. Rainbird: "Don't you remember?" Music stops. Cut back to Blanche: "Not a blessed thing." Cut back to Mrs. Rainbird: "It doesn't matter now . . . listen . . . listen" (she gets up, camera follows). Mrs. Rainbird remembers that the dying chauffeur wrote her that a parson who baptized the baby promised to keep track of him. Cut back to Blanche listening. Cut back to Mrs. Rainbird, who, after finishing her sentence, sits down, then adds: "And there is an additional thing I can tell you. . . ." End of scene, without a full resolution of the separation; the last words become a transition to the next scene.

Note that the positioning of Blanche's left profile (facing screen right, the same way as Mrs. Rainbird) defies the realistic arrangements of separation in which, in general usage, the A and the B face each other. Hitchcock always resented such restrictions. In *Notorious*, he had already introduced a profile "facing" a frontal shot. In the above separation it is only in shot 19 that Blanche turns her face to screen left to face Mrs. Rainbird, thus "justifying" her previous profile shots.

Scene 14 lasts 2 minutes, 10 seconds, and has 22 shots, including the introductory two shot. As expected, the scene is funny and satirical and, though it brings out new information about the pastor, it nevertheless delays the resolution of the new dramatic focus, namely the danger looming around George from Maloney and Adamson.

Scene 15. Starts with a two-shot of George and Blanche riding in their taxi: George is picking up on Mrs. Rainbird's last sentence ("An additional thing I can tell you . . .") from the previous scene, by saying "Don't tell me, let me guess . . . Five hundred." Blanche answers: "Not a penny until we can produce his name and address." She tells him about Bishop Wood of St. Arthur's Cathedral, formerly the pastor who baptized the baby and who might know of his whereabouts. It looks as though George has received a new assignment. He starts protesting; she pinches him on the cheek (still in the two-shot). The scene lasts only 30 seconds without cuts.

This simple scene unexpectedly generates a most complex transition to the next one: the inertia of the taxi's movement (from the outgoing Scene 15) is forward on a slight screen right diagonal.

Scene 16. The opening shot: a very high long shot of George climbing, by skips, an elegant formation of steps that leads, as the shot continues, with a camera panning and craning up, to an opulent cathedral.
George's ascent is toward screen left diagonal, in the opposite direction, in contrast to the taxi's movement. The horizontal lines of the
steps ending on the perpendicular tower of the cathedral gives the transition a burst of energy after the slack of the taxi scene. Curiously
enough it also leads to a most improbable event: the kidnapping of
Bishop Wood, whom George has just come to see—by whom else but
our pair of kidnappers. The narrative's credibility is tampered with, yet
Hitchcock gets away with it thanks to the black humor permeating
the entire scene and the quickness and precision of the operation of
the kidnapping itself.

Fragmented in 17 shots of less than 2 seconds each (four are less
than one second each), the event is presented with such skill in the
use of film language that the suspense thus created absorbs the slight
weakness in plausibility. The four-shot transition from the previous
scene is rather slow, taking about one half of the screen time. George
runs up the steps (shot 1) and enters the cathedral; the camera continues to pan to the top of the neogothic tower (31 sec.). George is inside
the church (shot 2), where a service is in progress (2 sec.). Cut (shot 3)
to a long shot of the congregation singing hymns; the altar is seen in
far background (4 sec.). Cut to (shot 4) George in medium two-shot
approaching a priest and asking how to see Bishop Wood. The priest
reprimands him for smoking a pipe in church and in a hushed voice
suggests he wait for the end of the service for an appointment. This
shot lasts 33 seconds, the longest one in the scene. The total length of
the introduction is 70 seconds.

Cut back (shot 5) to the long shot of the congregation (10 sec.). Cut
(shot 6) to a medium long shot of the bishop in a red robe walking
from left to right as camera follows (3 1/2 sec.). The fast-moving action
of the kidnapping starts here. Cut to (shot 7) a medium long shot of
Fran disguised as an elderly widow, all in black, with a veil, glasses,
and a false nose and neck. She moves resolutely from behind a balustrade walking to screen left, as camera pans with her; she passes the
bishop who keeps walking right; at this point, she feigns a fainting fit,
and falls in front of the bishop. He kneels down to help her (10 sec.).
Cut to (shot 8) a long shot of Adamson, dressed as a deacon with glasses,

moving fast, from a church pew, toward the accident. The crowd of worshippers is heard Ohing and Ahing (5 1/2 sec.). Nine shots of very short duration follow. Note that the quickness of these shots covers up a significant number of brief deletions between them. Shot 9, extreme close-up of Adamson's hand jabbing a needle into the bishop's arm (1 1/2 sec.). Shot 10, tight close-up of the bishop's face looking up in reaction to the needle entering (1 sec.). Shot 11, close-up of the withdrawn needle (1 sec.). Shot 12, close-up of bishop's face as the drug starts working (1 1/2 sec.). Shot 13, close-up of Fran's face, still on the floor, but readying to get up (1 1/3 sec.). Crowd is heard murmuring offscreen. Shot 14, close-up of Fran's bottom leg and shoe as she rises (1 sec.). Shot 15, close-up of Adamson's face as he moves quickly out of frame (3/4 sec.). Shot 16, close-up of Adamson's hand comes into frame and grabs the bishop (1/2 sec.). Shot 17, close-up of Fran's hand comes in from the bottom of the frame grasping the bishop (1 sec.). Crowd heard murmuring all the time. Shot 18, long shot of the congregation grouped on screen right, reacting slowly to what they start perceiving (1 sec.). Shot 19, long shot of the altar part of the cathedral with priest and attendants (1 sec.). Shot 20, medium two-shot of George and priest watching intently (1 sec.). Note that George, who, one should assume, is the principal onlooker, is shown only once, and only for one second, during this action. Shot 21, long shot of the congregation in the left side pews (1 sec.). Shot 22, long shot from the back of the retreating group of Adamson and Fran, holding Bishop Wood between them, heading for the back exit (3 sec.). The noise from the crowd is louder. Shot 23, long shot of the congregation on the right (repeat of shot 18) as people start getting up (1 1/3 sec.). Shot 24, long shot of the crowd on the left as people are leaving their pews (repeat of shot 21) (1 sec.). Shot 25 (repeat of shot 9), long shot of the altar as priest moves to the right (1 1/2 sec.). Shot 26, long shot (same as in 22): towards the exit we see Adamson, the bishop, and Fran reaching the doorway (3 1/2 sec.). Shot 27, third repeat of shot 18, this time the people have moved closer to camera in a medium shot, watching. We hear one parishioner: "Where do you think they're taking him?" Another: "I don't know. Do you think he's sick?" (3 1/2 sec.). Shot 28, third repeat of shot 22, the kidnappers have left through the door (2 sec.). Shot 29 (the longest deletion): high long shot of Adamson's car pulling out of an alley with tires screeching (2 sec.). Shot 30, medium long shot, parishioners coming out of the church door into the alley (2 sec.). Shot 31 (same as 29), long shot, as car turns out of the alley exiting the frame to the right (2 1/2 sec.). Shot 32, repeat of shot 30, more parishioners coming out of the exterior door watching. End of Scene 16 (2 min., 14 sec.). The last salvo of short shots contains 16 cuts of less than 2 seconds each. The audacity of the kidnappers matches the inability of the crowd to comprehend or act quickly enough.

The parallelism in the film's action between the duos of Adamson-Fran and George-Blanche is now one notch closer to converging since George has seen them for the first time; however, he still does not realize who they are. Complete convergence of the actions will have to wait till the end of the film. It should be noted, nevertheless, how diligently Hitchcock is preparing for that convergence. For example, the next scene, 17, is in symmetry with Scene 15, each representing the principals of the parallel action in a similar setting: in Scene 15 George and Blanche are riding in a car in a frontal shot. In Scene 17 Adamson and Fran are riding in a car (with their victim hidden in the back) also in a frontal two-shot. Sandwiched between these two scenes is the one of the kidnapping (16).

Scene 17. Starts with a frontal medium two-shot of Fran and Adamson in their car; the linearity of the narrative again sustained. The two kidnappers are returning from the "job," their victim somewhere behind their seats. The trigger release of the Hitchcockian time clock is also working with precision: Scene 15 a release, Scene 16 a trigger, and now Scene 17 a release again. Fran is in the process of taking off her make-up, glasses, and cloak; she looks behind her and, referring to the bishop, says: "He's moving. Are you sure you gave him enough?" Adamson shrugs it off: "The usual dose . . ."; and says, turning toward the seat: "He looks so harmless" (10 sec.). Cut to a close-up of Fran as she strips off her false nose and neck and takes off her wig. A separation begins containing 27 single close-ups; it is never resolved (as in Scene 15), as we no longer see both in the same frame. The framing is static, without change except for head turns to profile, as they speak to each other. After congratulating each other on the neat and successful job, they turn to the subject of George. As it turns out, they have both seen him in the church, and they suspect, quite naturally, that he had come with the purpose of spying on them. Adamson cannot understand how in the world George could have known of their kidnapping plans. Fran hints at the possibility that Blanche possesses the power of ESP. Adamson, covering with his devilish smile a build-up of fury, informs Fran that he's not going to do anything about it, that "Maloney is itching for that job and he's got it . . . I'm afraid our quarrelsome lovers will have to share a fatal accident." Fran is visibly shaken. She doesn't want to know anything about it. Adamson laughs at her: "Come on, dear, that's what makes it so exciting. We move on it all together, nothing held back." The last shot in the separation (shot 27) is of Fran as she looks horrified; the theme music begins again. Cut to a long shot of an uphill street. We see Adamson's large black car coming around the corner and down the street toward the camera; it then turns to the entrance of a garage. Cut to a medium shot of the car from the side; through the window we see Fran pointing a remote control device and the garage door opening (10 sec.). Cut to a medium long shot of the same as the door finally opens and the car drives into the dark garage; the garage door closes slowly, a natural fade out with strong funereal overtones (10 sec.). The scene contains 31 shots and lasts 3 minutes.

Scene 18. The transition is, as nearly always with Hitchcock, an energetic and startling one. From the blackness of the garage door an eye blinding cut to a sunlit kitchen in medium long shot, with George fixing hamburgers and Blanche at the table eating one. Such continuity, the return to the parallel action, is as if in answer to the mounting anxiety about the fate of our "quarrelsome lovers." George joins Blanche at the table and the camera moves in closer to a medium shot over George's shoulder (12 sec.). Now starts a series of five over-the-shoulder shots from one side of the table to the other as they talk about the kidnapping. Blanche eats avariciously; she wonders why in the world anyone would want to kidnap a bishop. George: "For the ransom, dummy, it's worth a million dollars." Blanche is worried about the chances of getting their reward of ten thousand. They argue. George insists that his most pressing obligation for now is to drive the taxi. At this point (45 seconds into the scene) the telephone rings. George shouts to her to answer the phone. Cut to the last over-the-shoulder shot toward Blanche; she leans over to pick up the phone; camera follows her (losing George from the frame). Maloney is on the line. George comes to her side of the table. Both huddle by the receiver as the camera moves in to a tight close two-shot (one minute into the scene).

Note how elegantly Hitchcock handles this over-the-shoulder sequence (at best, a clumsy form to get in and out of). He enters into it by following George, who sits down at the table opposite Blanche, and resolves it by having Blanche lean out of the two-shot far enough to reach the phone.

George joins her again next to the receiver in a two-shot. Both, in a funny way, try to listen to what Maloney has to say, unaware of the cloud of danger gathering over them. Maloney says that he has traced them through the plates and offers now to give information on the Shoebridge fellow they are looking for. Blanche in her frolicky manner asks why Maloney has changed his mind and wants to talk? The answer over the phone is that he wants a thousand for the information. They bargain; Blanche tells him that her lawyer is next to her and offers a hundred; Maloney suggests two hundred; George mimics an OK; they make a date, at Maloney's suggestion, to meet at Abe's Diner on Route 22. Blanche wonders why so far away. Maloney explains that he will be there on business. They set a meeting in two hours; to Blanche's final inquiry "Is Eddie Shoebridge still alive?" Maloney's answer is that he will not talk until he "sees the color of their money" and hangs up. George made a note of the address. He gets up, saying that it smells fishy to him, and walks out of frame. Blanche in close-up, with mouth full of food, mumbles: "What have we got to lose?" Cut to medium shot of George by the closet asking: "You got 200 dollars on you?" Cut to high medium shot of Blanche, who answers: "You know me better than that. Of course not." She asks for another hamburger. Cut back to George (as before) who points out that she already has one in her hand. Cut back to Blanche stuffing her mouth with food: "I'll eat it in the car." Cut back to George (brief): "Come on." Cut back to Blanche, in a hurry, taking food from the table, adding: "You're impossible." End of scene. The last six shots in separation show again how Hitchcock smoothly changes key within one scene from over-the-shoulder to separation. (Total length 3 minutes.) The transition, in both its pictorial and audio content to the next scene, is perhaps the most spectacular so far.

Scene 19. Begins with a very high long shot of Blanche's white car on a highway, the horn blasting rhythmically in tune with the theme music, while the camera pans and cranes up following the car; momentarily we lose sight of it behind some trees, then regain it from high up on a curve where the road goes around a steep hill (15 sec.). Cut to the interior of the car; Blanche looking morose, George at the wheel in a medium two-shot (3 sec.). Cut to a reverse long shot of Blanche's car coming around the corner toward the camera, approaching closer as camera pans to the right with it and past it. Camera eventually stops on the back of a parked car on the right side of the road, in close foreground. We see Blanche's car in the distance making a turn out of frame. The theme music (with the punctuating horn sounds) stops; in the dead silence a silhouetted back of a man's figure emerges, sitting in the front seat of the parked car. We recognize Joe Maloney watching Blanche's car passing out of the way (22 sec.). Cut to a long shot of Blanche's car driving toward the camera (reverse from previous direction), turning to the right as camera follows it, and parking at the side of Abe's Diner. Blanche and George slowly get out of their car, leisurely walk to the diner, with George, as always, favoring his back. (The slow pace seems to anticipate some crisis.) The scene lasts 75 seconds.

Scene 20. Picks up on action: Blanche and George enter the diner, sit down at a table covered with red and white oilcloth, both with their backs to the camera. A middle-aged waitress comes forward. George orders: "A couple of beers, please." The camera moves a bit closer. George looks at his watch, saying: "He must be late" (28 sec.). Cut to the exterior, we see a big green car, resembling Maloney's, drive in (camera pans with it) and park next to Blanche's car outside the diner (10 sec.). Cut to a side medium shot as Maloney emerges from his car; camera tilts as he stands up and looks over Blanche's car, the white roof of which is in the foreground (20 sec.). Cut back to the interior of the diner: reverse medium shot of Blanche and George this time facing the camera with the waitress' back to the camera. We hear George thank her for bringing the order. She turns and moves out; two new beers are on the table in front of Blanche and George (7 sec.). Hitchcock's use of the above reverse shot is an excellent example of his touch: he sandwiches Maloney's arrival outside the diner between the two views inside the diner, one from the back and the other from the front, with our protagonists sitting at the table (the axis is crossed). Included also is an ingenious deletion, allowing time for the new order of beers to be carried out (while the sense of danger hovers over). The structure here is original, thought-provoking, and cinematically elegant; and, it gives the viewer the kind of subliminal jolt that has to be seen for it is hard to put it in words.

Cut to a medium long shot of the door opening; a group of four children and a pastor enter the diner (4 sec.). Cut back to the same medium two-shot of Blanche and George; they look suprised since they, as well as we, expected Maloney (1 1/2 sec.). Cut back to the medium long shot of the children and the pastor as they file in and sit down at a table in the back of the diner. The owner behind the counter asks them how was Sunday school? The pastor: "Noisy." They order five Cokes (18 sec.). Cut back to the same two-shot of Blanche and George observing the group (2 1/2 sec.). Cut back to the group of kids (2 sec.). Cut back to our protagonists as George finishes his beer (2 sec.). Cut back to the group as the Coke is served (2 1/2 sec.). Cut back to Blanche and George getting restless (6 sec.). Cut to the entrance door (1 1/2 sec.). Cut back to the same shot of Blanche and George. He looks at his watch (5 sec.). Cut back to the medium shot of the entrance door, this time opening; but, instead of Maloney, a young woman enters, dressed in red. She is greeted by the pastor who settles her at a separate table (next to the one with the kids) (15 sec.). Cut back to the same medium two-shot of our protagonists. George smiles, pointing at the others, saying: "Look at that, nice arrangement." Blanche looks at them, then: "Don't be obscene, George" (9 sec.). Cut to the exterior. Maloney in a medium shot moves between the two cars (Blanche's and his), wiping his hands on a cloth in the way mechanics do after finishing a job, and quickly starting to enter his own car (6 sec.). Cut back to Blanche and George at the table, a wider shot than before. The waitress stands with two new beers. George thanks her loudly (perhaps the beers have started to work on him). The waitress moves away; camera moves in closer to the two. George drinks his beer and burps. Blanche leans on him: "Just try to keep your head screwed on, will you?" George downs the beer (21 sec.). Cut back to the exterior (as before). Maloney's car is gone; the space next to Blanche's car is empty (2 sec.). Cut back to the two-shot by the table. George finishes his beer and grabs Blanche's. She gives him a dirty look and both get up to go. George produces a few after-beer sound effects and gestures. Camera pans with them as they leave the diner and slowly approach their car (camera follows). They enter, start the motor, back up, and drive away (42 sec.). The light humor, by now necessarily stamped into the behavior of our two protagonists, makes us temporarily forget the impending danger, signified by the occasional appearances of Maloney and his mysterious doings. It is in the flavor of a "comédie dangereuse" that Hitchcock zigzags here between humor and suspense. These elements eventually culminate, hilariously and suspensefully, in the next scene. The length of Scene 20 is 4 minutes, 5 seconds—a rather long silence before the storm.

Scene 21. Shot 1: cut to a medium close-up of the rear of their car in motion. Camera dollies with them, then moves in closer to the undercarriage; we clearly see dark oil leaking out of the broken brake line (12 sec.). As often in Hitchcock's narrative strategies, the facts of a danger are laid out before the viewer, leaving no doubts about its nature. Later comes the elaboration showing how the characters handle the situation. Shot 2 is a frontal medium two-shot inside the car. George, with a sigh, glancing at Blanche: "Eh, that's the end of that" (3 sec.). Cut (shot 3) to exterior view of the empty road (in movement) (1 1/2 sec.). Cut (shot 4) back to the close-up of oil dripping under the moving car (4 1/2 sec.). Cut (shot 5) back to the same medium two-shot of Blanche and George inside the car; they look indifferent (1 1/2 sec.). Note that the above repeated two-shots are going to be the only stable images in size and angle throughout the scene. Cut (shot 6) to a fast-moving shot of the road, on a downhill curve (4 sec.). Cut to (shot 7) the same two-shot inside the car (third repeat). Blanche gets worried, says: "George, what's the big hurry?" (4 1/2 sec.). Cut (shot 8) again to a fast-moving shot of the road, to a downhill curve, and then to another curve, passing close to rocks on the left side, tires squeaking (6 sec.). Cut (shot 9) back to the interior (fourth repeat). George tenses up; Blanche implores: "Just slow up will you, please!" (3 sec.). Cut (shot 10) to a fast-moving road shot going around another curve (1 1/2 sec.). Cut to (shot 11) the interior of the car (fifth repeat). The two look ahead intensely. Blanche, hysterically: "I told you not to drive so fast, George." He: "Something's wrong with the accelerator, seems to be sticking" (4 1/2 sec.). Cut to (shot 12) a fast-moving shot of the road receding with the trunk of the car in frame. The oil is dripping onto the road behind (3 sec.). Cut back (shot 13) to the two-shot in the car (sixth repeat), Blanche gets more hysterical: "For God's sake, George, slow down. My hamburger is coming up" (6 sec.). Cut to (shot 14) a close-up of the accelerator and brake pedal. George's hand is trying to pry up the pedal. His voice offscreen: "The accelerator is stuck"

(6 sec.). Cut (shot 15) back to the interior two-shot (seventh repeat). Blanche shouts: "Try the brake" (1 1/2 sec.). Cut to (shot 16) a close-up of the brake pedal. George's foot pumps it twice; it goes all the way down to the floor (3 sec.). Cut to (shot 17) the two-shot (eighth repeat). Both look tense and scared, George trying desperately to make it around a curve (3 sec.). Cut to (shot 18) a moving view of the road on the curve (1 1/2 sec.). Cut to (shot 19) the two-shot (ninth repeat), both closer to each other, eyes glued ahead; Blanche moans: "What do you mean?" (3 sec.). Cut to (shot 20) a moving downhill view, curve to right, close to a barrier, another curve to the left, tires squeak loudly (3 sec.). Cut (shot 21) back to the two-shot (tenth repeat). Blanche grabs George's tie. He shouts: "Don't grab me. It's not my fault. It's the brakes that don't work." She still pulls at his tie: "I'm getting violently ill, George" (10 sec.). It is the first shot that is longer than 5 seconds in duration since the disaster, also the beginning of the hilarious displays of Blanche's hysteria. Cut to (shot 22) a moving road view on curve to the left (1 1/2 sec.). Cut (shot 23) back to the two-shot (eleventh repeat). Blanche is holding George by the neck, then turns away again, and pulls on his tie. He exclaims: "For Christ's sake" (3 sec.). Cut (shot 24) to the road, curve right, then left, as a big black sedan comes up toward them and passes by, then still another curve left. We hear Blanche's screams (4 1/2 sec.).

Cut to (shot 25) a fast close-up of their wheels hitting stones (in the opposite direction from the previous car movement) and stirring up dust at the edge of the road (2 sec.). Cut (shot 26) back to the two-shot (twelfth repeat), Blanche's legs are around George's neck (1 1/2 sec.). Cut to (shot 27) the road view, taking a curve to the left (2 sec.). Cut to (shot 28) the two-shot (thirteenth repeat); Blanche thrown by the leaning car to left. George begs her to try the hand brake (4 sec.). Cut to (shot 29) a close-up of Blanche's hand desperately pulling the parking brake (4 sec.). Cut to (shot 30) the two-shot (fourteenth repeat); George struggling with the steering wheel as Blanche throws herself on it (6 sec.). Cut to (shot 31) the road view, a dangerous curve to the left (2 sec.). Cut to (shot 32) the two-shot (fifteenth repeat), George desperately steering and shouting: "Get your hand off the damned wheel" (3 sec.). Cut to (shot 33) the road view; they seem to have hit the road barrier by the precipice on the right (1 sec.). Cut to (shot 34) the two-shot (sixteenth repeat), Blanche horrified by what she sees (1 sec.). Cut to

(shot 35) the road view curving left, with mountains across (1 sec.). Cut (shot 36) back to the two-shot (seventeenth repeat), Blanche looking ahead with horror (1 1/2 sec.). Cut (shot 37) back to the just seen mountain view (3 sec.). Cut back (shot 38) to the two-shot (eighteenth repeat), Blanche collapsing on the seat, her legs up against George, who is struggling to push them off (3 1/2 sec.). Cut (shot 39) back to a road view, two cars ahead going in the same direction (1 sec.). Cut back (shot 40) to the two-shot (nineteenth repeat), Blanche throwing herself against the steering wheel (1 sec.). Cut to (shot 41) the same road view as the two cars are overtaken (by George), then a right curve, a left, and another car is in front (5 sec.). Cut to (shot 42) the two-shot (twentieth repeat), George's eyes practically popping out (1 sec.). Cut (shot 43) back to the road view; they pass another car, then two cars, one in the opposite direction; finally they take a curve to the left (2 1/2 sec.) Cut to (shot 44) the two-shot (twenty-first repeat), Blanche struggling with George; he pushes her away (1 1/2 sec.). Cut to (shot 45) the road view, a brush against the right side of the hill (1 1/2 sec.). Cut back (shot 46) to the two-shot (twenty-second repeat), Blanche practically on top of George (1 sec.). Cut to (shot 47) road view, George's car apparently hitting the rocks on the left side of the road (2 sec.). Cut to (shot 48) George desperately trying to steady his listing car, Blanche out of frame (1 sec.). Cut to the road view (shot 49), rocks on the left; a car comes speeding up the hill, another pair of curves, left and right (3 sec.). Cut back (shot 50) to the two-shot (twenty-third repeat), Blanche's legs swinging over George's head; he pushes them off (1 1/2 sec.).

Cut back to the road view (shot 51) as they pass two cars. Then after a curve a group of eleven motorcycles appear suddenly, going uphill; George races down between them as they split in panic to one side and the other (10 sec.). Cut back (shot 52) to the two-shot (twenty-fourth repeat), Blanche saying, with her back to the camera: "We've got to get off this road" (3 sec.). Cut to (shot 53) the road view, a steep downhill curve to the left (3 sec.). Cut to (shot 54) the two-shot (twenty-fifth repeat), Blanche still with her back to the camera, her arm around George's neck. He implores: "Blanche, sit, hang on, baby" (1 1/2 sec.). Cut (shot 55) to the road; they hit a big bump beyond the right side of the road (1 1/2 sec.). Cut back to the two-shot (shot 56—twenty-sixth repeat). Blanche climbs over George, covering his face (2 1/2 sec.). Cut to the road view (shot 57); they seem to be off the road. After a big bump they run over some wooden sticks or sign in the form of a cross which, when hit by the car, flies up in the air (4 1/2 sec.). Cut to the two-shot (shot 58 and the last, twenty-seventh repeat). The car rocks violently. George tries to steady it and it slows down a bit (3 sec.). Cut to the view in front (shot 59) over uneven terrain, rocking from one side to even more of a list on the turn (2 1/2 sec.). Cut to (shot 60) a reverse medium shot of the car (this time seen from the front) as it slowly tilts, falls, and then rests on its side (1 1/2 sec.). Cut (shot 61) to a closer shot of the resting car (with one front headlight in the lower part of the frame).

After a few seconds of stillness, Blanche's head appears from what seems to be the side window of the car. She looks bewildered; the dust is still in the air (9 sec.). Cut to (shot 62) a close-up of George's face on the ground distorted by Blanche's shoe stepping on it (1 sec.). It is truly remarkable that Hitchcock, after such a short release (the fall of the car and the appearance of a living and, most likely, well Blanche), dares to jump directly to such an obviously comedic shot of George, with Blanche's foot on his face. Cut to (shot 63) a side medium shot of Blanche's face as she moves a bit higher, slowly, trying to free herself from the car (2 sec.). Cut back (shot 64) to the close-up of George's face with the shoe pressing harder (1 sec.). Cut to (shot 65) the same medium shot of Blanche coming out (2 1/2 sec.). Cut to (shot 66) George's face (same as before) as the shoe leaves him. He wipes his cheek with his hand (1 1/2 sec.). Cut back to (shot 67) Blanche as she climbs to the top of the overturned car and sits down (3 sec.). Cut to (shot 68) medium close-up of the top of George's head under the car (at ground level). He starts pushing out, crawling backward toward the camera and finally getting up on his feet (camera moves up with him), revealing Blanche's sitting figure; when she sees George she throws herself on him (36 sec.). Note that the above is so far the longest duration shot in the scene and, accordingly, the first release for the previous build-up of tension.

Cut (shot 69) on action to a closer two-shot of Blanche falling on George; she slides down to her feet, next to him. Camera moves back to a wider medium two-shot. George, staggering a bit, remarks: "Wasn't that fun?" Blanche hysterically hits him with a swing of her purse, saying "Damn you, George." George: "What's the matter with you? It wasn't me, *it's* Maloney." Blanche shouts: "He wasn't driving." George: "Of course he wasn't driving. He screwed up the car and broke the brakes." Blanche: "Maloney?" George: "Yes, Maloney. What do you think . . . it was a coincidence? Blanche, your car will be out of commission, it looks like, for a couple of days. We better go find us another way to get home." They start staggering to screen right, camera follows. Blanche: "George, are you all right?" Theme music starts again, this time in a minor key. George: "I think so. How about you?" She: "I'm sick. George . . . I'm sorry. [He kisses her on the cheek] You really think Maloney wanted us dead?" George nods; they keep walking closer to the camera in a high medium two-shot. She continues: "But why," she almost shouts, "Why in the name of God would anyone want to do that to us?" George, helping her walk: "I don't know. You can bet it has something to do with your friend Eddie Shoebridge. Maloney probably has him buried in his back yard, and doesn't want us to find out." They walk out of frame screen right (longest duration shot in this scene—66 seconds).

Cut (shot 70) to the two entering the frame from screen left, slightly from the back; they walk away from the camera. George picks her up and carries her slowly a few steps down an embankment toward the paved road (13 sec.). Cut (shot 71) to a reverse frontal two-shot (crossing the axis). George, after two more steps, puts her down, straightens his ailing back; they look to the right (7 sec.). Cut to a (shot 72) long shot of an empty road (3 sec.). Cut back (shot 73) to the two-shot. They keep looking. Blanche points to her right, asking: "Is that the way?" (2 sec.). Cut to the road again (shot 74); no cars (2 1/2 sec.). The theme music fades out. The above represents the final release from the build-up of tension. Consequently, since another, violent, trigger is coming up, I shall designate the above as the end of Scene 21 (total length 4 minutes).

Considering the frantic pace of the fragmentation during the hair-raising car ride, one should keep in mind that it is simply a checker-boarding of the 29 shots of the road view with the 27 repeated shots of our protagonists inside their car. The latter shots are sandwiched, each time, between two road views. Not a single shot contains both the car and the downhill road in the same frame (in itself a comment on the subject of cinema reality). Hitchcock, rightly, counts on the strength of his fragmentation to create a sufficiently believable illusion, and thus refuses to provide any additional proof that Blanche's white car is actually there on that neck-breaking ride. Contemporary films, on the contrary, present us, as we know, with spectacular car disasters that contain all the bloody ingredients and always with full exposition. Yet here Hitchcock, in addition, complicates his drama by injecting so much humor; as a result, the viewer is virtually split between worrying and laughing. Still, there is no question about a credible reality.

Scene 22. Starts an unusual separation, a two-to-one kind, between our two protagonists and one car with its occupant. This time it is not a humorous scene at all. Shot 1 is a medium two-shot; George and Blanche walking to the right, away from the camera. They stop; we hear a car in the distance; they look back (14 sec.). Cut to (shot 2) a long shot of the empty road, a speck of a car seen in the distance (3 sec.). Cut back to the two looking (shot 3, 1 sec.). Cut back to the road; the car is coming closer (shot 4, 14 1/2 sec.). Cut back (shot 5) to George and Blanche as they try to stop the car (2 sec.). Cut back (shot 6) to the car approaching; it turns out to be Maloney (3 sec.). Cut back to the same (shot 7) medium two-shot as Blanche and George drop their outstretched thumbs (1 sec.). Cut back to (shot 8) Maloney driving into a medium shot as he stops his car and says through the open window: "How are you? Sorry I'm late" (4 1/2 sec.). Cut back (shot 9) to the two; George, with irony: "Congratulations on the job you did on our car, Maloney" (3 sec.). Cut back to (shot 10) the medium shot of Maloney; he rubs his nose (3/4 sec.). Cut back to the two (shot 11), Blanche mumbles: "You're proud of it, are you?" (1 1/2 sec.). Cut back (shot 12) to Maloney. He tries to dismiss the serious tone: "You must be Blanche Tyler. Pleased to meet you. Eh, where is your car?" (3 1/2 sec.). Cut back (shot 13) to the two. George: "Eh, let's say it ain't exactly in running order, you know what I mean" (2 1/2 sec.). Cut back to Maloney (shot 14): "Hop in. I'll give you a lift to the station" (1 1/2 sec.). Cut back to the two. George: "No, thank you. We don't ride in hearses" (2 1/2 sec.). Cut back (shot 15) to Maloney, who for a moment looks at them, then: "What do you think I came for—the fun of it? And you wanted me to take you to that party that knows Eddie Shoebridge?" (5 sec.). Cut back (shot 16) to the two. George continues: "Why don't you go there by yourself this time, Maloney? We'll skip it" (4 1/2 sec.). Cut back to Maloney (shot 17). He looks at them penetratingly, lets his hand brake go, and drives off (8 1/2 sec.). As his car leaves the frame it wipes in the repeated medium two-shot of George and Blanche. After a moment they start walking, Blanche murmuring: "So charming" (shot 18, 4 1/2 sec.). Thus ends this minutely fragmented, 18-shot separation, again without an introduction and without a resolution. It is again sandwiched between shots of longer duration, as we shall see.

Cut to (shot 19) a dramatically high long shot of a car (Maloney's, as it turns out) on a highway, reminiscent of the similar shot of Blanche's car going to the diner, except this time Maloney goes in the opposite direction (to screen left). Similar music, a variant on the main theme (but more threatening), also contributes to the symmetry. We lose sight of the car momentarily behind some trees (also similar to the former shot), but regain it as the car slows down and makes a dust-raising U-turn (by now it is recognizably Maloney's) and starts racing back (22 sec.). Cut to a low long shot (shot 20) of the highway. In the far distance a car seems to be coming (as if in slow motion) to the accompaniment of drums (10 sec.). Cut to (shot 21) a similar long shot but more on eye level. Again we see in the distance the car coming (6 sec.). Cut to (shot 22) a frontal medium two-shot of George and Blanche walking toward camera; they see something (1 1/2 sec.). Cut back (shot 23) to the long shot of the approaching car (1 1/2 sec.). Cut back (shot 24) to Blanche and George. They recognize the car. George, as he grabs Blanche's arm: "It's Maloney, he's after us." They start frantically running back (2 sec.). Cut to (shot 25) a reverse medium two-shot (with crossing of the axis) of George and Blanche running toward camera. Behind them we see Maloney's car (2 sec.).

Cut (shot 26) to a quick shot of another car, a blue convertible, coming around the bend (1/2 sec.). Cut to (shot 27) Blanche and George
shouting and running (forward) with Maloney's car behind (3/4 sec.).
Cut to the two jumping to the side and throwing themselves against
the high side of the road (1 sec.). Cut to (shot 28) a high medium long
shot of the blue convertible coming from the bottom of the frame, while
Maloney's car comes in from the top of the frame and is forced to veer
off, screen right (1 sec.). Cut to (shot 29) a low medium long shot of
Maloney's car going over the embankment; we hear screaming (1 1/2
sec.). Cut to (shot 30) a medium shot of Blanche and George lying on
the ground; George turns around to see what happened (2 sec.). Cut to
(shot 31) a high medium long shot of the blue convertible with young
people in it. They are looking down at the embankment. We hear one
of them: "Gee, let's get the hell out of here," and they speedily drive
away (4 1/2 sec.). Cut back (shot 32) to Blanche and George still on
the ground looking (1 1/2 sec.). Cut to (shot 33) a long shot of the
empty road (1 sec.). Cut back to (shot 34) Blanche and George turning
their faces, searching for Maloney's car (2 sec.). Cut back (shot 35) to
the same long shot across the road: above the embankment appears a
cloud of black smoke (3 sec.). Cut back (shot 36) to Blanche and George
as they get up and start moving forward; the camera dollies back, keeping them in a medium close two-shot (12 sec.). (This long duration shot
releases tension.) Cut to (shot 37) a very high long shot looking down
the embankment, where Maloney's car is in flames (2 sec.). Cut back

(shot 38) to George and Blanche looking horrified; Blanche turns away, hiding her face on George's chest. She: "You better get the police" (4 sec.). Cut back (shot 39) to the fire (reminiscent of the fire at the gas station in *The Birds*) (2 sec.). Cut back (shot 40) to the two looking down. George: "And lose our ten thousand dollars?" (4 sec.). Cut back (shot 40) to the roaring fire (3 1/2 sec.). The scene lasts 3 minutes, 3 seconds. This suspense scene, the second in a row, ends with a tour de force, precise fragmentation remains the major strategy.

What contributes to the smoothness and flow in this scene is the singular rhythm in the first part of the separation: shots 1 and 19 are of longer duration, the eighteen shots in between are very short. In the second part, again the same rhythm: shots 20 and 36 are longer; the fifteen shots in between are short, some very short. The above is definitely a pattern in Hitchcock constructions and is one of his secrets.

Scene 23. Shot 1, in Adamson's jewelry store, brings us over to the parallel action. In a long shot we see Fran in a large hat entering through the glass doors and walking toward camera (5 sec.). Cut to (shot 2) a medium close shot of Adamson smiling; he notices her; the smile fades (2 sec.). Cut back to (shot 3) Fran waiting (1 1/2 sec.). Cut (shot 4) back to Adamson; he takes his fingers out of his vest pocket, starts walking to meet her, and leaves the frame (2 1/2 sec.). Cut on action (shot 5) as Adamson enters Fran's frame in a medium long shot. He pretends that she is a new customer, asks what he can do for her. (End of teaser separation.) She asks for a turquoise bracelet; he invites her to sit down at the display counter (13 sec.). Cut on action as Adamson walks around the counter and settles down (shot 6) in a medium two-shot in profile across from Fran. Here, in comparative privacy, he asks if there is anything wrong with their house guest. All is well, she says; she gave him a nice meal and a bottle of wine. Adamson, while displaying some bracelets for her, asks sternly what she is doing there (22 sec.). Cut to a frontal low close-up of Fran (shot 7). (Begins a 25 shot separation.) She tells him that a message has come through on (radio station) KAFG that they have located a stone (for the ransom) in New York (4 1/2 sec.). Cut to (shot 8) Adamson, also in a frontal close-up, listening (1 1/2 sec.). Cut back to Fran (shot 9). She adds that the stone weighs fifty-three carats (3 sec.). Cut back (shot 10) to Adamson's close-up; a smile is born, his rabbit teeth showing (2 1/2 sec.). Cut to Fran (shot 11) in a profile medium close shot; she returns to role playing, asking for the price of the bracelet that she likes (3 sec.). Cut to (shot 12) a symmetrical profile, medium close shot, of Adamson, who gives her the price: $315 including tax (5 sec.). Cut back (shot 13) to Fran's profile shot, acknowledging (1 sec.). Cut to the frontal close-up of Adamson (shot 14). Again confidentially, he asks when they are to make the pickup (1 1/2 sec.). Cut back to Fran's frontal close-up (shot 15). She tells him tomorrow night at 9:30 (1 1/2 sec.). Cut to (shot 16) the same close-up of Adamson, who agrees and quietly suggests that she go home (3 1/2 sec.). Cut to (shot 17) the same profile shot of Fran, who asks if the bracelet can be put aside so she can show it to her husband (3 sec.). Cut (shot 18) to a profile of Adamson, similar to the one before, who assures her: "Of courrse, Madame" (1 1/2 sec.).

Cut (shot 19) back to the frontal close-up of Fran, who with a sigh is just about to announce the bad news (2 1/2 sec.). Cut (shot 20) to a high close-up of a newspaper she slips in (1 sec.). Cut to (shot 21) the frontal close-up of Adamson looking down to read (1 sec.). Cut (shot 22) to a close-up of a headline (her voice: "Take a look at this"): "Man dies in a freak highway accident" (3 sec.). Cut (shot 23) back to the frontal close-up of Adamson who reads quietly, with a devilish smile on his face (6 sec.). Cut to the frontal close shot of Fran wondering what could be so funny in the paper (1 1/2 sec.). Cut back (shot 24) to Adamson's close-up; the smile changes into a furious outburst: "Incompetent bastard, he blew it!" (4 1/2 sec.). Cut back (shot 25) to the close-up of Fran, who listens to Adamson's harangue [offscreen]: "Now we'll have to eliminate those two ourselves." She: "Ourselves?" (5 sec.). Cut back (shot 26) to Adamson's close-up as before. He: "Yes, that's right. Tomorrow night" (2 1/2 sec.). Cut back (shot 27) to the close-up of Fran, while we hear Adamson's voice: "Right after we return our guest." She, incredulous: "I can't" (4 1/2 sec.). Cut back (shot 28) to Adamson, who says, emphatically: "You must" (1 sec.). Cut back (shot 29) to the close-up of Fran, reacting (1 sec.). Cut back (shot 30) to Adamson saying in a measured tone: "Remember, share and share alike" (4 sec.). Cut back (shot 31) to Fran (as before): "Stop it." She bites her lips; and again: "Stop it." She starts to get up (4 sec.). Cut (shot 32) on action: as Fran gets up in a long shot, her chair is overturned; the whole store witnesses it; she walks out in a hurry. Adamson cleans up after her (10 sec.). A new and equally grave threat is hanging over Blanche and George.

Past the first six introductory shots, the above separation races through twenty-five quick fragments to be finally resolved in the last long shot of the scene. This would indicate a rather usual structure since it has an introduction and resolution; yet the amount of fragmentation, the generosity of repeated shots in the context of what there is to communicate, makes it a rather unusual one. A conventional filmmaker would probably plan for (at the most) twelve shots for the whole scene, which lasts, as it is, 2 minutes, 24 seconds. Many of the details could have been executed with a camera movement instead of fragmentation (the shots with the newspaper, for example). Hitchcock uses fragments primarily for rhythmical emphasis; it is the way he orchestrates. He needed here a staccato rhythm, a sharp and steady beat. Reserving, in almost all cases (except three), the frontal close-ups for the private talk between Fran and Adamson, and the profile shots for their make-believe of customer and salesman, Hitchcock plays on those two variants as on a piano with four hands, and magnificently so. A small scene in his hands becomes an expression in high virtuosity.

Scene 24. Structurally an antidote to the previous few scenes: contains long duration shots and camera movements. Dramatically it is a pivotal scene, since our protagonist finally finds out about the new alias under which Eddie Shoebridge now lives. The contrapuntal arrangement continues. Shot 1: a long duration panning shot in the Barlow Creek cemetery; a priest's voice officiating at a funeral is heard offscreen. At the eighth second he utters the name of Joseph Maloney as the deceased; the pan goes beyond the small crowd of mourners, eventually coming up on a medium close shot of George in profile, cleaning his pipe and listening to the high praises the priest bestows on the character of the late Maloney (19 sec.). The above is a classical slow disclosure. Cut to (shot 2) a medium long shot of a group of mourners with Mrs. Maloney in the center; the sermon is still going strong (5 sec.). Cut (shot 3) to another group around the grave. We see the priest speaking (4 sec.). Cut to (shot 4) a medium close shot of Mrs. Maloney among a group of mourners, looking across from her, toward the priest. She listens to the priest's rhetoric about what a wonderful human being her husband was, without a sign of emotion. Even at this moment Hitchcock does not give up his irony (7 sec.). Cut to (shot 5) a medium close shot of the priest. Camera immediately racks focus to George, who stands just behind him (the first time in the film such a

device is used; the priest in the foreground goes out of focus) (5 sec.).
Cut back (shot 6) to the medium close shot of Mrs. Maloney, who apparently has noticed the presence of George (hence the focus). She is
visibly upset, reaches for her handkerchief, and nervously leaves, pushing herself out between the mourners (10 sec.). Cut (shot 7) to a medium shot of George (alone in the frame); he watches Mrs. Maloney's
movements (2 1/2 sec.).

Cut to (shot 8) an extremely high long shot of long duration, we see
from a bird's eye view the funeral on the right and two small figures
moving to the left as camera pans with them: Mrs. Maloney on the
upper part of the frame, George on the lower, as in a mythical labyrinth
among the graves, she trying to avoid him, he pressing on to corner
her (41 sec.). Cut on action (shot 9) to a medium two-shot of Mrs.
Maloney, with her back to the camera, and George, who has just entered the frame, approaching in profile. She mumbles: "Can't you leave
me alone? Isn't it enough that you killed him?" George: "It's not so,
Mrs. Maloney, it was the other way." She turns to him: "You started
it all, coming here and messing into things that are none of your business. Now go away, please." She turns to go. George grabs her arm:
"Mrs. Maloney, I have to talk to you." She tries to break away. He is
holding her. Turning to George, she shouts: "He's dead and buried.
There is nothing more to talk about." George talks over her voice: "Why
don't you help me find Eddie Shoebridge?" She: "I'm not helping you.
. . . Now get away." She tries to hit him; he holds on: "Mrs. Maloney,
your husband tried to kill me. You were in on it, weren't you?" She,
desperately: "No." George: "Then, why are you always running away
from me?" She: "No." George continues pressing: "Is that why?" She
repeats "No." George: "Do you realize that you're an accessory to an
attempted murder?" She tries again to run out to the left; George pulls
her back (camera delicately adjusts to their positions). She: "I had nothing to do with that." George: "But it happens that the police would
think you do have something to do with it. Do you want me to go to
the police about it?" They face each other in profile, but by now she
is on his left. She, imploringly: "For God's sake, you wouldn't do that?"
George: "Just tell me where is Eddie Shoebridge?" She is desparate:
"No, I can't." George, softly: "Mrs. Maloney, where is he? Please tell
me." A painful pause, she seems to be ready to talk. She turns away
from him toward camera and starts walking: "There is no Eddie

Shoebridge. He went up in smoke twenty-five years ago and came down in the city, and calls himself Arthur Adamson." She's scared of her own words and looks back at George, who repeats (the theme music fades in again): "Arthur Adamson?" She, as if voicing her thoughts: "If he finds out I told you he'll kill me. Now go away, and don't come near me ever again." She runs out of frame to the left. George stands alone, stupefied (86 sec., the longest duration shot so far).

Cut to (shot 10) a medium long shot of Mrs. Maloney running in the frame toward the two Shoebridge gravestones. She kicks Eddie's stone several times shouting "Fake, fake." The stone falls backward. She runs to left (5 1/2 sec.). Cut to (shot 11) a low medium close-up of George, watching her departure in total astonishment. The theme music loudly accompanies his thinking (a rather long 9 sec.). Cut to (shot 12) a close-up of Eddie Shoebridge's tilted headstone. Music fades out. The scene lasts 3 minutes, 12 seconds.

The most amazing configurations are shots 8 and 9, the former for its originality in breaking away from the conventional framing of the previous shots, soaring high into a bird's eye view of the cemetery, a signal of important events to come (like the high shots of the cars), and thus a perfect introduction to shot 9, the long conversation. The latter, without cuts and contrapuntal to the fragmented separation we had until now, is an example of a directorial decision made to conform to the overall orchestration, rather than for serving immediate needs. The orchestration at this point requires a release from the intensity of the fast beat of a separation; accordingly, Hitchcock arranges shot 9, the longest duration shot so far, to be without a single cut, in a floating two-shot.

Scene 25. A medium long shot brings us back to the domesticity of Blanche's kitchen. George is on the phone. Without a shirt, but with his taxidriver's cap on, he is animatedly defending himself. His boss is accusing him of truancy on the job. Blanche stands by listening and prompting. His language is juicy. After five seconds, a separation starts, with Blanche in low medium close shot, George in a high medium shot. Blanche whispers that he should stand up to the boss. George nevertheless surrenders and promises his boss to be on the job. Blanche walks away. He tells Blanche that he must put some hours on the taxi, otherwise he will certainly lose his job. Blanche accuses him of not putting up much of a fight. They argue as usual and are funny as usual.

After nine single shots the brief separation is resolved by Blanche running up to George in a medium long two-shot, kneeling in front of him: "You won't have to drive a cab, if we can get this thing done and over and collect the money." George: "If, if, you're always giving me the ifs, I can't eat them. Neither can you . . . look, honey, the least I can do is to show up at work every now and then, after all didn't I give you the name?" Blanche, still on her knees, reaches for the phone book: "Yes, but the phone book is full of Arthur Adamsons . . ." George assures her that all she needs to do is to locate the right one, "One that's close to forty years old and trembles at the name of Shoebridge. It's very simple. We'll do it tomorrow." Blanche still implores: "No, it's much better . . . A bird in the hand . . ." George interrupts her: "No, sweetheart, the only bird in my hand tonight, and I'm sorry to say that, will be a steering wheel, from four to midnight." He tries to kiss her; she rejects him. He, buttoning up his shirt: "Why should I get a kiss?" Blanche walks away telling him that he is impossible. She starts examining the phone book: "Maybe I'll do it without you." They argue again. He warns her that Adamson may be dangerous. Finally he comes over, tries to soothe her, pats her behind, complimenting its shape and promising, after a sexy hug, that tonight he will take care of her and devise the strategy. She does not even turn to him. He walks away. Camera follows him to the door as he leaves for work. This brief interlude is the most lyrical and sensual moment between them so far.

Cut to Blanche still at the kitchen counter examining the phone book. She finally tears out one page and energetically moves to leave as music starts with a strong accent, changing into a variant of the main theme (which continues through the next three shots). She leaves the same way George did, with camera following her in a medium long shot. A search for the right Adamson begins. (So far the scene has lasted one min., 40 sec.). Cut to a medium shot of Blanche ringing a bell at an entrance door with a prominent sign: A.M. Adamson, MD. A woman doctor opens the door; Blanche excuses herself saying: "You wouldn't be Arthur . . ." She walks away reading her telephone page (10 sec.). Cut to a close shot of the back of a workman with a sign on his overalls: A. L. Adamson, air conditioning. Camera pulls back quickly to reveal in a low medium long shot Blanche standing and shouting "Excuse me" to the man working on a section of the ceiling. He turns to her. She sees that he is black (6 sec.). Cut to a medium shot of Blanche with her back to the camera facing an auto mechanic under a sign: "Adamson Garage." She asks him if he is Arthur Adamson. The man calls to the back: "Hey, Arth"; in comes his identical twin brother. Blanche looks at the two, turns to the camera, confused (15 sec.). Cut to medium long shot. Blanche rings the bell at the door of an establishment: Palm Apartments, A. A. Adamson. The door is opened by an old man in his eighties. Blanche asks "A. A.?" and slowly withdraws from the frame. The man looks after her (15 sec.).

Cut to a night exterior long shot of Adamson's sign over his jewelry store. Camera moves back with a swing down to reveal Blanche approaching the glass entrance door. The strong music fades; she sees the saleswoman at the door. Since, as we know, she has finally reached the "holy grail," this, unlike the previous four episodes of the search, will be a mini scene with cuts. Cut to Blanche in medium two-shot talking to the saleswoman (she is familiar to us) who is just about to close the store. The next nine shots are of the over-the-shoulder variety from the back of Blanche's head to the frontal shot of the saleswoman and vice versa (to be followed by a separation). Blanche would like to see Mr. Adamson tonight. No, he is not in. He left early, most likely he has a party tonight. After learning that he is about forty years old, Blanche assures her that this is a private matter and agrees to leave him a note as the saleswoman suggests. Both enter the store. Camera follows on a close-up of Blanche. Cut to a medium two-shot at the counter. Blanche starts writing the note. A nine-shot separation sequence begins here between a low close shot of the saleswoman and a high medium close shot of Blanche. Blanche procrastinates in writing the note. She would rather . . . send a telegram, tonight. What is his address? The saleswoman hesitates. Blanche: "It's all right . . . We're friends." The saleswoman pauses a moment in an expressive close-up and finally gives her the address: 1001 Franklin Street. Blanche, in total disbelief, repeats the address, as in a dream. Then, coming a little closer to the camera (in a full close-up), challenges the saleswoman: "You're a Capricorn, aren't you?" Cut to the close-up of the saleswoman: "No, I'm a Leo." Blanche, taking a few steps back, already on her way out (now, in medium close shot): "That's what I thought." Cut on action to a long shot of the store as Blanche exits and the saleswoman latches the glass door. The last shot represents the resolution of the separation. Music starts again with a variant of the theme of the film. Note that all nine shots of the above separation cut exactly on dialogue without any voice overlap.

With the music triumphantly continuing, cut to a long shot of Blanche's car arriving at the canopy of a big residence. She stops and a corpulent doorman comes to her window. Cut to a medium two-shot of Blanche telling the doorman (apparently a friend of George's) to inform George when he sees him that she "found it" and she is going to 1001 Franklin Street. The doorman faithfully repeats the message and promises to deliver it: "George will for sure stop by before long." Music ends. Total length of the scene is 5 minutes, 48 seconds (the jewelry store sequence alone lasts 2 min., 35 sec.). What started as a rather funny search scene with four individual episodes ends happily with a real find, certainly to the satisfaction of the viewer. Curiously enough, Hitchcock needed a separation sequence at the "kill" and, without losing any of his sense of humor, delivers one at the jewelry store as sharply as ever, reaping the most striking benefit separation can deliver: a burst of extra energy, well fitting the moment of success in the drama. Presently, as our protagonist gets closer to her goal, Hitchcock's strategy will be to delay and complicate.

Scene 26. Brings us back to the parallel action: Inside the Adamson household, in a medium long two-shot, Fran is getting dressed, as a blond this time, ready to do the pickup. Arthur Adamson enters and asks her to repeat the instructions. She retorts that she knows them by heart. Adamson, busy with preparations, asks if she is all right. She: "I will be." She puts on her boots; he slips the familiar revolver into her purse, incidentally shown in a quick close-up (the only insert of this sort in the entire film). Cut back to a long shot. Adamson suggests they start moving since it's getting late. They leave the room, turning off the light (24 sec.). We shall now be offered another tour of their lair with all the technical tricks of the trade of professional kidnappers. Cut to a reverse medium long shot. They walk into a hallway; camera follows as they approach; they turn and go down a stairway. On the way down we see the elegant chandelier (the camera comes down with them) (18 sec.). Cut to an eye level long shot as they go down some steps away from the chandelier (7 sec.). Cut to reverse medium long shot as they descend into a basement. Camera follows them to a brick wall. Fran pulls out one of the false bricks under which there is a switch to an intercom. Adamson starts talking into the device: "Bishop Wood, it's time to go" (10 sec.). Cut to a high close-up of Adamson with his face close to the wall as he continues: "Have you got your vestments on?" A voice answers: "Yes . . . but I haven't finished my chicken." Adamson smiles, then switches a contact and speaks: "I'm sorry, your excellency. Here's what I want you to do. Place the armchair in the middle of the room facing away from the door and seat yourself in it. You'll be comfortably put to sleep. It will last only a short while." A voice from the other side: "Thank you very much; you're most considerate." Adamson again turns a switch and talks: "Let me know when you're ready." Voice from the other side: "By the way, I haven't yet finished the book you kindly lent me. May I take it along?" (32 sec.). Cut back to the medium long two-shot of Fran and Arthur smiling at the request. Adamson speaks into the intercom: "With our fingerprints on it? Nice try, your Excellency." Voice: "Thank you very much. I'm ready." Adamson: "I'll be turning the lights off on you." Fran walks over to the opposite wall (camera pans with her) and turns off the light. In semi-darkness they both open a large door in the brick wall and in silhouette enter a room inside. We see a shadowy outline of a head, with one on each side of it. Fran hands Arthur the syringe; he administers the injection; we hear a brief moan of pain. A doorbell is ringing loudly. Adamson, to Fran in silhouette: "We mustn't be late. See who it is. Be careful." Fran walks out, camera follows as she walks up the few steps (52 sec.). Cut to a reverse medium shot on action. Fran walks down the entrance hall to the door. Camera follows and moves into a tight close-up of her profile looking through the small door visor. The musical theme that started at the first doorbell is now frantic. Again the bell rings, loudly (7 sec.). Cut to the view through the visor: a round image of Blanche pressing the doorbell in medium shot size (3 sec.). Cut back to a medium shot of Fran turning from the visor (2 1/2 sec.). Cut to a medium long shot of Adamson coming up the steps (1 sec.). Cut back to Fran in a close shot as she runs toward Adamson, camera panning with her. She reaches Adamson and in medium two-shot tells him in whispers that Blanche Tyler is at the door. Adamson loses his temper. He hysterically repeats that they have to make the pickup in thirty-five minutes. Fran desperately: "What are you going to do?" Adamson: "Nothing . . . until later tonight." Fran runs back to the door; camera follows her; she looks through the visor again (33 sec.). Cut back to the view seen in the visor. Blanche is not there (7 1/2 sec.). Cut back to Fran in close-up, she turns toward where Adamson is: "She's gone" (1 1/2 sec.). Cut back to the same medium long shot of Adamson who says, energetically: "Com'on, let's go" (2 sec.). Cut back to Fran who runs toward him (3 sec.).

Cut to an exterior medium long shot of Blanche going down the steps outside Adamson's entrance door (the theme music continues). She stops and seems to be hesitating, then turns around and goes up again with a small note in hand (15 sec.). Cut on action of her turning to the door, in medium shot, holding the note (2 sec.). Cut to a close-up of the note; one can read: "Dear Mr. Adamson, if the name Shoebridge means anything to you, please call me;" a telephone number is given (8 sec.). Cut back to Blanche in medium shot attaching the note to the door with tape. She turns to go down and leaves frame (7 sec.). Cut on action in medium long shot as Blanche continues on the way down, then walks around the building, and looks around (20 sec.). Note that shots are of a much longer duration. Hitchcock nevertheless goes back on occasion to a more detailed fragmentation, as in the above segment of Blanche and the note, where he takes six shots for this simple action, in order to create a rhythmical preparation for an upcoming crisis. The musical theme, this time with a solo piano, fades out. The scene lasts 3 minutes.

Scene 27. Starts with a darkish close shot of Fran activating a remote control for the garage door (2 sec.): cut to a wide shot of the garage door lifting and revealing, in a long shot, unexpectedly, Blanche standing just in front of it on the street (2 1/2 sec.). Cut to a medium two-shot of Adamson and Fran inside their car, amazed at what they see. Adamson with fury whispers to Fran: "I thought you said . . .?" Fran defends herself: "I didn't know . . ." (2 1/2 sec.). Cut back to the long shot of Blanche as she takes two steps forward calling out: "Mr. Adamson" (1 1/2 sec.). Cut back to the two in the car. Adamson, ready to get out, snaps to Fran: "Watch him." Fran also comes out on her side (7 sec.). Cut back to Blanche, who with childish enthusiasm runs to the garage, ending in a medium three-shot: "Oh, Mr. Adamson, oh how wonderful I didn't miss you. I'm Blanche Tyler the spiritualist." She extends her hand toward Adamson, who does not budge. She cheerfully swallows the insult, then turns to Fran: "Good evening, honey" (16 sec.). Presently Hitchcock cuts to a series of eight over-the-shoulder shots from 1 1/2 to 5 seconds in length each, in fairly close two-shots, looking at Adamson over the back of Blanche's head and vice versa. Adamson, in his vitriolic voice, asks her to kindly move her car, it is blocking the driveway, he's late for an appointment. Blanche, giggling, assures him that if he hears why she has come he wouldn't mind being late, "Mr. Adamson, or should I call you Shoebridge?" She teasingly pinches his cheeks. Adamson, grinding his teeth, cuts in that he knows very well why she and her cabdriver friend have been sniffing around them in the past few weeks "like two little eager bloodhounds." At this point there is a cut to a close-up of Fran who worriedly listens and moves to the side. Back to the over-the-shoulder shots. Adamson continues: "So you found me, Madame Blanche. And I'm perfectly willing to listen to your demands, but not . . . right . . . now." Blanche triumphantly announces that there are no demands. "Hardly that. Julie Rainbird wants nothing from you but the privilege of making you heir to the entire Rainbird fortune." (The series of 8 over-the-shoulder shots last 50 sec.). As already observed, in this film Hitchcock often moves from the latter structure to a separation, and so he does here. Thus follows a close-up of Adamson, who is incredulous. Then cut to a close-up of Blanche: "The whole lovely millions and millions of it." Cut to a close-up of Adamson, who turns to Fran. Cut to a close-up of Fran suppressing a half smile. Cut back to the close-up of Blanche, who continues: "If she made any demands at all, they were on me to find you . . . through psychic means of course." Close-up of Adamson, who is totally puzzled: "Let me get this straight. Is that the only reason why you and your friend have been, shall we say, investigating me?" Cut to Fran who looks down at something. This shot is a transition from the seven-shot separation to a sequence of fragmented action shots.

Just a hair from a possible happy ending, a major narrative complication ensues: cut to a close-up of a piece of red vestment (the bishop's) sticking out of the car door (1 1/2 sec.). Cut to a low medium close-up of Fran worried by what she sees (2 1/2 sec.). Cut to a close-up of one hand reaching down to the car's door handle (1 sec.). Cut to a close-up of her other hand reaching down to the bottom of the door, where the red cloth is protruding (1 1/2 sec.). Cut to a very low medium shot of Fran squatting by the lower part of the door, her left hand trying to catch the red cloth in order to push it in, her right hand attempting to open the door slightly to help. (In the background we hear all this time Blanche's effervescent bubbling about how difficult it was to trace

Adamson.) We see the car door opening, unfortunately too far (2 sec.). Cut to the Bishop's head, still drugged, falling out in close shot, to the accompaniment of a strong musical accent (1 sec.). Cut to a low medium shot of Blanche who sees this (1/2 sec.). Cut back to the close-up of the bishop's head hanging out (3/4 sec.). Cut to a reverse medium long three shot from the back of Blanche toward Adamson and Fran attempting to hide the bishop (3/4 sec.). Note the drumbeat of very brief shots. Cut back to the medium frontal shot of Blanche (as before). She panics. Turning to the doorway she tries to run, as the big garage door is suddenly lowered. Blanche is thus trapped inside. She settles on the floor holding on to the doorway (5 sec.). The music stops. Cut to a low medium two-shot of Fran and Adamson, who is still holding the remote door control. He puts it aside, takes a step forward (music comes back), and asks: "Does anyone know that you've come here?" (8 sec.). Cut back to the squatting Blanche, as we saw her before; she repeats his question; then, as she slowly gets up to her feet and starts slowly walking sideways to screen left, she keeps repeating: "No, no, no one, not even George." Camera follows her in a medium shot; she lifts her finger to her mouth and in a measured tempo speaks: "You have nothing to worry about, Mr. Adamson. I promise, I won't breathe a word . . . to anyone . . ." Her shadow on the wall walks with her, in this most remarkable shot (31 sec.). Its long duration generates a temporary release. Cut to a medium shot of Adamson in 3/4 profile. He sizes her up, then with a slight smile on his face starts walking toward her, coming closer into a profile close-up.

Camera makes a fast pan to a close-up of Blanche; his hand sweeps through the frame; we see and hear a slap (4 sec.). Cut to a wide medium shot; he pushes her; she falls and a can of white paint overturns (a plant) (3/4 sec.). Cut to Fran watching in horror (2 sec.). Cut to a high close-up of Blanche's head leaning on a gasoline can; she slowly turns her face and looks up (6 sec.). Cut to a very low close-up of Adamson glancing down with that murderous smile, then turning to where Fran probably stands: "It looks like Miss Tyler will need some rest" (5 sec.). Cut to a medium long shot of Fran by the car. She shakes her head in disagreement (2 1/2 sec.). Cut back to the low close-up of Adamson in fury: "Will you do as I say?" (2 sec.). Cut back to Fran in a medium shot, who slowly leans into the car and brings out the syringe (3 sec.). Cut on action to a close-up of the needle in her hand, a

small amount of fluid in it; his gloved hand enters the frame and takes the needle (4 1/2 sec.). Cut on action to Adamson in a low medium shot, the syringe in his hand, he takes a step forward (1 1/2 sec.). Cut back to a close-up of Blanche (as before) still resting on the gasoline can; frightened, she gets up, tries to defend herself (2 1/2 sec.). Cut on action to a medium two-shot of Blanche at the moment Adamson pushes her to the wall (3 1/2 sec.). Cut to a fast zoom into a close-up of Fran's face, in horror (3/4 sec.). Cut back to a tighter medium two shot of Blanche and Adamson locked in struggle (1 sec.). Cut on action to a close-up of her head swung around, followed by six masterly orchestrated very brief shots (1/2 sec. or less): a low shot of her arm twisted, a high shot of her foot pushing, then a low shot of a sleeve pulled, a high shot of hand with needle, again arm twisted, finally the needle strikes in close-up (total 3 sec.). Cut to a high close-up of Blanche's face with mouth open; a shout of pain is heard (2 sec.). Cut to her bloody sleeve sliding down (1 1/2 sec.). Cut to a close-up of Fran turning her face away (1 sec.). Cut to a medium two-shot of Adamson lowering Blanche's limp body to the floor; we see several paint cans overturned (7 1/2 sec.). Cut back to the close-up of Fran turning her head to see (2 sec.). Cut to a long shot of Fran and Adamson; he hands her back the needle and asks her to unlock the door (to the secret chamber), then picks up Blanche from the floor and carries her limp body up the few steps. He talks to Fran as he walks: "Cheer up, dear, let's go get the new diamond for our chandelier." They leave. There is a brief pause in the empty garage (the entire shot lasts 25 sec.). The last line, spoken casually, in the context of a long shot, in a darkish interior with their backs to the camera, does not necessarily beg for special attention. Hitchcock, with a naughty design in mind, pulls the viewer's leg, since the above line is important and the only clue for understanding the small mystery of the finale of the film (how Blanche knows that the diamonds are taped to the chandelier). Having done so, Hitchcock leaves the inattentive with an unsolved puzzle. In addition, this proves how stubbornly he refuses to serve the narrative with special shots: in the above case a close shot would certainly help to single out the clue, but the scene at the closing requires a long duration long shot, without cuts, as a release after an animated action sequence.

The action of the scene guards a believable reality, yet, at the same time, is presented with gusto; it is stylized in the kind of shots, their placement and rhythm. There are several shots that would normally defy a test of veracity but are here gracefully absorbed (like the zoom into Fran's face, and the exaggerated and slightly distorted low shots). The scene has a solid structural plan: a relaxed and funny introduction of Blanche at the garage, followed by a series of over-the-shoulder shots, then a short separation sequence with an almost happy ending, then an unexpected crisis, a struggle with quick fragmentation and, finally, a long duration release shot (with the clue). The transitions to the next scene involve considerable time deletions. Also, the parallel actions are about to merge and shots will be of longer duration in contrast to the previous scene.

Scene 28. Starts with the time deletion: in a medium two-shot Fran and Adamson are riding in their car (a frontal shot); through the rear window we see passing urban lights of the night traffic. Adamson brings up to his eye a gleaming, oblong diamond (apparently they have made the pickup of the ransom). He examines it, watching the road occasionally. His mouth is watering; finally, he bursts out with his kind of smile that chills. Fran holds a silk cache, he drops the diamond in (23 sec.). Cut to the roadway in movement (1 1/2 sec.). Cut to a close-up of Adamson, who with deliberate cadence says: "And now for Madame Blanche" (4 1/2 sec.).

Cut to the primary parallel action of George in medium shot emerging from his taxi with urgency; he wears a cabbie's hat (2 sec.). Cut to a fast zoom shot into Blanche's white car parked in front of Adamson's house (2 1/2 sec.). Cut back to George at the taxi, looking; he starts walking in medium shot, camera follows; he crosses the street and starts up the steps to the entrance door (32 sec.). Cut on action to a low medium long shot of George from the back approaching the door; he rings the bell, sees the note Blanche has left, picks it up, and starts going back (18 sec.). Cut on action to a long shot of George descending the steps; camera follows as he keeps walking along the building; occasional cars pass on the street (18 sec.). Cut on action to a medium shot of George walking in profile; he comes upon Blanche's car (in foreground), looks into it (12 sec.). Cut to a close-up of Blanche's car keys in the ignition (1 1/2 sec.). Cut back to tighter medium shot of George emerging from the car after he concludes that since her keys are still in it, she must be in the house. He looks around, walks over to the black garage door, tries to open it without success, then looks down (23 sec.). Cut to a close shot of a streak of white paint on the cement coming from inside the garage. Musical theme starts (1 1/2 sec.). Cut back to the medium shot of George leaning down (9 1/2 sec.). Cut on action to a close shot of the paint and George's finger touching it (1 1/2 sec.). Cut on action to a medium close-up of George lifting his finger with wet white paint to examine it; he gets up and tries the door again; he walks along the garage door and looks around (27 sec.). Cut toward the corner of the house, leaves are blowing out of an alleyway (1 1/2 sec.). Cut back to the medium shot of George who notices the existence of the alley, walks toward it (camera follows to the corner only); George makes a turn and enters it. In the background can be seen two garbage bins. He examines the walls and stoops down to a basement window (by now he is in a long shot) (36 sec.). Music continues strongly. (Note that from the time we see George, his movements and progress are deliberately shot in slow, almost real time, with cuts on action, without deletions, and in perfect linearity, as part of the delaying tactic I spoke about before.) Cut on action to a medium close shot of George leaning toward the small basement window. He tries to open it, feels it out, takes a knife out of his pocket, opens it (29 sec.). Cut on action to a close-up of the knife as it is pushed by George's hand (2 sec.). Cut to a reverse close-up; from inside the basement we see the blade of George's knife prying the catch of the locking mechanism, poking several times and finally unlocking it (9 sec.).

Cut on action to a medium shot of the window opening as seen from inside the basement. George pushes himself head first through the small opening and with difficulty manages to slip in; he lowers himself to the floor (camera adjusts down) and looks around (18 sec.). Cut to the secondary parallel action; in a medium frontal two-shot we see Fran and Adamson continuing their ride home (2 sec.), an insert-type shot mainly because of its brevity, merely a reminder of the upcoming danger. (I don't remember seeing any similar shot in Hitchcock's films, especially since the insertion is into a shot of long—real time—duration). Cut back to the medium shot of George retrieving his knife, then walking cautiously along a wall and up the steps leading to the main floor of the house (16 sec.). Cut on action to a medium close shot of George energetically coming up into the frame, looking in one door, then attempting to open another one (8 sec.). Cut to a reverse medium shot from the other side of the door opening; George's hand seeks out a switch; he puts the lights on and looks stupified (7 sec.). Cut to what he sees: a panning high shot of the empty garage, camera stops on Blanche's purse lying on the floor (4 1/2 sec.). Cut to a medium close shot of George looking in disbelief (1/2 sec.). Cut to a quick zoom shot toward Blanche's purse (1 1/2 sec.). Cut back to George in a wider medium close shot. The theme music starts again. He walks down the three steps to the garage; camera dollies back with him; he stoops down to the purse (7 sec.). Cut on action to a close-up of the purse with George's hands picking it up, drops of blood are clearly seen on the leather. George examines them, exclaiming (offscreen): "Oh my God" (8 sec.). Cut to a low frontal close-up of George looking intensely, then turning his face to the door (he may have heard something) (3 sec.). Cut back to a close-up of his hands putting down the purse (1 1/2 sec.). Cut back on action to a wide medium shot of George placing the purse on the cement floor, turning back to the door, going quietly up the few steps, turning off the lights, and exiting the garage (15 sec.).

Cut to a reverse medium shot of George on the other side of the door entering, on tiptoe, the house proper (4 1/2 sec.). Cut to a low medium shot of George turning right, entering another open door, looking around; the theme music continues; he reaches around the wall (12 sec.). Cut on action to a reverse shot from the other room; George, reaching for a switch, puts the lights on, calls out "Blanche," then turns the lights off and leaves (5 sec.). Cut on action from a very high angle long shot of George emerging from the room he just left. He tiptoes over to a pair of sliding doors as camera pans with him; he opens them and calls out for Blanche again, then across the large entrance hall to another open room and calls her again; finally, upon seeing the stairway, he starts up, noticing the splendid chandelier on the way. He is about to reach the upper floor when he hears the garage door noise. He stops, listens at the half landing. Upon hearing voices he starts up again; camera pans down to reveal Fran and Adamson entering (George is out of frame by now). Fran, as she passes, says: "My stomach, you know, doesn't agree with murder." Adamson, who follows her to a side room: "Do you think I'm looking forward to it?" (38 sec.). Cut to a low medium shot of George stooped at the upper railing, listening. Offscreen voice of Adamson: "If Joe Maloney had been efficient, they would be dead by now" (6 1/2 sec.). Cut to a high medium shot of a pair of feet (Fran's) walking on a tile floor; the voice of Fran: "You can have my share, keep it all to yourself" (6 sec.).

Cut back to the medium close shot of George at the stair railing, listening and reacting with his funny mimicking. Adamson's voice: "I'll tell you what I'll do. You help me to take sleeping beauty out of the cellar and load her into your car where I'll drive her to some deserted road where a 'suicide' can take place . . . I promise you we'll talk this thing over" (14 sec.). Cut back to the high shot, with Adamson's feet walking the floor; Adamson's voice: "OK?" Fran's voice: "What about the cabdriver?" (4 1/2 sec.). Cut back to same shot of George reacting strongly to what he hears, especially since it is about himself. Then Adamson's voice: "Well, if she was able to find us, he can too. He'll walk right into our hands." Fran's voice: "Your hands Arthur, not mine." Adamson's voice: "Don't you think we ought to have a look at her?" (6 sec.). Cut back to the high shot of Adamson's feet on the floor. He continues: "It's been a while since we gave her that shot." Fran's voice: "You do it." Adamson: "OK." He starts walking out (5 sec.). Cut back to George, still at the balustrade, quickly going up, out of the way (1 1/2 sec.).

Cut to a high long shot of Adamson slowly walking out of the room toward the basement stairs. He puts on the lights (6 sec.). Cut back to the medium shot of George quietly descending the stairway (6 1/2 sec.). Cut on action to a close-up of George's feet. He takes off his shoes, to walk silently (2 sec.). Cut back on action, to the medium shot of George walking down, shoes in hand (3 1/2 sec.). Cut on action to a medium close shot of George in profile sneaking by an open door of the room where Fran is sitting (with her back to the camera) at a table (3 1/2 sec.). Cut to a reverse medium close shot of George stepping forward from around the corner, coming closer and hugging the wall, looking up intently (8 sec.). Cut to a high long shot of Adamson in the process of opening his brick wall/door (2 sec.). Cut to a low close-up of George, his eyes penetrating what he sees (1 1/2 sec.) Musical theme starts again.

Cut back to Adamson entering his secret room (3 sec.). Cut back to a medium close shot of George, who has already started moving, shoes in hand, down the few stairs (camera follows) to the open door of the secret room; George sneaks a look inside as Adamson stands by the bed, then quickly moves to the other side of the door (7 1/2 sec.). Cut on action as George continues in medium shot to move into a shadow by the brick wall (3 1/2 sec.). Cut to a long shot (through the open door) of Adamson walking forward, presumably leaving the room (2 1/2 sec.). Cut to an insert of George (medium shot) jumping back into the shadow the instant Adamson approaches the door (1/2 sec.). Cut back to Adamson continuing his walk, he reaches behind the door for a rubber hose (3 sec.). Cut to George peeping out for a moment (1/2 sec.). Cut back to Adamson carrying the hose up the stairs. He addresses Fran loudly: "You'll be happy to know that she's still unconscious" (7 sec.). Cut back to the medium shot of George; he quickly slides sideways, making sure Adamson has left, and enters the secret room (9 sec.). Cut on action to a low medium close shot of George approaching Blanche, lying asleep on the bed. The shot turns into a medium two-shot with Blanche in the foreground. He touches her with a finger, whispering her name. Suddenly she opens one eye, lifts herself slightly, and hushes him (8 1/2 sec.). Even in the most suspenseful moments, humor stays like an aura around this couple. The sequence, so far, is composed of mostly longer duration shots in real time with cuts on action; yet, still, it is peppered regularly by bursts of fragmentations.

Characteristically, the shot in the secret room where George discovers Blanche safe and sound is left hanging (by Hitchcock), with a return to the parallelism. Cut to a low long shot of Fran coming toward the doorway leading, as it turns out, to the garage (at first one thinks

she is going to the basement where George and Blanche are). She walks slowly, in a daze. She comes down the few steps (17 sec.). Now begins a short separation sequence. Cut on action; she stops at a door and rests against a beam (3 1/2 sec.). Cut to a high medium shot of Adamson cutting the hose. He addresses Fran: "I'll put one end in her exhaust pipe, the other in her window. That way it will look like suicide." Adamson assembles the hose and leaves the frame (8 sec.). Cut back to Fran standing as before. She looks at him morosely (3 1/2 sec.). Cut back to the high long shot of Adamson, who walks over close to his car. Using the remote control, he opens the big garage door; we see Blanche's white car parked there. Adamson walks toward it (6 1/2 sec.). Cut back to Fran (as before) observing him (1 sec.). Cut back to the long shot of Adamson going toward Blanche's car, and throwing the hose through the window. He quickly returns, closes the garage door, opens his own car and tells Fran: "You better get her now." He walks over to the stairs, and goes past Fran. Since we see them in one frame this is a resolution to a brief six-shot separation.

Adamson continues: "I'll take her in our car, you follow in hers." He leaves the garage (23 sec.). Cut to a medium long shot of Adamson rounding a corner and entering the basement. Fran joins him; they go down the steps and head toward the secret room. Camera follows with a pan (8 sec.). Cut on action to a reverse medium two-shot as they enter the room. Blanche's bed is in the foreground. Adamson reaches out to lift her (3 1/2 sec.). Cut to a close-up of Blanche's hand on our side of the bed (unseen by Adamson) clutching the frame tightly (preventing herself from being lifted) (2 sec.). Cut back to the medium three-shot of Adamson struggling to lift her out of bed; he exclaims to Fran, who stands just behind him: "Jesus, she's heavy." At this moment Blanche jumps out of bed with a howl (2 sec.).

Cut on action to a tighter medium shot from the direction of the door as Blanche pushes Fran out of the way and runs, screaming, toward the camera that swiftly dollies back; Adamson is just behind in pursuit. One more step and she is out of the door as George slams it shut, the kidnappers are locked inside. Both Blanche, out of breath, and George turn the key. (The above takes only 2 sec., and the shot continues without a cut). George: "We got them. You, Blanche, are still the hero." They lean against each other; Blanche, still out of breath: "Thank you. Do you realize how much reward is waiting?" She covers her face and rests her head on his chest. George: "Yes. But do you realize how much more the reward would be if we could find the diamonds and turn them in?" Blanche, upon hearing this, straightens up and takes up the posture of a medium, with one hand stretched out ahead of her. George: "What's the matter Blanche, what's the matter?" (celestial music starts in the background). She walks slowly toward the steps, as camera pans with her; she approaches, in a profile close-up, and starts climbing the steps (58 sec.). Cut to a medium shot of George left alone at the brick wall: "Blanche, what's the matter?" He too starts walking, camera pans with him; eventually he reaches Blanche at the top of the steps: "What is it?" (9 sec.). Cut on action to a reverse medium two-shot (again the axis is crossed); the two continue walking, Blanche ahead of George, camera dollies back with them. Blanche heads toward the big stairway; she turns and climbs five steps. Camera moves in to a close-up of her profile, turning to the chandelier. Heavenly music intensifies. She points a finger to the left, to the chandelier. Camera pans left and moves into an extreme close-up of the round diamond hanging among the crystals of the chandelier (29 sec.). Cut to a close shot of George in profile (looking to the left). He exclaims, delighted: "Blanche you did it. You are psychic." He smiles sincerely, camera backs away to a close two-shot. Blanche asks, as during her séances: "What am I doing on the stairs?" George cuts in: "You're not a fake." Blanche repeats "What am I doing on the stairs?" George, pointing toward the diamond: "You actually found one"; Blanche looks innocently to the left and asks: "I did?" George: "Now I get the police on the phone and give them our good news and call Mrs. Rainbird and give her the bad." Cut to George running away from the camera to a long shot; he enters a room on the main floor, picks up a phone, dials, and excitedly asks: "Operator, can I have the police?" (20 sec.). Theme music starts again. Cut to Blanche in a beautiful close-up. She turns from profile to camera, slowly lowers herself to a sitting position (camera adjusts to a central framing), and, looking straight at the camera, flashes an extraordinarily charming wink. (Theme peaks, credits roll up.) Thus ends with a touch of burlesque this charming farce. It started with a farcical psychic séance and closes with a farcical wink directly at the audience. Blanche, the delightful fake, gives a signal that she has performed one more naughty trick.

The film leaves us with a bagful of unfinished business that is, to be sure, charming to contemplate; such as, how Blanche and George will bathe in their riches, how Mrs. Rainbird will take the bad news, how the kidnappers will look when led by the police out of their secret room or, for those who missed the well-hidden clue, how Blanche knew about the diamond on the chandelier. To answer this question they will, I'm sure, scramble to see the film again to take another flight in the winsome fictionality that Hitchcock offered as his last wink to his audiences.

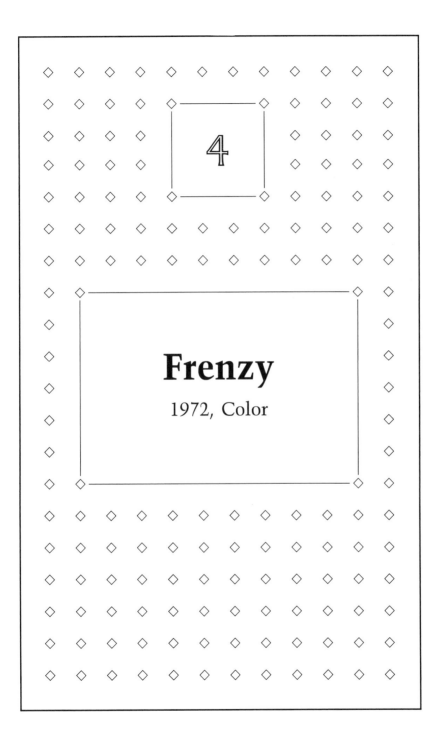

4

Frenzy

1972, Color

T HE FILM STORY of *Frenzy* carries within it an unmistakable symmetry since, in essence, the plot reminds us of *The Lodger*, a film Hitchcock made, also in London, about a half century before. *Frenzy* is perhaps the most "Hitchcockian" film of the three I selected for this book, both in subject matter and in the manner of execution. The story is set in London. A sadistic sex maniac is at large; he rapes and murders women by strangling them with a necktie, his peculiar signature. The naked body of a woman is found floating in the Thames, a tie around her neck. The town is buzzing; people demand that the necktie murderer be apprehended. When the protagonist of the film, Richard Blaney (Jon Finch), is first introduced, he is putting on a tie in front of a mirror. By the magic of Hitchcock's humorous ambivalences, a shadow of suspicion falls upon Blaney. But soon the viewer learns that this former squadron leader and presently unemployed bartender, down on his luck, is just a victim of circumstances. As often with Hitchcock, in the first part of the film the audience learns who the killer is; in this case he is none other than the best friend of Blaney, an apple-munching, toothpicking, potato and produce firm manager Robert Rusk (Barry Foster). The above is of course privileged information for the viewers of the film only, who are given a shocking demonstration of the rape and murder. Rusk's victim this time is Mrs. Brenda Blaney (Barbara Leigh-Hunt), Richard's divorced wife. The police get a good share of ridicule in this film; Chief Inspector Oxford and his wife, incidentally, provide the major comic relief. The police suspect Richard Blaney since he was seen at the scene of the murder and was heard arguing violently with his ex-wife the day before. Blaney attempts to hide, witn the help of his girl friend Babs Mulligan (Anna Massey), who sincerely believes in his innocence. She, in turn, becomes Rusk's next murder victim. Rusk loads her body into a sack, then onto a lorry full of potatoes. Meanwhile a major complication creeps in: Rusk has lost his monogrammed tie pin, most likely during the struggle with Babs, who apparently bravely defended herself. Since, if found, this may implicate him, he goes back to the truck and tries feverishly to retrieve his pin from the hand of the dead Babs, in what turns out to be the most striking tragicomic scene of the film. Richard Blaney ironically seeks shelter with Rusk, who quickly turns him over to the police. Implicated in the two murders, Blaney is sentenced for life. At the sentencing, Blaney desperately shouts out that Rusk is the guilty one. Chief Inspector Oxford (Alec McCowen) is sufficiently impressed to begin a new investigation into Rusk's role in the affair. Blaney, who has succeeded in escaping from jail, is on his way to avenge himself on Rusk. Chief Inspector Oxford, who by now has received convincing evidence against Rusk, rushes to Rusk's flat where he finds Blaney standing over another woman victim sprawled on Rusk's bed, a tie around her neck. A moment later Rusk comes up the steps dragging a large trunk into which, one assumes, he plans to stuff the victim. Upon entering the room he is faced by Blaney and Inspector Oxford, who comments in an ironic tone: "Mr. Rusk, you're not wearing your tie"; and so ends the film.

Frenzy, seemingly a film within the genre, is, in fact, ascending to a finesse and ambivalence that satirizes and questions the rationale of the genre. Most importantly, Hitchcock's exquisite film language reaches here such heights of expressiveness that it becomes a showcase for cinema art.

Scene 1. The film starts with a roll up of credits superimposed over a high dollying shot (most likely from a helicopter) overlooking the river Thames, slowly approaching the Tower Bridge, with its roadway gates open; as the credits of screenplay writer Anthony Shaffer, followed by the director Alfred Hitchcock, come on the screen the camera is nearing the bridge; it soon passes under the span into open water, where a large brown tug spouting black smoke is crossing the river from right to left (90 sec.). Dissolve to a high long shot zooming slowly to the left (the direction of the tug) into a small crowd of people gathering by the river's quay, listening to a speech (40 sec.). Cut to a low medium long shot of the speaker, with the crowd in the foreground; he is an elegant gentleman, evidently addressing a political rally (8 sec.). The next 27 shots are short (between 2 and 7 sec. in duration), at first alternating between the speaker and the crowd; in flowery oratory, quoting from Wordsworth, the politician promises his constituency to

clean up the polluted environment around the river bank and restore it to its natural beauty: "Clear of the waste of our society, with which for so long we have poisoned our rivers and canals." The succession of shots is ingeniously arranged, in contrast to the introductory moving camera shots, by minute fragmentation, as if anticipating a sudden change of mood. The speaker, who at first is shown in a high long shot and then intercut with the crowd in medium long shots, is presently seen in stages closer and closer (low medium shot, low medium close shot). The crowd at first is composed of journalists who take notes, later of some photographers, a local official with his wife, then, in a longer low shot, the common people of the neighborhood with Hitchcock in the back row, in a bowler hat.

On the twelfth shot, just as the gentleman in his grandiloquent manner speaks of how soon everything will be clean and pollution will disappear from the river, we see a medium shot of a working-class man shouting out: "Look," pointing to the river. This Hitchcock follows with a triad of shots on the same axis, each wider and wider. The medium single becomes a medium two-shot, then a group medium long shot, embracing a small crowd with our man still pointing down. The three shots last only 3 1/2 seconds. Cut to what they see, a high long shot of what appears to be the body of a naked woman floating by the river bank.

The above triad is a deliberate move by Hitchcock to simulate a pull back, yet still retain the benefit of rhythmic cuts. He has already used a similar triad of shots in the *Birds* (with the first victim, the farmer); here it acts as a counterpoint to the dolly shots seen in the beginning, as a reverse symmetry to closer and closer shots of the speaker, and also as a delay in showing the body of the strangled woman.

What follows is a series of 18 shots, intercutting between the dead woman floating closer to the shore and the crowd reacting: rushing forward, looking at the police activity, gossiping; for the latter, Hitchcock reserves the longest duration shot of the series, 15 seconds. The episode is a satire on the reputed British love for the morbid. (Incidentally, Hitchcock appears in this shot for the second time: a rare double cameo.) The rest of the shots are between one and three seconds. The last two shots of the scene are funny: we see in a medium two-shot our politician-speaker, who, by the way, is addressed by his companion as Sir George, exclaiming after watching the dead woman: "Say, it's not my club tie, is it?" Cut to the only close shot of the upper part of the floating woman's body, with a clearly visible brown and white striped tie around her neck (2 1/2 sec.). In this first scene Hitchcock sets forth the subject of the film and, with his few touches of humor, the tone of the film, but most importantly he presents the iconography of his structures: complex camera movements in conjunction with rapid fragmentation. The scene including credits lasts 4 minutes, 20 seconds.

Scene 2. Starts with a direct simile on the theme of ties, indeed similar ties. In the first shot we see Blaney, the protagonist, in a medium close-up putting on his brown and white striped tie. He seems to be sympathetic enough; still, the viewer, always on the lookout for hints and signs, here picks up a veiled suspicion that perhaps Blaney is the killer. The shot is leisurely in pace, considering the speedy cuts in the outgoing scene. A touch of cinematic elegance is added when Blaney moves to the side and the camera, with a slight pan to the left, reveals the real Blaney walking. What we have seen so far was only his image in the mirror. Such quid pro quos of walking out from a mirror are extremely gratifying to the viewer, thus it is shrewd of Hitchcock to introduce his protagonist in such a manner (16 1/2 sec.).

Cut to Blaney still walking via stairway and beaded partition, camera tracking with him, in medium shot. In a gracefully floating motion he reaches behind an empty bar and pours himself a drink, which he

downs with intense pleasure (18 sec.). Cut (shot 3) to a low medium shot of Felix Forsythe, the bar owner, who also enters the area with camera tracking until he stands in a two-shot with Blaney. He greets him sarcastically as "the squadron leader," reminding him that "this establishment is for selling liquor, not stealing it" (12 sec.). The above two shots with fastidious camera movements are a subtle introduction to an 18 shot separation sequence, a verbal duel between the two men. Blaney in medium close-up (framed on the left side of the frame) categorically denies the accusation, insisting that he intended to pay (2 sec.). Forsythe (framed a little closer and on the right) cynically refuses to believe him and fires him from his job as bartender (3 1/2 sec.). Back to Blaney, who repeats that he always puts the money in the till, even when he drinks Forsythe's watered down gin; he turns and walks to the opposite wall (8 1/2 sec.). Cut back to Forsythe (as before) who repeats that Blaney is fired (1 1/2 sec.). Cut to (shot 7) a medium close shot of Blaney who turns toward Forsythe (1 sec.). Cut to a close shot of Forsythe (who remains in the same framing all the time), barking back some vulgarity (1 1/2 sec.). In shot 9 the separation is momentarily interrupted by the entry of Babs Mulligan, Blaney's girl friend and the barmaid (the camera pans with her as in the other entrances); she stops close behind Forsythe in a medium two-shot, and asks what is going on (2 1/2 sec.). Cut back to the medium close shot of Blaney (as in shot 7), he tells Babs what happened (2 1/2 sec.). Cut back to

the two-shot (Forsythe and Babs). Babs defends Blaney, testifying that she saw him put money in the till whenever he took a drink (8 sec.).

From the above we see a shift to a two-to-one separation (Forsythe and Babs versus Blaney). Cut back to Blaney who listens to Babs' testimonial. Cut to a medium close-up of Babs. (Now the separation shifts to A, B, C singles; the two to one is terminated). Babs is adamant, accusing Forsythe of unfairness (2 sec.). Cut to a close-up of Forsythe; he turns his head to Babs who stands behind him. Forsythe tells her to shut up or she too will be fired (7 sec.). Cut back to Babs listening (1 sec.) (the separation is now between Babs and Forsythe). Cut to Forsythe bidding Babs to stay out of this dispute (2 1/2 sec.). The next 3 shots (Babs, Forsythe, Babs) continue with salvos of bitter accusations; among others Babs reminds him how he often "fingers her"; each shot is less than 2 seconds. Cut (shot 20) to a medium shot of Blaney, who takes some change from his pocket and throws it toward Forsythe, then takes his jacket from the hanger on the other side of the beaded curtain. He returns, camera panning with him, to a three-shot, saying that he'll send for his things shortly. Thus the separation is presently resolved. Forsythe shouts that there is still a small matter of ten pounds he advanced Blaney on his salary (20 sec., the longest duration shot in the scene). Cut to a close-up of Blaney taking two five pound notes from his wallet and crumbling them with fury (3 1/2 sec.). Cut to the three-shot with Blaney in the foreground throwing the money at Forsythe, then walking out of the bar with desperate energy; camera pans with him (7 1/2 sec.). Cut to the exterior of the bar; Blaney walks out followed by Babs in medium two-shot. She asks him what he intends to do; he thinks that he'll look for another pub job (9 sec.). Cut to a medium close two-shot from the right, a 90° angle change; she asks him if he is all right, if he needs money (2 1/2 sec.). Cut to a two-shot from the left (opposite side); Blaney assures her that he has some money left (3 1/2 sec.). Cut back to the two-shot from the right. Forsythe joins them (making it a three-shot), reminding Babs that this is Covent Garden, not the Garden of Love, and she should start work. He returns to the bar (3 1/2 sec.). Cut to a frontal two-shot of Babs and Blaney; she kisses him warmly on the cheek (1 1/2 sec.). Cut back to a wider medium two-shot; Blaney thanks her and promises to call. She goes back to the bar. He turns vigorously to the right and walks away into the crowded street; camera follows with a pan (6 sec.). Total length of Scene 2 is 2 minutes, 40 seconds. So far Blaney, who behaves in a rather short-tempered and choleric manner, carries the stigma of suspicion planted on him at the opening of the scene.

The above separation, with its ingenious variants of one-to-one, then two-to-one shots, with the intense eye contacts between the participants during the fast-paced exchanges and with its symmetries of camera movements (in the beginning, middle, and at the end) is an example of Hitchcock's brilliant use of this element of structure. The few touches of environmental reality Hitchcock affixes during the exterior shots, in front of the entrance to the pub, such as a passing pedestrian or a blurred carton of goods crossing the frame in the foreground, or a bag of fruit carried the other way, are effective; even though they appear only at the end of the scene, they seem to carry their weight back over the entire scene, giving us some sense of the neighborhood.

Scene 3. Shot 1: Blaney in reverse low medium shot approaches a news vendor; in the near foreground a news display has a handwritten, clearly readable sign: "Another necktie strangling" (6 sec.). Blaney buys a paper and walks out of the frame. Cut to an extremely high long shot above the entire intersection of streets with stalls of produce, trucks, and warehouses. We hardly see the little figure of Blaney crossing the street. The camera keeps panning to the left covering almost the whole geography that later will become the stage of many actions of the film

(28 sec.). Cut to a medium moving shot of Blaney walking amid crates with lettuce and similar merchandise in a crowded path in front of a warehouse. Camera pans, then he exits the frame again to the left (15 sec.).

Since the above two medium shots of Blaney walking bracket the extremely high long shot, one admires Hitchcock's audacity in joining linear shots of such antipodal size, to which a conservative filmmaker would surely be allergic, to say the least. A gradual descent from a very high long shot to an eye level or low medium close-up (or vice versa), as shown in the opening scene of *Frenzy*, is fairly digestible (on a reality level). But the extreme switches during Blaney's walk require the viewers to adjust and reorient themselves to the geography. Hitchcock, in so doing, energizes the scene and also telegraphs the beginning of the dramatic part of the film. In whatever other way one interprets this high long shot, it points to Hitchcock's originality and his constant striving to extend the limits of cinema language.

In the next shot we see Blaney in medium shot walking over (with camera panning with him) to greet his friend Bob Rusk at his fruit and vegetable establishment. They face each other in a medium two-shot profile. They exchange pleasantries; Blaney walks to the left and, leaning on some crates, says: "I've just been given the push." He tells Rusk about his dispute with Forsythe. Blaney is restless and walks away as he talks (34 sec.). Cut on action to a close shot of Blaney as he settles

with a cigarette, leaning against a wall inside the warehouse; a ten-shot separation follows between the medium close shot of Blaney and a silhouetted medium long shot of Rusk (with the unloading trucks in the background). Rusk jokes about Forsythe, asks Blaney what he wants to do next. Blaney has not decided as yet. Rusk reminds him that if he needs something he knows where to come; Blaney thanks him. After attending to an order at the shop, Rusk walks over to Blaney (23 sec.). The separation is thus resolved. They stand again in a middle two-shot, profile to profile. Rusk suggests that Blaney visit his ex(wife). Blaney sees no point in that since he has not seen her in ages. Rusk hesitates, then approaches Blaney again: "You can always rely on me." Then, extending his hands with some paper money, he offers it to Blaney, who adamantly refuses, assuring Rusk that he just got paid (30 sec.). Rusk walks away to get him some grapes. By directing his actors to move around even during separation, Hitchcock gives the viewer an opportunity to scrutinize the behavior and the physiognomy of the characters, especially when they approach the camera. Here, for instance, we notice how shifty-eyed Rusk is; although at this moment it does not yield any suspicion, it plants some seed for future reflection. Blaney walks over and picks up his raincoat. Just then Rusk comes into a medium two-shot with a box of grapes; he makes jokes about how his mom used to ask him to peel her a grape when he was a kid (30 sec.). Cut to a closer medium shot. Rusk asks him again if he is sure he does not need any money, is there anything else the matter? Blaney refuses again and denies that there is anything wrong. In this exchange, that also includes a mention of Babs, Hitchcock has made four cuts of a semi over-the-shoulder type (total 23 sec.). Finally, as Blaney is about to leave, Rusk grabs his paper. For a moment we think that the headlines are to be revealed, but Rusk wants to give him a racing tip (6 sec.). Cut to a close-up of the racing page. Rusk circles the name of the horse "Coming Up" (10 sec.). Cut back to three more of the over-the-shoulder two-shots as Rusk explains that the horse will come in first on a 20 to 1 bet (4 sec.). Blaney, in disbelief, asks: "20 to 1?" Rusk assures him that his little birdie told him, and she's reliable (total: 11 sec.). Just then a voice is heard: "Good morning, Mr. Rusk." Both turn their heads (17 sec.). Cut unexpectedly to the face, in close-up, of a helmeted London policeman, framed as a significant image (it will eventually become a familiar image later in the film) (3 sec.). Cut back to Rusk; "Hello sergeant" he says, as he moves in medium close-up, with camera panning, to join the policeman in a two-shot. The sergeant complains about the necktie case giving him a headache. Rusk suggests advertising; the sergeant replies: "Very funny." He asks Rusk to keep his ears open in case he may get a "line on it." Rusk keeps joking; he wants to introduce his friend and so turns to where Blaney was standing (31 sec.). Cut to the place by the crates: it is empty; Blaney has vanished; instead we see only some handlers walking by with crates (3 1/2 sec.). Cut back to the two-shot. Rusk, wondering what happened, says: "Funny fellow." Then to the sergeant: "Don't worry, sarge, I'll put a word about it." He picks his teeth (as is his habit). The sergeant leaves, walking across the frame in front of Rusk (10 sec.). Note how Hitchcock likes to move people out of the frame by making them pass in front of a character who remains in the frame. The scene lasts 3 minutes, 15 seconds.

    Scene 4. Starts with a high long shot of a busy street: Blaney walks toward camera, then turns left into an alley (5 sec.). Cut to an interior of a crowded pub; we see Blaney entering in a medium long shot. Camera pans with him as he approaches the bar (5 sec.). He orders a large brandy, in a medium shot (1 1/2 sec.). Cut to two business or professional men entering the pub; camera pans with them (7 sec.). Cut to a reverse medium shot from behind them toward a corpulent barmaid who tells them what she has for lunch (4 sec.). Cut to a medium two-shot of the businessmen ordering two shepherd pies and two pints (2 sec.). Cut to a close-up of the barmaid who takes the order and goes to the back (1 1/2 sec.). Cut back to the medium two-shot of the men. Presently Hitchcock, who started the scene with seven brief shots, introduces a rather leisurely conversation, over two minutes in length, between the two men about the necktie murder. Blaney is seen sitting in the background, reading a paper by the window. The conversation is laced with Hitchcockian irony and a few jokes while they talk about the psychological and legal aspects of the murder cases. The lengthy conversation is interrupted twice: first, when the barmaid brings the beers and is told (by one of them) that they are talking about the necktie murders. Cut to her in medium close-up as she confides: "He is raping them first, isn't he?" Cut to the two-shot of the men: "Yes," says one with a chuckle, "I believe so." The other adds: "It's nice to know that every cloud has a silver lining." Cut to a baroque-like close-up of the barmaid filling the frame; she laughs with a touch of horror and walks away. Cut back to the two-shot (as before) of the conversing gentlemen. The second interruption takes place shortly after when Blaney comes forward to the bar for another drink; he stands (in a medium three-shot) next to the two who continue their conversation about how the murderer may on the surface appear "as a normal, likeable adult but emotionally remains a dangerous child" and "is particularly dangerous when his desires are being frustrated." Just then Blaney gets his drink; he furiously protests to the barman that he ordered "a large drink, not something that scarcely covers the bottom" (of the glass). He looks into his wallet, there is only one green note. Cut to a medium shot of the barman, with a frustrated look on his face. Cut back to the three-shot, Blaney now orders a triple brandy and pays with the last note. Cut back to the barman taking the money. (Note the sudden intrusion of the intense fragmentation.) Cut back to the two men who talk about how "on the one hand the scandal of the necktie murders is good for the tourist trade . . .," as Blaney goes back to his seat by the window.

In addition to the satirical underpinnings, Hitchcock is weaving in more suspicion against Blaney, yet does it ambivalently enough so that, when the changed venue comes, he will be able to manage it without shock. Despite the lengthy conversation, Hitchcock builds in a sufficient number of occasional cuts to give it the form of a staccato construction, thus keeping up the kind of cinematic energy needed in preparation for the explosive scene soon to come.

Next we see Blaney, after a deletion, in a slight high long shot, going through a busy street still in Covent Garden; when he reaches a medium shot size he hears someone calling him from above (6 sec.). Cut to a low medium long shot of Rusk leaning out of his second story window, greeting Blaney and asking: "How about coming up?" Cut to a high close-up of Blaney who refuses because of time. Cut back to Rusk: "No, I meant the horse 'Coming Up' who did come in first and paid 20 to 1." The exchange continues in a 17-shot separation between Blaney and Rusk, many of the shots no more than one second in duration, another drumming up of the rhythm. Blaney swallows the news about the horse and lies that he made a fortune. (We know that he had not followed through because of a lack of money.) Rusk wants to introduce his mother to him; a funny old lady with red hair looks down from the window; she is pleased to meet Blaney whom her son has called the best pilot on earth. Blaney finally bids them good bye, thanks Rusk for the tip, and walks away, furiously repeating: "20 to 1." He grabs the box of grapes Rusk had given him, throws it to the ground, and steps on it. The grabbing, throwing and stepping on are done in a triad of quick extreme close-ups, of details of the action, as a final pitched accent of the scene. The total length is 3 minutes, 35 seconds.

Scene 5. Starts in a strong visual chord as a cluster of double-decker red London buses moves toward the camera in a low long shot (with robust musical support) (3 sec.). Cut to a moving medium shot of Blaney on a crowded sidewalk, approaching the camera from the opposite direction, then turning left into an alley (8 sec.). Cut to a reverse medium long shot, looking from inside the alley, of Blaney looking at a hanging shingle with "Blaney's Bureau, Friendship and Marriage," on it; he turns to the house (8 sec.). Cut to another reverse medium shot as Blaney steps in and, with a slight stagger, starts climbing the steps (another important plant of the stairs to be used in the future) to the second story office with camera craning up with him in a frontal medium close shot (12 sec.). Cut to a low medium long shot (looking up) of an odd couple being escorted out by Monica, Mrs. Blaney's secretary. In this comical episode, a humorous release before an upcoming storm, we learn that the couple's marriage was arranged by the bureau. The bride, a huge, resolute woman, her new husband, a tiny, dried-up man, and

Monica, with big, horn-rimmed glasses, pouring out the sweet phrases one expects to hear from a matrimonial establishment, exchange pleasantries. There are five close-up shots of Blaney, who is the onlooker in this interlude, intercut between the medium three-shots of the couple with Monica. Blaney reacts with amusement at what he sees, with an occasional chuckle at their expense. Monica assures the couple that: "The agency's ultimate satisfaction is to make two lonely people happy." The shots now are closer. Monica is extremely comical here, with her funny appearance and personality; she is also a plant for a more extensive role later, a characteristic strategy of Hitchcock's constant anticipatory planning. The odd couple say their goodbyes and start down, on the way passing Blaney. The bride starts telling her little man that her late husband used to serve her a cup of tea in bed. (The episode has 17 shots and lasts 1 minute, 20 seconds.)

Cut back to Blaney's medium close-up as he turns toward the glass entrance door to the office and nonchalantly pushes the door with his fingers (5 sec.). Cut on action to a reverse medium shot of Blaney entering the secretary's office with a generous "Good afternoon." Camera pans with him as he throws his raincoat on the table, remarking to Monica that she is new here; by now they are in medium long two-shot. She: "I've been here for over a year now. What can I do for you?" (13 sec.). Cut on action to a medium two-shot over-the-shoulder from Monica's back toward Blaney: "You can inform Mrs. Blaney that one of her less successful exercises in matrimony has come to see her" (6 sec.). Cut to an over-the-shoulder toward Monica: "And who shall I say is calling?" (2 sec.). Cut back toward Blaney: "Mr. Blaney, or if you prefer ex-squadron leader, late of RAF and Mrs. Blaney's matrimonial bet" (6 sec.). Cut back toward Monica: "Oh, I see. Is Mrs. Blaney expecting you?" (3 sec.). Cut back toward Blaney: "I think so. Everybody expects a bad penny to turn up sooner or later." Monica announces him over the intercom; a voice says send him in. Blaney gets up, carelessly throws his paper on Monica's desk, and goes in a medium long shot through the inner glass door (18 sec.). Cut on action to Blaney in a medium close shot as he goes through the door in profile with a terse greeting: "Hello, Brenda." (Note the change in size of the image from a medium long shot to a medium close shot during an entry through a door, a seldom seen cinematic maneuver). The impact is visceral: the image of Blaney is bigger after the cut, consequently his entry through the door is extensively energized, promising something of import (3 sec.). Cut to Brenda in a medium shot; then, as she walks toward the camera she shares an intimate medium close two-shot with her ex-husband; she greets him, he kisses her on the cheek and, with the camera panning, walks around her to a chair (12 sec.). Cut to Brenda in a medium shot; she circles around her desk toward her chair with camera also panning, saying in a friendly voice: "It's good to see you, Richard" (5 sec.). The above two shots, with the semicircular movements of the characters and camera are, again, anticipatory forms that Hitchcock will use forcefully in an upcoming pivotal scene where they will pay what will turn out to be their morbid dividend on recall.

A small detail worth mentioning: both Brenda and Richard are about to sit down after their semicircular walk to their respective chairs, but Hitchcock delays the sitting by one shot each; the sequence reads: (1) Richard walks, reaches the chair, is just about to sit; (2) Brenda walks to hers; (3) Richard in medium shot sits down comfortably; (4) Brenda also in medium shot is already sitting, attending to some papers on her desk, as she continues talking to him. Such a layout (and delay) helps to tie together the separated single shots by spreading the act of sitting down over several shots in a fragmented linearity, yet still retaining the important rhythm of the cuts.

The above four shots, incidentally, start a lengthy separation sequence of 41 shots (with one interruption). After a few pleasantries they start sparring, with Richard Blaney the aggressive partner. He begins with irony about her business successes: "I'm amazed that, in an age when everybody considers marriage as hell, you can find any clients." Brenda, a little taken aback, asks him if he came here to insult her; he interrupts with a shout: "I'm not insulting you, for Christ's sake." She: "Would you please lower your voice." She gestures toward the glass door; Richard keeps shouting; he doesn't care if (Monica) listens. "By the way, why don't you have her married off, preferably to a 700-pound Japanese wrestler. That should iron out some of her creases a little." Brenda gets up and walks quickly to the glass door. Reverse medium shot of Brenda at the open door; she suggests that Monica take the rest of the day off since it's already late. In the far background we see Richard Blaney getting up and turning to the window (technically this would represent a resolution to the separation, but here it is casual and thus not consequential). Cut to a medium long shot of Monica at her desk asking if Mrs. Blaney is absolutely sure she doesn't need her. Cut back to Brenda by the door: "No, I'm sure." She closes the door; for a moment we have the opportunity to see through the patterned glass to the inside of the secretary's office (an important plant). Cut back to a medium moving shot of Monica looking intently toward that glass as she dresses to leave; we hear the argument from the inside. Brenda mentions that after a few drinks he usually gets violent. Cut back to the interior office; Blaney defends himself. He would never get violent toward Brenda, "the goddess of love. What Brenda Blaney brings together, let no man pull asunder!" He bangs his palm violently on the desk. In the background, through the glass door, we see Monica's silhouette listening. Brenda tries to quiet Blaney. She gets up and walks over to him (into a medium two-shot) with the words: "Look what a state you are in"; he brushes her off with: "Bachelors are supposed to be untidy." Finally he calms down, walks over to the desk and tells her he has had a bad day, he lost his job. This two-shot, in fact the resolution of the separation, is of the longest duration in the scene, 26 seconds. Hitchcock disregards this resolution and successfully restarts the separation for another 15 shots.

As I have said on a few occasions elsewhere, my studies have convinced me that separation as an element of cinema resists continuation after a resolution; it loses its charisma after a full expository shot, with both the participants together in one frame. Even as great an artist as Ozu, who uses separation profusely, is not able to successfully rewarm one after an interruption. Yet Hitchcock succeeds. In the above case two factors help; for one, the short digression from the A, B, A, B between Richard and Brenda to a separation between Brenda and Monica; second, the brief glimpse of Richard during that digression. When Hitchcock restarts the separation, the framing of Richard is slightly tighter and higher, while Brenda's is lower and wider. In this exchange Richard tells her that he was accused by his boss of stealing brandy; Brenda hears for the first time that he worked as a bartender; he also tells her about his bad luck, for lack of money, of not following up on a tip from his friend Bob Rusk on a horse that came in at 20 to 1. Brenda is sorry to hear all that. She invites him to have dinner with her (and on her) at her club at 7:30 this evening. She walks into his frame to write down the address of the club, in a medium two-shot, both with backs to the camera: the final resolution to the separation.

The shots in the A, B, A, B were between 2 and 5 seconds long, on average. The whole scene (Scene 5) has 66 shots and lasts 5 minutes, 50 seconds.

Scene 6. Transition here seems simple, yet one should not miss the details of positioning, always important in Hitchcock's arrangements: in the last shot of the outgoing scene Brenda is on the right, leaning down over the desk, her back to the camera, while Richard is on the left, also with his back to the camera; he turns his face to a three-quarter profile, watching her with a touch of sentimentality. The transitional first shot here has the same configuration in a frontal shot: Richard on the left, Brenda on the right, but both facing the camera as they sit at a table in the club's restaurant at the end of their dinner, in a medium two-shot. Richard (here too) turns his face to Brenda in a three-quarter profile and says: "Thanks for a lovely evening. It was great, I mean that." Note that even though the symmetry of the arrangements is inversed (from back to front), the screen directions or positionings are preserved, a well justified move since we switched locations and jumped (deleted) a few hours.

In the same two-shot, Brenda suggests that Richard should get married again (18 sec.). Cut to a medium close shot of Richard Blaney, who protests that he is "not good at it, you ought to know that." The above is the first shot of a 23-shot separation. The conversation starts on a mild tone but soon edges into sharper repartee as Richard, after a few drinks and thin-skinned as he is, becomes more and more aggressive. As exchanges intensify the shots get shorter and shorter, from a range of 8 seconds down to 1 1/2 to 2 seconds at the end. Richard remarks about their ten years together: "It's a good job that you got out when you did." She is not sure—she is "lucky that her agency worked out so well." Richard: "What you mean is that you didn't have to rely on me all those years." She: "I didn't say that." He snaps back, "But you meant it." He reminds her what "filthy luck he had" with his business projects; she knows and is sorry for that, but, she reminds him that he never used to be sorry for himself. At the 14th shot of the separation the single shots become close-ups. Brenda quotes from his citation as squadron leader in the RAF. Richard, in his close shots (even tighter than Brenda's), gets worked up and, speaking too loudly, complains that in this world good leadership doesn't count. She gets embarrassed, tries to hush him, people are listening; he blasts out: "Let them. They never

had to turn out their livelihood with their own hands. It's all right for you. You're good at business. They're all good at business. I'll bet you make a fortune in the agency, and why not? If you cant't make love, sell it. The respectful kind of course . . . the married kind." Cut to an extreme close-up of an empty wine glass crushed in his hand (1 sec.). Richard's last tirade is intercut with four brief, silent shots of Brenda listening, horrified and ashamed (in close-up as before). After breaking the glass there is one more, the 24th shot of the separation, of Brenda, who says: "Now look what you have done." Cut to a medium long shot that includes neighboring tables. This resolution to the separation is wider than the introductory two-shot. An older waitress comes over, attempting to help; Richard snaps at her: "Leave me alone." She promptly does so. After a painful pause, Richard, while wiping his bloody hand with a napkin, tells Brenda that he is sorry. She wonders how he does with money. They start leaving, moving among the tables, watched by the mostly middle-aged, respectable crowd (32 sec.). Cut to a reverse medium shot as they enter the cloakroom to get their coats. Only a very observant viewer will notice that Brenda slips something into his raincoat pocket before handing it to him. They exit. (No cuts—18 sec.).

Cut to exterior night, long shot of a London taxi coming to a curb. Brenda and Richard get out (7 sec.). Cut to a medium two-shot of Brenda saying good night. Richard wants to stop by, he wants to see how she lives. She resists, "It's late for a working girl." He insists, promising to be only a few minutes. She agrees. They enter, lights go on in the ground floor window (38 sec.). End of scene. (Total time: 3 minutes, 30 seconds.) Somewhere in the corner of the viewer's consciousness there must linger a grain of suspicion and worry when Richard enters Brenda's flat.

The above scene 6 is, indeed, simple, especially the separation with its classical construction: introduction, symmetrical resolution, stable shots, closer shots in the middle, and a climactic shot (broken glass at the end), without any filigrees or oratory. Indeed there is a lot of wisdom in this kind of construction, in the context of the drama. The underlying aim here, the real undercurrent beside the business at hand, is to permit the viewer to observe Brenda, to get to know her better, to see her reactions, attitudes, to see her face, the anatomy of her expressions. All this in preparation (anticipatory again) for the tragic violence that comes shortly after, when our sympathies for her will be called to hand.

Scene 7. The shortest scene in the film, 55 seconds, and the simplest, five shots only: starts with a slow disclosure: a close-up of the Salvation Army sign in the center of a blanket, camera pans up to Richard Blaney's face; he is sleeping on a cot (6 sec.). Cut to a high long shot of the enormous shelter with hundreds of cots (5 sec.). Cut to a medium two-shot of Blaney's and a neighboring cot where an older man reaches out toward Richard (6 sec.). Cut on action to a close shot of the older man's hand digging into Richard's raincoat pocket (7 sec.). Cut back to the medium two-shot, the older man withdraws his hand with some money in it; Richard wakes up, grabs the money out of the man's hand. He tries to cover up by insisting that he picked it up from the floor; Richard, furiously: "You keep your hands out of my pocket or I'll break your arms." Richard examines the few five pound notes, wondering; the camera moves in to a close-up of his smiling face (30 sec.). The scene performs a minor narrative function but its most important reason for being here is to delay and bridge, with its neutral mood, into the next, most tragic and disturbing, scene, of rape and murder.

Scene 8. The longest scene in the film and probably the most complex: composed of 139 cuts basically in a separation mode with an interruption at the epicenter of the struggle (from shots 51 through 81). At the end of the scene there is a clean-cut resolution and a closure.

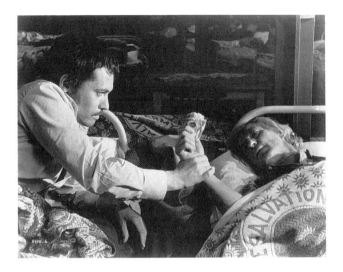

It is clear from this scene that Hitchcock was not restricted by the censorship that existed at the time of the filming of *Psycho*. From the pictorial strategy it is also clear that Hitchcock stays away from voyeurism per se. Separation, with its fragmentation, is definitely less voyeuristic than open expository shots. As an arbiter evaluating his directorial choices, I find it awkward to use superlatives here as not appropriate in such a gruesome part of the drama; nevertheless I must state that the scene is, without question, a masterpiece.

Shot 1 starts in a medium close shot, from a slightly high angle, of Brenda Blaney behind her desk touching up her makeup (3 1/2 sec.). The shot has a two-pronged impact: on the one hand it connects directly with the end of the previous scene, in answer to Richard Blaney's thoughts about who put the money in his coat pocket; on the other, it is a perfectly logical start to a scene where Brenda is the heroine and the unfortunate victim. Cut to (shot 2) a medium shot of the glass door and Bob Rusk's unexpected entry (3 sec.). Cut back to the same medium close shot of Brenda Blaney (a framing that will remain stable for 11 shots), surprised: "Oh, it's you again, Mr. Robinson?" (3 sec.). The viewer takes note of the subterfuge (Rusk's name). Cut back to (shot 4) Rusk, still at the glass door. He answers innocently: "Yes, I'm afraid so" (3 sec.). Note the steady beat of shots of 3 seconds each. Cut to (shot 5) the same shot of Brenda; she is short with him, stating that

she is on her lunch hour now and he will have to make an appointment
with her secretary (7 sec.). Cut back to Rusk, her voice offscreen: "By
the way, how did you get in?" He starts walking to screen left with
camera moving with him (reminiscent of the panning in Scene 6 of
Richard Blaney's visit in the same office). He says: "Oh . . . no problem, really" (4 sec.). Cut back to Brenda listening. Camera makes a
brief panning move to the right in sync with Rusk's previous walk (2
sec.). Cut back (shot 8) to Rusk, who reaches the filing cabinets and,
while fiddling with an open file, continues: "I was waiting in the courtyard, till I saw her go out to lunch." Brenda's voice, after a pause: "It
all seems so elaborate." He looks at her and he says: "Yes . . . but
. . ." (11 sec., first break in the rhythm of short shots). Cut back (shot
9) to Brenda listening, slightly perturbed (1 1/2 sec.). Cut to (shot 10)
Rusk as he walks toward her: "You are the one I want to see" (3 sec.).
Cut back to Brenda (shot 11): "I've already explained to you that we
cannot help you" (4 sec.). Cut back to Rusk (shot 12); he keeps walking
to the left, camera panning with him, he insists that she can be most
helpful when she tries (5 sec.).

Cut back (shot 13) to Brenda as the camera again moves slightly to
the right, synchronizing with Rusk's walk: "Look, Mr. Robinson . . .
you want women of a specific type" (4 1/2 sec.). Cut to (shot 14) a low
medium close shot of Rusk; he quickly turns his face to her in strong
reaction to what she says (2 1/2 sec.). Cut back to (shot 15) Brenda,
who continues: "How shall I put it? Certain peculiarities appeal to you"
(3 sec.). Cut to (shot 16) Rusk who sinks into the easy chair (in which
Richard Blaney sat previously) listening (camera adjusts to his position), as we hear her voice offscreen: "And you need women who sub-
mit to them" (4 sec.). Cut to (shot 17) the same shot of Brenda as she
continues: "Here, I'm afraid, we have a very normal clientele, and as
I've said, we can do nothing for you" (5 sec.). Cut to (shot 18) Rusk in
medium shot still sitting in the chair, biting his fingers. Her voice continues: "And now if you will allow me to get on with my lunch." Rusk
springs to his feet (camera pans up with him) pointing his finger at her,
then moving back, with camera panning, to the filing cabinet; nearly
shouting, he complains that she did not do as much for him as she
most likely did for the others, pointing to the files. The shot lasts eleven
seconds, again a break in the rhythm of shorter shots. His half circling
of the room, in addition to being familiar from the Richard Blaney scene,

now becomes threatening. Cut to (shot 19) Brenda (the same shot): "I've explained, you're different"; a shadow of fear can be seen in her eyes (3 1/2 sec.). Cut to (shot 20) a medium shot of Rusk walking slowly toward Brenda's desk. He asks, in an almost Shylockian speech: "How come? I have my good points. I like flowers . . . and quiet . . . people like me; I have things to give." We see him closer and closer in four shots intercut with four shots closer and closer of Brenda; in his shots the camera is low and static, it is he who moves closer; hers are of high angle and the camera moves in closer. He says that he thought matrimonial agencies are supposed to bring people together. She: "Not people like you." He stops and adds: "I'm getting along with all sorts of people." She: "Good, then you don't need us." The total amount of time for the above eight shots is 28 seconds.

Presently Rusk leans on the desk in the first close-up (shot 28): "You are not the only agency in town" (2 sec.). Cut to (shot 29) a tight close-up of Brenda looking up: "Then go elsewhere" (2 1/2 sec.). Cut to Rusk's (shot 30) close-up: "I've been elsewhere" (2 sec.). Cut to (shot 31) Brenda listening, in fright (2 sec.). Cut back to Rusk (shot 32) who leans even closer and speaks slowly and softly: "But this one to me is the best . . . because . . ." Cut (shot 33) to Brenda closing her eyes (2 sec.). Cut back to Rusk (shot 34) who continues: "Because I like you." Cut to (shot 35) Brenda looking up, incredulous (3 sec.). Cut to (shot 36) Rusk, who as if in a trance: "You're my type of woman" (4 1/2 sec.). Cut to Brenda (shot 37); after a moment of pregnant silence, she tries to dismiss him by saying: "Don't be ridiculous" (5 1/2 sec.). Cut to Rusk (shot 38), still leaning close: "I'm serious . . ."; after a pause, "I respect a woman like you." He backs away a bit, turns and sits down on the desk in medium close shot profile (6 sec.). Cut back to (shot 39) the close-up of Brenda, listening, thinking fast (2 sec.). Note that Brenda's picture size does not change when Rusk sits down.

Cut back to Rusk's profile (shot 40) as before; he tells her that in his trade there is a saying: "Don't squeeze the goods until they're yours." Cut to (shot 41) Brenda's close-up, a bit lower angle, she listens (2 sec.). Cut back to Rusk's profile (shot 42) as he continues: "That's me . . . I would never do it"; his eyes roll up, insanely (3 sec.). Cut back to Brenda's close-up (shot 43). She listens, looks into his eyes (2 1/2 sec.). Cut back (shot 44) to Rusk's profile: "You know that, don't you?"; he looks at her with shifty eyes (5 1/2 sec.). Cut back (shot 45) to Brenda looking (1 1/2 sec.). Cut back to Rusk (shot 46) looking (1 1/2 sec.). Cut back to Brenda (shot 47). She seems to have made a decision: "Excuse me, I've just remembered a call I have to make" (5 sec.). This is the end of the series of eighteen close-ups. Cut to (shot 48) the phone; we see his hand jumping on her finger as she starts to dial (3 1/2 sec.).

So far into the scene we can delineate two distinct acts, both on the narrative as well as the structural side: the first act is the stalking by Rusk, the ominous walking around, eighteen shots in all—the eighteenth shot, as pointed out, is the longest in duration and it interrupts the rhythm of the short shots; the second act, shots 19–47, is the coming forward, the slow steps of advance, the bearing down of Rusk upon poor Brenda. A break comes at the end when Brenda attempts to use the phone, shots 47 and 48. The first act, accordingly, is staged in medium shots, the second act is done in close-ups that progressively increase in size. Both acts are in the separation mode, with the telephone introducing a partial resolution, since we see in shot 48 both her hand and his. Incongruous as it may seem, the telephone incident affords a certain pause in the tension that is built up during act two with the menacing close-ups of Rusk. Here is an example of how even a partial resolution of separation can produce a slight release. This partial resolution eases in a more substantial one, since a couple of shots later Hitchcock introduces two-shots, at first intercut with singles of Rusk. Act three, then, starts at shot 48 with Brenda beginning to dial as Rusk briskly prevents it.

Cut to (shot 49) a medium shot of Brenda with the phone receiver in her hand; Rusk's arm enters the frame, he rips the receiver away from her; his voice: "There's no reason to call the police." She recoils, collects herself, and asks innocently: "What made you think I wanted to call the police?" (8 sec.). Cut to (shot 50) a medium close shot of a smiling Rusk, who answers: "Oh, just intuition I suppose." He moves to the left, sits, and takes an apple from her lunch; camera follows his movement. The shot ends as a two-shot (of the over-the-shoulder kind) with the back of Brenda's head on the right (9 sec.). This shot, since it is the real resolution to the separation and because it is larger in size (a two-shot), longer in duration (9 sec.) and with Rusk's suddenly relaxed smile, represents a more substantial yet still temporary release from the trigger of suspense of act two. Cut to (shot 51) the same medium two-shot, but this time with Brenda facing camera and Rusk in

profile, still sitting on the desk, eating her apple. There are altogether seven such over-the-shoulder shots, with a median length of eight seconds each, from shot 50 to 57. Dramatically the mild release is still sustained. Rusk jokes about how frugal her lunch is, is she on some sort of a diet. He suggests that he take her out to lunch, the best lunch in town. She refuses at first, then quickly agrees. In shot 56 Rusk disbelieves: "You're going to have lunch with me? You mean it?" Cut to shot 57, camera aiming at Brenda: "Of course . . . Just let me wash my hands." She gets up and starts to walk to the glass door. Rusk grabs her and presses her to the wall. Now it becomes a medium two-shot. They struggle. Brenda defends herself; she mutters that they're supposed to have lunch; he says: "That'll be after." He twists her hands behind her; he tries to kiss her; she struggles. She finally agrees to do what he wants, but not here. She warns him that her secretary might be back any minute. He brutally twists her arms again, calls her a liar and "a wicked little girl." After a scuffle, he overcomes her and with a swing lays her on her desk. The camera follows this action ending with a close-up of Brenda's head hanging down in a faint. The above (shot 57) is the climax of act three and is of the longest duration, so far, in the film (59 sec.). Note that, unlike the other Hitchcockian pattern of using the over-the-shoulder series of shots as an introduction to a separation, here, instead, it follows a separation and in turn is followed by a series of two-shots, as we shall see.

Shot 58: an extreme close-up of Rusk's sweaty face hanging over Brenda's (who is out of frame). He whispers: "Don't worry . . . You have nothing to worry about." This eight-second close-up is a bridge to the series of two-shots that follows; it also predicts a type of close-up of Rusk that will dominate later in the scene. Presently a desperate struggle ensues; for twenty-three shots (from shot 59 through 81) we see raw action of the brutal force of a rapist and superhuman efforts by Brenda to extricate herself, 86 1/2 seconds of a nightmare.

Briefly: In a medium two-shot (shot 59) Brenda with both legs pushes Rusk off her body, throwing him to the opposite wall. She attempts to run; in two brief shots we see Rusk catch her by the leg and pull her back (shots 60, 61). He picks her up (shot 63) and throws her into the lounge chair (shot 64). He jumps on top of her and kisses her; camera moves closer to a tight close two-shot (shot 65). Rusk presses her down; she offers him money. The following six shots are tight close two-shots from four different angles, alternating high and low as Rusk forces his kisses on her: "It's you that I want, not money . . . you are my type." The shots are between two and six seconds each. During shot 71 the telephone starts ringing. She begs him to let her answer; he assures her they won't be disturbed, he locked the door downstairs. In shot 73 we see her arm only, reaching desperately in the air; again three tight two-shots with multiangularity, the latter only three seconds long. Shot 77 shows his legs as he tries to push. In shot 78 he begins to rip her dress; she promises not to struggle; he likes her to struggle; she begs him not to rip her dress. Her head is dangling on the other side of the chair. He is pressing forward. The shot is a bit longer in duration (11 sec.). In shot 79, from a high angle, we see him rip off the upper part of her dress, revealing her white breast (8 1/2 sec.). Then follows two brief cuts: shot 80 with her legs kicking in the air (1 1/2 sec.); shot 81, the most explicit of them all, Rusk's hand pulling down her panties (a fraction under 1 sec.). In my perhaps arbitrary divisions of the scene into acts, I propose to call the above shot the end of act three, the only act without separation, having instead close two-shots and, most importantly, multiangularity. This is the act of struggle.

Act four starts with a low frontal close-up (shot 82) of Rusk by now already in a crazy trance, looking down at her, and repeating rhythmically, as he will continue until the end of actual sex act: "Lovely, lovely, lovely . . ."; his face also moves rhythmically back and forth

(6 sec.). Presently starts another, most intense separation. Shot 83 is a tight close-up of Brenda's head, looking to the side; she is reciting the ninety-first Psalm: "Thou shalt not be afraid for the terror of the night." In the background we hear the "lovely, lovely" mutterings of the rapist (10 1/2 sec.). Shot 84 is a close-up of Brenda's bare breast (the same shot we have seen before). She tries to cover it by pulling up her slip. A small diamond-studded medallion cross is seen on her chest (4 1/2 sec.). Cut (shot 85) back to the close-up as in shot 83. She continues reciting. Rusk's shadow moving back and forth is seen on her right shoulder (11 1/2 sec.). Shot 86 is a low frontal medium shot with Rusk on top and part of Brenda's head at the bottom of the frame (technically this interrupts the separation). He increases the volume of his exclamations: "Lovely" (4 1/2 sec.). Shot 87 is back to the tight close-up of Brenda, now looking forward (at him), a martyr's look (5 sec.). Cut to (shot 88) a low close-up of Rusk who by now shouts at the top of his voice: "Lovely, lovely" (6 sec.). Cut back (shot 89) to the same close-up of Brenda, her head is more upright, she has almost a look of compassion (3 1/2 sec.). Cut back to (shot 90) Rusk (the same close-up). He looks at her as if suddenly awake (having climaxed) with hatred: "You . . . bitch!" He lunges forward (3 1/2 sec.). Cut to (shot 91) high angle close-up of Brenda with Rusk's hands grabbing her around the neck. (A plant for brief shots soon to come; 1/2 sec.). Cut back to (shot 92) Rusk, low medium close-up. He withdraws his grip and speaks through his teeth: "Women, they all are the same" (5 sec.).

Cut to (shot 93) a close shot of Brenda looking with horror (2 sec.). Act five of the murder starts here. Cut to (shot 94) a tighter close shot of Rusk, who adds "I'll show you" (6 sec.). Cut to (shot 95) a tight close-up of his hand removing a tie pin from his tie and sticking it in his lapel as camera follows. There is a prominent letter R on it (an important plant for future use, 6 sec.). Shot 96 is the start of a series of thirty very brief shots (planted in shot 91). Close shot of Brenda as she looks (second repeat) at what he is doing (1 1/2 sec.). Cut back to Rusk (shot 97) (same as before). He starts removing his tie (2 sec.). Cut to (shot 98) the same close shot of Brenda (third repeat), this time with a flash of recognition in her eyes (1 sec.). Cut to a closer low shot of Rusk, he finishes taking off his tie (1 1/2 sec.). Cut back (shot 100) to Brenda (fourth repeat) horrified as she realizes the meaning: "My God, the tie" (3 1/2 sec.). Brief cut to Rusk (shot 101) (1/2 sec.). Cut back to Brenda (fifth repeat, shot 102); she screams (1 sec.). Cut to (shot 103) medium two-shot from the side, as Rusk loops the tie around her neck (1 sec.). From now on, in this series, we shall see extreme close-ups only. Rusk's face is filmed on a diagonal, low close-up, Brenda's in a high close-up of the face or neck. Most shots are one second, some 1/2 second in duration, the exception is shot 108 of Brenda begging "Please, help me"—a wide close shot (3 sec.). The sequence is a classical example of minute fragmentation. The act of strangling is horrific in itself; Hitchcock arrives at a reality of a peculiar kind that does not beg for more elaboration of naturalistic details. Its veracity is indisputable and what we see is the essence of the thing. Devastating as it is, it represents some sort of an extract, a stylized rendition.

At first Rusk's diagonal close-up (a stylization in itself) is alternated with Brenda's shots. In her frame we always see his hands tightening the loop, or her fingers desperately trying to loosen it. After six A, B, A, B's of this sort, Rusk's face appears only after four shots of Brenda's tossing around, the next time after five shots of Brenda's; then from shots 120 to 133 it starts again to alternate between Rusk's and Brenda's one to one. As she is dying, Brenda's close-ups start to slow down (shot 121—2 1/2 sec., shot 123—2 3/4 sec., shot 125—3 sec., shot 127—3 1/2 sec., shot 129—face—plus shot 130—neck only—4 1/2 sec., and finally shot 132—a startling and also stylized close-up of her fading eyes, still with some movement of the pupils, then still—5 sec.). Rusk's diagonal close-ups alternating with the above are less than a second long, except in the last two shots (shot 131—2 sec. and the final—133—13 1/2 sec.). The last shot of Rusk (133) is less a close-up, the stylized diagonal is gone; we see him breathing heavily, he seems to be lying on her (she is out of frame). He gets up exhausted, straightens up and starts backing away (13 1/2 sec.); and then suddenly, although every cut is in a sense sudden, this one is shockingly so, we see in a medium close shot Brenda, tongue out, tie hanging down her neck (strange how orderly it is arranged), eyes popped, dead, a stylized image perfectly centered in the frame (2 sec.). Cut to a medium long shot (shot 135); Rusk continues backing up, opening his collar; camera dollies back revealing Brenda lying dead in the soft chair (in profile). Rusk leans on the desk, picks up the apple, and takes a bite; then, from Brenda's open purse he takes out a bunch of notes, pockets it, looks around, reaches for his pin (35 sec.). Cut on action (shot 136) to a medium shot

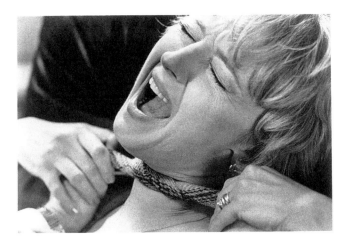

as Rusk takes out his pin and uses it as a toothpick (also a plant for a future scene) (8 1/2 sec.). Cut back on action (shot 137) to the medium long shot (as in shot 135), Rusk turns toward the door, looks around (5 sec.). Cut (shot 138) to an insert close shot of Rusk picking up the rest of the apple left on the desk (1 1/2 sec.). Cut back (shot 139) also on action to the previous medium long shot as Rusk pockets the apple and leaves the office through the glass door. Camera holds a couple of seconds on the glass partition (8 sec.).

The most striking aspect in this pivotal scene is its architecture, the predetermined design of structures that are built one on the other. If one scrutinizes the narrative content it is not difficult to conclude that the individual shots are, in fact, not designed to fit exactly each occasion. There is, for example, a total lack of so-called deep focus set-ups that would make more explicit the act of rape and the murder. The absence of full shots is tantamount to giving up on the reality of what happened. Closer shots are traditionally structured gradually from long shots, thus giving the viewer a context and reference point. Hitchcock, instead, starts Scene 8 with close shots in separation. The only reference to the geography of the place is by recall from previous scenes. Hitchcock always plants shots for future use, for the context; he forces the viewer to remember, to be actively involved in thinking, figuring out, recalling, and even predicting—a process similar to that in human language. After the first separation Hitchcock switches to two-shots, at first mildly via a release from tension, then moving into multiangularity for the violence. This he follows again by a stylized separation for the act of rape, and a minutely fragmented separation, also stylized, for the actual murder. Thus, as the narrative approaches the climax we get less explicit reality and instead more fragments, for Hitchcock knew the value of repetitions and symmetries. He also knew that naturalism is not the ultimate goal of the art of cinema; on the contrary, as in the other arts, its aim is to touch upon the essence of a given situation.

By now we already know who the necktie murderer is; accordingly, the viewer releases Blaney from the shadow of doubt, although society, as we shall learn, thinks otherwise.

Scene 9. Shot 1: Rusk in a medium shot exits the downstairs door into the alley; he walks hastily, sucking his middle finger; camera pans with him when he passes in a close shot; Rusk goes toward Oxford Street in a long shot where he turns to the right and out of frame; the camera then does a remarkable swish pan, without a cut, to the opposite entrance of the alley where in a long shot we see Blaney walking toward us and turning to enter the familiar downstairs door to his ex-wife's bureau (22 sec.). This fairly long duration shot is both a release from the previous buildup of tension and a surprising introduction to a new and serious worry about Blaney's fate. Shot 2 connects linearly as Blaney climbs the stairs, knocks at the glass door, and, after a few attempts to call for Brenda ("Brenda . . . this is Richard . . . any one there?"), turns to the stairs to descend (30 sec.). Cut to an exterior long shot of the alley; we see Monica, the secretary, on her way back to the office (5 sec.). Cut to what she sees: Blaney in medium long shot coming out of the building into the alley (3 sec.). Cut to a medium shot of Monica, walking steadfastly, although we see in her eyes a gleam of recognition. This time the camera pans with her as she walks by and finally enters the building. Camera stops dead on the plain brick wall with the entrance on the left of the frame; in the far background is the empty alley's other access. (Pedestrian traffic is minimal each time we see the alleyway.) From the moment Monica enters the building, for a painstaking 23 seconds, we wait for her to react to what we are well aware she will encounter upstairs. Hitchcock makes this enormous delay more unendurable by showing us nothing but, literally, a blank wall. He thus reveals a singular, anti-voyeuristic phrase in cinema language: the power of not showing that which can be imagined. (In addition, in this case full exposition would be morbidly snoopy). After 22 seconds of this spellbound silence we see two young women approaching in the alley and they, as well as we, hear a hysterical scream from upstairs (it lasts 4 sec.). The young women look around and up and continue walking on their way, paying little attention. The last shot lasts in toto 37 seconds.

To summarize so far: the shots are of much longer duration (except when Monica sees Blaney), in direct contrast to the scene before, with its mini-fragmentation; the rare "real time" shot, i.e., the 180° swish pan from Rusk leaving to Blaney arriving, Hitchcock devised especially to make the coincidence believable. And Hitchcock effectively follows the most explicit scene (the blood-chilling murder) with a most unexplicit shot, the blank wall and the long silence.

The next shot is a medium close shot of Blaney in a telephone booth; totally unaware of what has happened, he is calling his bar and wants to talk to Babs. Unfortunately, Forsythe, his former boss, answers the phone, furious at being disturbed at his busiest time. Babs, who is behind the bar in the far background, guesses who has called, comes over and takes the receiver from Forsythe. They make a date for four o'clock across from the Leicester Square Odeon—she'll bring him his clothes from the bar. This simple episode delays the crisis; we see Blaney at the beginning and at the middle of the phone conversation. It lasts one minute, 20 seconds. Total for the scene (Scene 9) is 2 minutes, 50 seconds.

Scene 10. Shot 1: a full long shot, almost a master shot, rare for Hitchcock: Monica is in the outer office being questioned by the police sergeant; detectives, photographers, and other personnel are roaming through the offices (6 sec.). Cut (shot 2) to a medium shot of the glass entrance door, Chief Inspector Oxford enters, greeted by the sergeant. Camera pans with him as he approaches the desk where Monica is sitting. The sergeant gives him some data; the inspector goes to the inner office for a moment, then comes back asking if Monica has any ideas. The sergeant tells him that she saw the murdered woman's ex-husband leaving the building when she returned from lunch. Monica: "I saw him clear as day. It was Blaney all right" (45 sec.). Cut (shot 3) to a medium two-shot of the inspector and sergeant listening (4 sec.). Cut (shot 4) to a medium close-up of Monica crying: "I saw him come out, the beast" (4 sec.). Cut (shot 5) to a low medium shot of Monica from the side, the inspector, leaning down, comes into the frame in profile, asking if she is sure it was Blaney. Monica: "Absolutely, I'd know him anywhere. He came yesterday in the afternoon and was positively horrid" (6 sec.). Cut to a tight medium two-shot, over-the-shoulder, camera toward the inspector. She describes the experience of the other day. (We see the benefit of the close-ups of Blaney in the telephone booth; they bring back, in a vividly visual way, his presence in this investigation.) Presently follows seven similar over-the-shoulder shots. Monica goes over the details of Blaney's visit and his violent behavior, adding that he had been drinking. The inspector asks her if he struck Mrs. Blaney. She: "Yes, I think so. There was the sound of a blow." The inspector gets up, camera follows him back into the medium two-shot next to the sergeant. He asks her to describe Mr. Blaney (36 sec.). Cut to a high medium close shot of Monica, who, in appearance and manner and the overly precise way she describes Blaney, snaps back to the comedic farcical mask of the previous day. Her monologue, which even includes such items as her opinion about the inappropriateness of Blaney's clothes for London weather, lasts only 21 seconds at her fast clip. Cut back to the two-shot of the two police officials. The inspector: "What an extraordinarily precise description, Miss Bartlette" (3 1/2 sec.). Cut back to the close shot of Monica: "In my job I've learned to keep a sharp eye on men, Inspector" (5 sec.). Cut back to the two-shot of the police officials (2 sec.). Cut to a medium long shot; a detective enters from the inner office with Brenda's handbag, saying he found no money in it. Monica protests that she had cashed a fifty pound check for Brenda that morning. The inspector gives instructions to his staff. End of scene (2 minutes, 55 sec.).

Scene 11. Essentially a funny scene, it follows Hitchcock's strategy of delaying, with humor and narrative complications, the next tragic turn of events. The structure too is rather simple. At first we see, in a long shot, Blaney waiting at a park fence (4 sec.). Cut to a medium long shot of an approaching taxi with Babs in it (3 sec.). Shot 3 is comparatively long in duration as we see Blaney in medium long shot crossing the busy street to enter the taxi (7 1/2 sec.). Here we see a small twist, a characteristic Hitchcockian maneuver: Blaney starts to enter the taxi (in shot 3) from right to left; in shot 4 (medium shot) he completes the entrance to the interior of the taxi from left to right, thus crossing the axis, the invisible taboo line between camera and subject, which, when crossed, confuses the viewer's sense of right and left, and is thus potentially disorienting. Not so in Hitchcockian application. Blaney's entry in shot 4 is dynamic, in a much closer shot than the crossing of the street; he penetrates the interior of the taxi on a diagonal, having crouched to avoid the ceiling. He bypasses Babs and sits down next to her, on the right. The shot thus becomes a medium two-shot. She wonders how Blaney can afford a hotel after he orders the driver to go to one. Blaney: "I'll tell you later."

Blaney's energetic entry is well justified since what follows is a lengthy taxi ride (67 sec.). Blaney tells her humorously about his night at the Salvation Army. His jacket will need fumigation to get rid of the smell. To Babs' insistent inquiries about why he orders the taxi to a hotel, Blaney finally answers that he collected an old debt. Cut to (shot 5) a low long shot of the tower of a building; camera pans down to a canopy with the sign Hotel Coburg. The taxi enters the frame, makes a U-turn, after waiting for the heavy traffic to pass, and stops in front of the hotel (15 sec.). Note that in this scene both the direct imagery (on location) and the rear projection during the taxi drive are vividly realistic. Cut to (shot 6) a low medium shot of Babs and Richard emerging from the taxi, paying and walking, with Blaney holding his bag, to the hotel entrance as camera pans with them (23 sec.). Cut to (shot 7) the lobby; with a panning medium long shot the camera follows the two as they approach the reception desk; the camera then moves in to a medium three-shot with a middle-aged receptionist facing us. Blaney orders a double room. Babs whispers: "What are you up to? Not here" (26 sec.). Shot 7 is an introduction to a three-way separation. Cut to (shot 8) a medium two-shot of Blaney and the receptionist, who asks him if he wants single beds or the matrimonial size (6 sec.). Cut to (shot 9) a close-up of Babs confused and furious (1 1/2 sec.). Cut back (shot 10) to the two-shot of Blaney and the receptionist. Blaney asks for a double bed. Cut to (shot 11) a tighter high two-shot of Blaney and the receptionist, who suggests room 322, the "Cupid room" (4 1/2 sec.). Cut back to (shot 12) the close-up of Babs (second repeat), whose eyes wander from where the receptionist stands to where Richard is (4 sec.). Cut (shot 13) to a new close-up of Blaney who, à propos the "Cupid room," suppresses a chuckle while the receptionist continues offscreen: "It's very cozy. Will you please sign the register?" Blaney:

"Yes, of course." He proceeds to register, saying loudly: "Mr. and Mrs. Oscar Wilde" (8 sec.). Cut back (shot 14) to the close-up of Babs (third repeat): "Look here, Richard Blaney" (2 sec.). Cut to (shot 15) the close-up of Blaney: "Oscar please, if you don't mind" (1 1/2 sec.). Cut back (shot 16) to Babs (fourth repeat): "Stop playing games" (2 sec.). Cut to (shot 17) the close-up of Blaney (1 1/2 sec.). Cut to (shot 18) the two-shot of Blaney and the receptionist who interrupts Babs and asks for ten pounds plus two for service (5 sec.). Cut to (shot 19) the close-up of Babs (fifth repeat) watching (1 1/2 sec.). Cut (shot 20) to the full medium long three-shot, the same as the introduction to the separation. We see Blaney paying the money; a funny porter comes around, picks up their bag, and asks them to follow him. Camera pans with them to the elevator (16 sec.). This orderly resolution to the separation (including the symmetry with the beginning) indicates how tame this scene is compared with the more turbulent ones. There is a charmingly funny epilogue to the separation: a close-up (shot 21) of the receptionist looking lustfully after the couple (1 1/2 sec.).

The comedic tone is augmented in a long shot (shot 22). We see Blaney, Babs, and the porter walking in the upstairs corridor toward the camera, joking about the Cupid room; they end by the door with camera panning to a close three-shot. The porter confidentially asks Blaney if he can get him something from the pharmacy: "No, thank you" (15 sec.). They enter the room and start settling down (shot 23) in a low medium long shot. Blaney gives the porter a tip (5 sec.). Cut to (shot 24) a high medium shot of the porter exiting the room into the corridor, playfully tossing and catching the coin in the air. Blaney calls out to the porter from behind the door, goes and hands him his jacket and then his pants, after taking them off in front of him, to be sent urgently to the cleaners for, as he says, "Spraying with DDT, if necessary." The porter is amazed. Blaney sends him off with a few jokes (30 sec.).

Cut to (shot 25) a medium two-shot of Blaney and Babs in bed asleep; one assumes it is morning (after a deletion). Babs starts moving; she looks around. Camera pans over to her head only (10 sec.). Cut to an insert-type medium shot (shot 26) of her clothes on a chair (1 sec.). Cut (shot 27) to a medium shot of her bare legs swinging out of bed to a sitting position; she starts putting on her short socks, stands up, and walks to the bathroom; as she retreats from the camera we see her

naked behind; when the light of the bathroom goes on she is naked in a long shot (the latter is another plant, important for a future scene). As she closes the bathroom door the camera quickly pans to the bottom of the entrance door where in a close shot we see a newspaper (pushed under) with a prominently readable headline: "Another necktie murder" (the entire shot 27 lasts 37 sec.). Cut to a medium close shot (frontal) of the porter reading the same headline in the newspaper at the reception desk. He calls out for Gladys, the receptionist. She comes into his frame; they both read; camera moves in for a close two-shot. He points out that the jacket he took to the cleaners is like the one in the description (22 sec.). Cut to an insert close-up of the newspaper (2 1/2 sec.). Cut back to the porter saying that the man in the Cupid room is the one the police are looking for. Simultaneously both look up toward the room in a clownish way. He picks up the phone and calls the police, asking them to come at once. The receptionist slips out of the frame. The porter warns her not to do anything foolish (30 sec.). Cut to the receptionist starting up the stairs (1 1/2 sec.). Cut back to the porter running to the main entrance. Camera pans with him as he runs out to the street; we see him through the open glass doors waiting for the police. As he waits there are two cuts back to the receptionist, 1 1/2 seconds each, standing restlessly at the elevator (these help create the needed deletion). Finally a white police car with two uniformed bobbies drives up; they get out; the porter runs ahead of them, camera panning again; they all enter the small elevator. The receptionist is left there after the elevator closes, wringing her hands nervously (38 sec.). Cut to a long shot of the upstairs corridor as the two policemen and the porter emerge and run toward the room. In spite of the potential danger to our protagonist the scene continues with a strong undertone of the satirical. They go through two sets of french doors and finally knock at room 322. There is no answer. After several attempts, the policeman opens the door, unlocked as it turns out (15 sec.). Cut to a long shot view of the empty unmade bed, camera swish pans to the window (2 1/2 sec.). Cut to a reverse long shot of the police followed by the porter running into the room and to the open window (5 sec.). Cut to a high long shot of a backyard metal stairway (2 1/2 sec.). Cut back to the three-shot. The porter tells the police that they must have gone out the back way (4 1/2 sec.). The structure of this part of the scene is that of a classical action episode.

The position of Blaney in the present constellation of the drama has changed: we realize that he is, unfortunately for him, the prime murder suspect. Not trusting the system of justice, he has decided to run (after reading the morning paper which identified him as the prime suspect).

In Scene 12 Blaney, on the run, will convince Babs and later his army friend Johnny that he is innocent in the necktie murders. Yet, as usual with Hitchcock, the pictorial information has a multi-hierarchical meaning. The scene will have a large number of close shots of Babs (listening to Blaney's explanations) with the subliminal purpose of familiarizing the viewer more intimately with her. Shortly after (as we know from the synopsis), she will be Rusk's next victim. The similarity with Hitchcock's handling of Brenda's image is striking; he also gave us an extensive number of her close-ups, shortly before her murder.

Scene 12. Starts with an extreme long shot of a park with a couple sitting on a bench in the distance (2 1/2 sec.). A cut to a medium two-shot reveals Babs and Blaney (still in his pajama top). He talks animately, defending himself: "I ask you, is it at all likely that I would murder a woman I was married to for ten years?" Babs: "If it was true it would be horrible." Blaney: "I raped her after ten years?" Babs: "Maybe you wanted to get rid of her?" Blaney: "But I got rid of her. We were divorced for two years. It wasn't a question of alimony, Brenda was making far more than I did" (23 sec.). Cut to a series of seven close two-shots of the over-the-shoulder type while dialogue continues in

the same vein. Babs is still suspicious because of his lying about the money Brenda slipped into his pocket (the total of the seven shots is 30 sec.). Babs gets up, upset. He defends himself vehemently. She points out that he sent clothes to the cleaner; and in sex cases the police always do a lab test. He circles around her explaining that his clothes stank to heaven. They sit down again (24 sec.). A series of seven close two-shots follow, slightly different from the previous ones: after every over-the-shoulder shot is a two-shot of both of them in profile, with the latter of longer duration. Babs softens her position; she believes him; they embrace and kiss. Babs is sorry that she thought of him even for a moment as a sadistic murderer. She suggests he go with his story to the police. Blaney resists; he insists the police will never believe him; he is most likely their only suspect (56 sec.). As they talk we hear from offscreen a voice calling Blaney; cut to a medium long shot as the two get up swiftly from the bench and start running (3 sec.). Cut to a man running toward the camera in long shot, shouting: "Dicko" (2 1/2 sec.). Cut back to Blaney and Babs, in long shot, stopping and looking back (2 sec.). Cut to a quick zoom shot from extreme long to a medium long shot of a woman on a high floor balcony looking down (2 1/2 sec.). Cut to very high long shot of Babs, Richard Blaney, and the man, Johnny (presumably what the women on the balcony sees). They talk. Johnny eventually suggests, with a gesture, that they go into the house (18 sec.). The change of tempo with Johnny's appearance reanimates the so far slow scene. The zoom to the balcony to Johnny's wife, Hettie, as it turns out, is a formal intrusion of some magnitude, promising something of consequence. However, since it is the strongest zoom in the film, it leaves me with an unanswered question as to Hitchcock's intention. In the rest of the scene Hettie plays the part of a satanic madame who believes Blaney guilty of murdering his ex-wife, and the whole situation is used by Hitchcock to satirize the new prosperous middle class, the precursors of the yuppies; still, the zoom, in this context, does not yield the promised big event.

The next shot is a medium long shot of Hettie in the modern apartment. She is pacing the floor, thinking, while waiting for the others to come up (14 sec.). Cut to the three walking up the stairs. Johnny tells Babs how he met Blaney during the Suez Canal invasion. They emerge on the proper floor but retreat stealthily, while someone is about to take the elevator. Eventually they cross over to Johnny's door (22 sec.). Cut to the interior, medium long shot, of Hettie to whom Johnny (off-screen) introduces the newcomers. She remembers "Dicko"; she greets Babs (camera moves in to a medium shot of Hettie). Cut to the three. Johnny explains that he bumped into them in the park. Cut back to a medium shot of Hettie who, with a slight irony in her voice, tells Blaney that they have not seen him in years, and then: "How is Brenda? Have you heard from her lately?" Cut back to the three-shot of the group, camera moves into Blaney for a close shot. He: "Well, she's dead, I'm afraid." (The total time from their entry into the apartment is 23 sec.). Cut to a long shot of the four; Hettie picks up a newspaper and hits Blaney with it adding: "And you killed her."

An elaborate three-way separation ensues, lasting 23 shots between three images: a two-shot of Johnny and Babs by the door, a single of Hettie standing, and a single of Blaney by the window, to which he walked over, passing in front of Hettie (in shot 2) (a crossing Hitchcock likes, especially to plant in the beginning of a separation). Hettie accuses Blaney of treating Brenda badly even before; she reminds her husband of the divorce petition, where Blaney was accused of extreme cruelty; she sits down on a couch, spreading her arms like a queen. Blaney defends himself, stating that speeded-up divorce procedures sometimes require the accusation of mental cruelty and even depravity. Cut to a medium long shot of the group, (as Blaney finishes), thus resolving the separation (63 sec.). In this medium long shot Blaney is on the left side

of the frame. Babs is on the right, with Hettie still sitting on the couch in the middle of a very symmetrical mis-en-scène. Hettie adds that she wonders if the police have a copy of it (the divorce decree). Cut to a close-up of Blaney, who mumbles: "My God." Babs sits down next to Hettie, trying to explain that Blaney after the divorce had no motive to kill his ex-wife. Hettie then asks why he is not going to the police instead of involving Johnny. Cut to Blaney who insists he did not plan to involve him; Johnny invited them to the apartment. Cut to a medium shot of Johnny (who so far has been out of frame); he confirms that he believes Blaney and will offer him shelter. Hettie warns him that he may be arrested for harboring a fugitive and for obstructing justice. She gets up and leaves the room saying that she washes her hands of it and will go shopping; camera follows her (1 min., 25 sec.). Cut back to the medium long shot of Blaney, Babs, and Johnny, who promises that he will calm Hettie down, and that Blaney can sleep there, on the couch. Camera moves into a medium three-shot on the group. Babs remembers that she is late for work. Johnny learns upon inquiry that she works in a pub, just as Blaney did. Johnny suddenly has the idea that they should slip out of the country and help him in the English pub he has just opened in Paris. Blaney likes the idea and tries to convince Babs, who has some doubts. Blaney and Johnny convince her. Blaney makes a date with her at Victoria Station next morning. There are five cuts in this part of the scene, mostly in the multiangle and closer shots as they talk. Finally Babs kisses Blaney before she leaves, with Johnny following her to the elevator. As Blaney is left alone Hettie leaves her room and walks past Blaney in eloquent silence and leaves (80 sec.). The whole Scene 12 lasts 8 minutes, 32 seconds.

Scene 13. Starts with a full shot of a turning giant cube with "The New Scotland Yard" sculptured into it, an appropriate transition from the worried figure of Blaney in the outgoing scene (5 sec.). Cut to a close-up of a plate loaded with a real British breakfast; someone is eating with vigor (a slow disclosure). Camera moves back slowly, revealing in a middle two-shot Chief Inspector Oxford, the eater, and Sergeant Spearman, a dead-pan comedic figure, looking attentively on. This breakfasting goes on in silence for 30 seconds; Spearman follows every move of his boss with his eyes, fascinated. A woman brings in more coffee and bread. Finally the sergeant remarks: "Enjoying that, are you sir?" The Chief Inspector tells him, without interrupting his meal, that his wife is a student of a continental school of gourmet cooking and for breakfast feeds him a "café complet." Sergeant: "I beg your pardon, sir?" Oxford: "A cup with one-half inch of coffee, full of hot milk, and a sweet bun full of air." His wife and her school of cooking do not realize that "a man here needs to eat breakfast three times a day, and an English breakfast at that." The sergeant remarks that he is a Quaker Oats man himself (30 sec.). Cut to a door as an assistant enters; camera pans with him as he approaches the inspector's desk in a medium long three-shot. He reports that the lab test determined that the ten pound note Blaney paid the hotel came from Mrs. Blaney's purse. As the assistant leaves the report, camera moves in closer to the same size two-shot we had before. The sergeant remarks: "That about does it for him." Inspector Oxford agrees. The sergeant wants to know more about that type of sex offender. The inspector gives him a brief lecture, while still eating his beloved meal, wiping himself occasionally with a napkin and eating again: "The main point is that they are impotent." The sergeant exclaims in wonderment: "Impotent?" Inspector: "Yes. They're also sadistic, as you well know." He gives him Blaney's divorce petition to read. A phone call interrupts the lecture. The inspector asks to put the caller on (this shot without cuts lasts 68 sec.). Cut to the pub where the owner Forsythe, in medium shot, is talking on the phone with Chief Inspector Oxford. In the background we see the normal pub activities. This conversation, similar to the one in Inspector Oxford's office, has comedic overtones in contrast to the seriousness of the business under discussion.

Forsythe, waving the morning paper, informs the Chief Inspector that the fellow they are looking for is Richard Blaney who worked for him. Muting his voice, as if conveying a secret, he tells the inspector that he is worried about the safety of the barmaid Babs who spent the night with Blaney, as far as he knows. There are two brief inserted shots of the inspector on the line (in a stable medium two-shot with the sergeant) during which Oxford asks Forsythe for some clarification, like a good description of Babs. Forsythe is concerned about her safety. The inspector assures him that she is safe as of eight o'clock this morning. Cut back to Forsythe, this time in close-up; he is disturbed, practically hysterical, about Babs leaving his pub without help; he repeats that she left her clothes there. Final cut back to the inspector who tries humorously to set him at peace by remarking that these days ladies would more readily abandon their honor rather than their clothes. He thanks Forsythe for the information and hangs up. He tells the sergeant that it was Forsythe, the manager of the Globe. (The whole phone conversation lasts 85 sec.). The entire scene (Scene 13) is 3 minutes, 40 seconds in duration.

Scene 14. A long shot: Forsythe's pub: we see Forsythe return to the bar, as if he has just finished talking to the inspector (3 sec.), a curious attempt to condense the events of one morning into a meticulously linear continuity spread over several places (the hotel, Johnny's apartment, Scotland Yard, Forsythe's pub). Cut to a medium shot of Forsythe moving to the left behind the bar; camera pans with him until it comes upon Bob Rusk standing in front of the bar in a medium shot, drinking beer with a man who is talking about the poverty-stricken potato business; Forsythe is seen in the background attending to the bar. Rusk is glad he is not in the potato business; he has troubles of his own (12 sec.). Cut to a medium close shot of Forsythe looking toward the entrance door (2 1/2 sec.). Cut to a long shot of the door; no one comes (1 1/2 sec.). Cut back to the same medium two-shot of Rusk with the man who tells him that he is sending a truck of potatoes to Lincolnshire tonight and worries about whether they will be able to sell them (8 sec.). Cut back to the close shot of Forsythe (second repeat) looking toward the door while filling a glass of beer (1 1/2 sec.). Cut to the door. A boy is entering (1 1/2 sec.). Cut back to Forsythe (same shot, third repeat). He continues filling the glass of beer and lifts his eyes to the door; in the background we hear the conversation between Rusk and his companion on the subject of potatoes (5 sec.).

Cut to the door. We see Babs entering in long shot (1 1/2 sec.). Cut to a medium close shot of Forsythe on the move to catch her (3 sec.). Cut to a medium shot of Babs walking fast, camera following her. Forsythe enters the frame just as she starts up some stairs, in a medium two-shot. Nine over-the-shoulder shots follow in A, B, A, B fashion. The shots are tighter, in close two-shots; the arrangement is helped by the fact that Babs is two steps above Forsythe. The exchange is snappy and sharp; the shots last between 1 1/2 and 3 1/2 seconds each. Forsythe accuses her of taking a hell of a chance by staying the night with a murderer. Babs snaps back: how does he know? Forsythe, in his stupid and clumsy way, tells her about the call to the police and how worried he was for her safety. She tells him to mind his own business. He retorts that Scotland Yard is sending a man to see her; her lover should be locked up so he cannot strangle any more women; at this point Babs bolts out of the frame. Cut to a long shot of Babs from the back, leaving the pub with a shout: "Oh bull!" The exchange between the two lasts 48 seconds. The next shot is an example of a spectacular use of film language with flair and originality: cut to a reverse exterior medium shot of Babs emerging from the pub (note that we are familiar with the site). She approaches the camera, which dollies in to an extreme close shot of her face (from eyes to chin). She is boiling inside, thinking what to do—a suspended 3 seconds in the void of helpless agitation. She looks beautiful. From behind we hear a quiet voice: "Got a place to stay?" Babs moves out to the side, revealing behind her the face of Bob Rusk in close-up, smiling. The camera makes a fast move back (a reverse zoom) to a medium two-shot of Babs and Rusk. He tells her that he heard her exchange with Forsythe. The strange tension built up since Babs' exit and Rusk's appearance is slightly released as the two start walking along the street between the parked cars. It should be noted that the two camera movements, the dolly in on Babs as she emerges from the pub and even more so the fast dolly back from Rusk, are complimentary. In addition one feels that they foreshadow the coming doom of Babs.

The last shot is without any cuts and lasts 22 1/2 seconds. Cut to a long shot of a doorway leading to a large warehouse for fruit and

vegetables; Babs and Rusk enter and walk toward camera which dollies
back keeping them in medium shot. Rusk offers her his place to stay
if she wants to since he is going north for a few days. He can take her
there right now. Babs would like to use it only for one night if he really
plans to have it free. Then he tries to find out where Blaney is hiding
out; he would like to help him; they are after all old buddies. She resists; she is keeping the secret (60 sec.). Cut to the two crossing the
street in front of Rusk's house (7 sec.). Cut to a reverse medium shot
as both enter and start going up the one flight of stairs. Camera climbs
up in front of them. Rusk, who is behind her, can be seen throwing
her lustful looks; as they turn the half flight Rusk lets her in and we
can hear him say, before the door closes, "I don't know if you know
it Babs, but you're my kind of woman" (the walk up takes 28 sec.).
Next, without a cut, in what amounts to a silent part of the scene, the
camera starts slowly retreating down the stairs, as if hugging the railing, from Rusk's white door all the day down, through the entrance
corridor to the street and across, until we see the whole house with
Rusk's windows and the geranium plants (that we saw with his mom
when she was looking down to greet Blaney). Workers with pushcarts
and wheelbarrows are going about their business, carrying produce of
all kinds; we hear the sound of the city and the warehouses only, no
music (the pullback alone lasts 52 sec.). The above shot is accomplished with extraordinary technical skill and precision (the camera

has to pass through two narrow doorways that most likely needed to be taken apart during the movement). For those interpreters who are prone to seek all sorts of meanings, the last shot is a rich field for speculation. In sum, it is the high point of the film, a requiem for Babs.

Scene 15. A quick-witted transition, to say the least: Chief Inspector Oxford enters his apartment with a newspaper in hand and walks forward (toward camera) in the same direction and at the same pace as the retreating dolly did at the end of the previous scene (out of Rusk's house). The inspector is a pleasant looking, civilized chap; his wife, as we already know, is a gourmet cook. She has a shrill but small voice and is totally preoccupied with her cooking and the foreign names of dishes. The scene is funny, as we expected. Subtextually Hitchcock desires to suspend and delay the worries about Bab's fate and Blaney's predicament. The scene is constructed elegantly, with light touches, almost like a dance. The dining table is positioned so that one can see the wife in the kitchen, but she cannot see her husband at the table. The mode seems to be always on the verge of becoming a separation but never does so, as the wife keeps coming and going to and from the kitchen with her exotic and elegantly served dishes, while her husband tries to cope with the food by simply cheating (that he eats). The chain of shots is arranged so that only every few episodes are of longer duration (shots 1, 5, 11, 15, 23, 30, 37). The rest are brief close shots of dishes, with fragments of food, close-ups of the inspector's reactions, or rather revulsions, and the wife's graceful servings. They talk about the case. When the inspector arrives he greets his wife, who announces "soupe de poisson"; he goes for his drink, to which he escapes several times. An elaborate camera dolly and pan around the lighted candles follow him to his seat at the table (on the right). She asks him what's new in the case. He tells her about Blaney. For the next 20 shots they converse about the details of the case while he struggles in close shots with different specimens of exotic fish swimming in the soup. Only in shot 30, the longest in the scene (31 sec.), is he able to dump his soup, surreptitiously, back into the sterling silver tureen. Just then his wife announces the entrée, quail with grapes, and finally joins him at the table (shot 37) in the widest, so far, long shot, each sitting at opposite sides of the formal table setting. In the last shot of the scene (shot 39) we see in close-up on his plate a tiny roasted quail. He tries desperately to cut it with his knife while explaining to his wife that

the police must find Blaney, "the psychopathic killer, before his ap-
petite is whetted again" (presumably for another killing). The scene
lasts 4 minutes, 30 seconds.

Scene 16. Takes us abruptly from the close-up of the roasted quail
to a night low medium shot of Rusk emerging from his house, slowly
pushing a hand truck loaded with a potato sack; he looks around con-
tinuously and leaves frame left (14 sec.). Cut to (shot 2) a contrapuntal
extreme high long shot of Rusk pushing the hand truck toward the
truck parking area (familiar from an early scene of Blaney walking into
this area), entering frame from lower right toward left center. A bell
tower starts ringing the hour; it's one A.M. (20 sec.). The leisurely pace
of this shot permits the viewer to contemplate the chilling thought of
what might be in the potato sack. Cut (shot 3) to another contrapuntal
low medium shot of Rusk, seen from the back, entering into the frame
from the right, pushing his load (4 sec.). Cut to (shot 4) a medium shot
in profile as Rusk enters frame from the left pushing the cart to the
back of a truck. Camera follows him with a pan and stops. Rusk, with
determination, picks up the load in the sack, by now quite obviously
containing the body of Babs. He has difficulty with its weight and after
a hard struggle manages to lift it and dump it over the tailgate into the
truck. He leaves frame to the right with the hand truck (45 sec.). Notice the Hitchcockian pattern of high and low shots as well as the opposites in direction. Cut to (shot 5) a medium shot; Rusk enters frame,

pushes the hand truck from the left, looks around, then leaves frame again to the left (5 sec.). Cut to (shot 6) a medium shot of Rusk entering frame from the right. He takes his apron off and tosses it into the back of the truck, looking around again. Music starts (7 sec.). Cut on action (shot 7) to a long shot as Rusk takes off his hat, walks to the camera, and tosses the hat into another truck as he passes it (5 sec.). Cut to (shot 8) an insert of his hat in flight (1 sec.). Cut on action (shot 9) to a medium shot of Rusk still walking toward the camera; he tucks his shirt in and pulls up his pants; he leaves his frame to the right (4 sec.). Note the reverse symmetry with shot 3; the same will be the case with the next two shots as Rusk returns to his house. Cut to (shot 10) a high long shot of Rusk coming from behind the trucks, crossing the street toward the right corner of the frame; camera follows with an adjustment. We hear distant laughter as if from a pub (13 sec.). Again, a reverse symmetry with shot 2. Cut to (shot 11) a medium low shot of Rusk entering frame left and disappearing in the corridor of his house to the right; reverse symmetry with shot 1 (4 sec.). Cut to (shot 12) a medium shot of Rusk climbing his steps quickly. Camera cranes up with him until he opens his door (8 sec.). Cut to (shot 13) a reverse low medium close shot of Rusk entering his flat; he takes his first deep breath, leaning against the door. Exhausted and sweaty, he throws himself on the couch (camera follows his movement throughout this shot); he pours himself some wine; drinks it lying down; then takes a piece of cake. He is restless. He gets up and looks out through the curtains (38 sec.). Cut to a high long shot of the exterior (shot 14) with the parked trucks (3 sec.). Cut back to (shot 15) Rusk at the curtain (as in shot 13). He needs to pick his teeth, so he reaches for his tie pin at its usual place on his lapel. It is not there. He tries to think where it could be; then, getting panicky, he starts looking for it on the couch, in the bed, in the drawers among Babs' possessions. Finally he stops, takes a few steps toward camera (to a close-up) and thinks hard, reaching in memory to events of the day (64 sec.). Cut to (shot 16) a flashback (the first in the film) composed of ten quick close-up shots of less than a second in length of Babs' murder: Babs' desperate face, choking throat, hand with spread fingers and, again, eyes in pain, mouth shouting, a tie knotted around the neck, eyes, a tightening grip of the tie, fingers fighting (10 sec.). Finally Babs' hand grasping for the tie pin on the lapel with the prominent letter R shining between her fingers (10 sec.). The flashback ends and the accompanying strong music continues. Cut back to (shot 17) the close-up of Rusk (as before the flashback) who, with a curse, runs out of the room. The next five shots are a speeded-up repeat in exact order of the first five shots of the scene (of Rusk leaving with Babs' body on a hand truck) (total length of the five shots is 10 sec.). Rusk, back at the truck, opens the tailgate and jumps into the back of the truck (12 sec.). End of Scene 16.

Note that shots 13 and 15 of Rusk inside his flat, half a minute and over one minute in length, respectively, are of long duration and without cuts, with an active mise-en-scène (Rusk and camera in movement). These shots are precursors of the upcoming scene that will, in contrast, have an exceptional number of cuts of short duration. The total length of the scene is 4 minutes, 27 seconds.

Scene 17. Inside the truck: Rusk is determined to retrieve his tie pin, which could implicate him in the murder. The scene is unique in many ways: for one, it has no dialogue (with the exception of a passing car whose driver informs the truck driver that potatoes are falling out on the road). For almost nine minutes the dramatic tension is maintained at high pitch. The murderer is the sole and secret performer in a chilling and repulsive drama, forced into an intimate relationship with the body of his victim. As is often the case with this genre, the viewer becomes progressively desensitized to the horror of the crime and temporarily suspends his sympathies for the dead victim. The attention at hand is whether or not Rusk will be able to retrieve the telltale pin. The scene consists of close to one hundred shots, mostly brief (4 sec. or less). In 1974 Hitchcock showed me a few pages of yellow pad with a list of, and particulars for, these ninety-six shots that he had prepared ahead for the shooting of this scene, a remarkable testimony to his method.

Although Rusk's face dominates the imagery, there are more medium and medium close shots of him than close-ups (about 30 of the former and about 20 of the latter). The next in frequency are his hands and parts of Babs' body. The truck has the smallest number of shots (around 15). The modality vibrates constantly in rhythm to the cuts of low and eye level shots that, toward the end of the scene, changes to high and low shots. And even though most shots are singles, the structure is not a true separation, since there is no living contact or interaction between participants. The well distributed interruptions, like the few shots of the truck driver, or the potato spill on the road, form the necessary pauses between the shots of the struggle going on inside the truck. The action, in fact, is simple. Rusk has terrible difficulties moving the stiffened body inside the sack of potatoes; and, after spotting the pin clasped in Babs' hands (shot 54), has great trouble opening her fingers (even with the help of a knife) (shot 55). The scene, despite the few touches of black humor, is ghoulishly morbid, suspenseful, and disquieting.

In the first medium shot we see Rusk opening the tailgate and jumping inside the truck (12 sec.). The tailgate becomes one of the complications that will plague him later. In shot 2 (low close-up in profile) he realizes that he can be seen with the tailgate open (7 sec.). In shot 3, a medium shot, he foolishly tries to close the tailgate while in the truck (4 sec.). Shot 4, back to the low close shot in profile, a light from the outside shines on his face; he moves back (6 sec.). Shot 5, also a low close-up three-quarter profile; he listens to outside sounds (1 1/2 sec.). Shot 6, an exterior long shot, we hear voices and steps approaching (2 sec.). Shot 7, back to a close-up of Rusk worried, listening, following the footsteps with his eyes, eventually realizing that the driver of the truck is mounting. The engine starts; the lorry is moving; Rusk, trapped, is in terror (the longest duration shot in the scene so far, 18 sec.). In the next four shots Rusk tries to hide in the rear of the truck, pulling his load behind other sacks. (Total length of the four shots is 32 sec.).

In shot 12 (close shot of his face) Rusk starts opening the sack that contains the body, the light of a passing car flashes over his face (5 sec.). Shot 13, a match-cut on action (most of the cuts in the scene are on action) to Rusk ducking the light and pulling farther to the back (7 sec.). Shots 14 to 21 are alternating close-ups of his intense face and close shots of his hands opening the sack and searching the body, with potatoes always in the way (total 31 sec.). From shot 20 we see the corpse's foot and Rusk's desperate pulling against the enormous power of rigor mortis. This series climaxes, with a bit of comédie macabre, when Babs' foot springs out into Rusk's face (shots 28 through 31). The shots become shorter, between 1 1/2 and 3 seconds in length. Finally Rusk succeeds in freeing himself from the oppression of the foot by putting it under his arms. Exhausted, he wipes his face. (Shots 32 and 33 are 12 sec.). Suddenly a cut to (the first of this kind) a frontal medium shot of the lorry driver, whistling, at the wheel; this breaks the scene for a needed pause (4 sec.). The next four shots alternate between Rusk just about to sneeze and the driver continuing to whistle, unaware of his secret passenger. On the fourth repeat of the image of the driver the lorry apparently makes a sharp turn; we see a medium shot of Rusk thrown to the side, a light from a passing car on his face; he takes cover inside the sack, swearing about the bloody pin. The driver makes another turn, presumably to avoid an obstacle; Rusk (in a wider medium shot) is again violently thrown back. Cut to an exterior long shot of a bag falling out of the truck, spilling potatoes all over the highway. The next two shots cover the incident of the spilled potatoes: a car passing the lorry informs the driver of the spillage. The lorry stops; Rusk listens in his hideout; the driver goes out to check, closes and secures the tailgate without seeing Rusk, then continues the journey. The "pause" with the truck episode lasts 75 seconds.

Back inside the truck, Rusk, by now totally exhausted, continues his search with the energy of desperation. The next series of shots (from shots 46 to 54) alternates between a low close-up of Rusk's face and a high close shot of his hands digging deeper into the sack, pushing aside piles of potatoes. Finally, after uncovering most of Babs' corpse he sees (shot 55, close-up) the end of his silver pin between the fingers of her hand (the above shots last 28 sec.). A series of 21 shots follows, again high and low close-ups, alternating between Rusk's face and the hands, including Babs', depicting the retrieval of the tie pin. It is the gloomiest episode in the scene. In the first nine shots Rusk tries to open Babs' fingers, without success (23 sec.). He takes out a pen knife; its blade breaks on the first trial. In the next ten shots he makes what appears to be a superhuman effort to open her fingers one by one (with loud cracks of the joints), finally succeeding in getting his pin free (30 sec.). He wipes his sweaty face and puts the pin in his lapel. The lorry seems to be slowing down. Rusk, in a couple of medium shots, looks out from under the tarp. A shot of the road surface shows it is too dangerous to jump. Just then the lorry, in a long shot, turns into a truck stop restaurant. The entire scene inside the lorry has 79 shots and lasts 5 minutes, 48 seconds.

Scene 18. Rusk's escape (16 shots) and the discovery of Babs' body by the police (16 shots) is in perfect linear continuity. A close shot: Rusk inside the lorry (shot 1) realizes that they have stopped; music is coming from a restaurant (3 1/2 sec.). Shot 2 is a repeat of the long shot of the lorry. The driver steps down and shuts the door (2 1/2 sec.). In shot 3 (the same close shot) Rusk is looking around and listening (3 sec.). Shot 4 is wider, a medium long shot. We seek Rusk peeping from under the tarp; then, while climbing over the tailgate, he trips the catch so both tailgate and Rusk fall down (10 sec.). Shot 5, a cut on action (of falling), is a high medium long shot. We see, from a bird's-eye view, Rusk hitting the ground; he quickly gets up, checks that no one has seen him, and starts walking away as camera continually adjusts by panning, lifting, or gently reframing. Rusk stops midway and looks (14 sec.). Cut to a long shot of the restaurant. We see through the glass door the lorry driver talking to the waitress (1 1/2 sec.). Cut back (shot 7) to Rusk looking, then moving on to the restroom (marked "Gents") where he looks out through a corner of a broken window (8 sec.). Cut to (shot 8) the same long shot of the restaurant; the driver picks up a bag (of coffee, presumably) and leaves (3 1/2 sec.). Cut to (shot 9) a close-up of Rusk looking through the broken glass of the restroom; he watches the movements of the driver (4 sec.). Shot 10 is a medium long shot of the driver mounting his lorry (5 sec.). Cut back (shot 11) to the close-up of Rusk (second repeat) looking through the broken window (3 sec.). Cut back (shot 12) to the long shot of the lorry moving out of the parking lot (8 sec.). Cut back (shot 13) to a third repeat of Rusk looking out in close-up; he moves to the right (1 1/2 sec.). Cut back (shot 14) to the lorry exiting the truck stop and turning to the road (out of frame) (3 sec.). In shot 15 Rusk still looks out in close-up (fourth repeat), then moves behind the frosted glass (we see his silhouette); camera follows him to the door (6 sec.). Cut to (shot 16) a medium long shot of Rusk coming out of the restroom; he dusts himself off on the run, then wipes his shoes while walking, and finally enters the restaurant (13 sec.). Note the generous number of repeats Hitchcock uses in a simple parallel action (Rusk's actions versus the driver's actions), his way to convey anxiety, a meaning beyond the need to communicate the actions only. One should bear in mind that this episode is also a plant, since Rusk's presence at the truck stop will be an important factor in the future investigation and eventually in Rusk's undoing.

Cut to (shot 17) a long shot of a parked police car, night traffic passing by (3 sec.). In shot 18 the camera pans as our lorry passes to the left; one can catch a glimpse of the corpse's foot sticking out of the open tailgate (2 1/2 sec.). Cut to (shot 19) a frontal two-shot of the two policemen behind the windshield; they notice the body; one of them exclaims: "Do you see what I see?" (1 1/3 sec.). The next seven shots are distributed between the lorry in medium long shot and the police car (mostly in the two-shot, as in shot 19) following it (the average length is 2 sec.). In the next shot (shot 26), a close shot of the lorry driver in profile, we hear the siren of the police car; he looks in the mirror and starts braking (5 sec.). Cut to a (shot 27) long shot of the lorry stopping, camera quickly moving in to a medium long shot. The corpse, rocked by the truck's movement, falls out on the roadway (3 sec.). The camera's forward movement partially simulates the forward thrust of the police car. Consequently, in the next shot (28) (a repeat of the two-shot), the policemen, shocked by what they see, brake their car abruptly (2 sec.). Cut to a side medium shot (29) (note the sudden change of angularity) of the police car coming to stop a few inches before hitting the corpse (2 sec.). Cut to another, significant change of angularity, this time to a long high shot (shot 30). We see both the lorry and the police car and the corpse between them. The policemen come over to the corpse; the driver asks: "What's wrong? Who is it?" (7 sec.). Cut on action to a close-up of dead Babs' contorted face (as it is being uncovered by the police). We hear the police answering: "Perhaps you can tell us?" (Total length of the scene is 2 min. 15 sec.) The Hitchcockian pattern here, as in many similar situations, is the fragmentation of the action into many repeated singles and then, after a change of angularity, a release in a high shot.

Scene 19. Starts with a medium shot of Blaney sleeping on the couch; camera lifts as Hettie comes into the frame with a shout, demanding (in a medium two-shot) that he move out. Hardly awake, he learns from her that Babs has been strangled (33 sec.). Note the sudden switch to longer duration shots after the fast tempo of the previous scene. Cut to Johnny, still in his robe, coming into the room (medium long shot). He walks over, camera pans with him, into a medium three-shot; he confirms the information, as reported on the radio. Blaney is stunned; he says he did not leave this room all night. Hettie accuses him of lying. Johnny defends him by repeating that Babs, according to police, had been dead for twelve hours and was found at 3 A.M., so it is clear that Blaney couldn't have done it, since he was with them all that time. Blaney, who so far has been sitting on the couch he slept on, gets up and walks over, as camera follows him, to the other side of the room, distressed, mumbling to himself "poor kid" (32 sec.). Cut to a medium two-shot of Hettie and Johnny; he is explaining to his skeptical wife that Blaney was after all with them, and the police could not make an eight-hour mistake in the time of death. Then, turning toward Blaney: "Hey, Dicko, do you know what that means? You're in the clear. We can give you an alibi." A separation is in progress. Cut to a medium long shot of Blaney who takes a step toward them and says: "Yes, I suppose you can." Cut back to the medium two-shot of Hettie and Johnny: "There's nothing to suppose. We will simply tell the police that you were here with us." Cut back to Blaney (presently in medium shot): "You'll do that, before you go away?" Cut back to the two-shot. Johnny: "We'll be delighted . . ." Hettie cuts in: "You'll do nothing of the sort, not unless you want to go to jail for harboring a wanted man." The next 15 shots continue alternating in this one-to-two separation between Hettie and Johnny on one side of the room and Blaney on the other side. Hettie heats up the situation by assuming that the announced hour of death could be a police ploy, that there is no assurance that Blaney did not murder Babs, and in any case their trip to Paris may be jeopardized by their mix-up with Blaney. Johnny slowly gives in to his wife's arguments. Blaney is furious, calling them "cowardly shits." Finally the separation is resolved by his walking over to pack his bag (in a long shot) with all of them in the frame, still arguing. Camera moves in to a medium shot. Blaney, with bag in hand: "Don't worry. I'm leaving." The scene lasts 2 minutes, 50 seconds.

The above scene is again an example of the sharp working of a Hitchcockian separation. After a leisurely start the shots become shorter and shorter, up to the climax of Blaney's leaving. We feel contempt for Hettie and Johnny, and burdened by Blaney's lot. The situation is believable, yet the magic lies primarily in Hitchcock's ability to inject and generate so much reality with a form (separation) that takes so much liberty with reality.

Scene 20. Starts with a very high long shot of the familiar Covent Garden fruit and produce market. The shot acts as a release from the tension of the outgoing scene and as a transition to the next. Cut to a medium long shot of a policeman with a German shepherd on a leash walking from right to left across the frame. The previous high long shot had a diagonal axis while this one is horizontal. (The two shots last 9 sec.). Cut to a medium two-shot of Bob Rusk talking with Forsythe, who has stopped by to tell him about his morning visit to the morgue to identify Babs' body. He thinks that Blaney is the killer: "It stands to reason." Rusk does not share this view, a rather ironic touch, saying that: "I'm not eager, as some, to turn on my old mates." Rusk keeps munching some fruit while they talk. He uses his tie pin, on one occasion, to pick his teeth. Forsythe is too obtuse to catch some of the digs directed at him. Rusk: "Some people have all the luck in the world, jumping up in the morning, running to identify all sorts of girls at the morgue." Finally they part. Forsythe leaves for his job where he expects brisk business, saying: "You know how morbid people are." The shot lasts 63 seconds, probably the longest duration static shot in the film, almost a proscenium construction. Again it is a release before the trigger of the next shots.

Cut on action to a close shot of Rusk entering the frame, from the left, in profile, and stopping in surprise at what he sees (2 1/2 sec.). Cut to a long shot of Blaney in a narrow doorway among crates, deep in the background in a vertical frame (2 sec.). Cut to a tight close-up of Rusk (starting with the back of his head, then turning to a profile) saying: "My God . . . Dick." He goes closer to Blaney. Camera moves with him to a high medium two-shot of both in profile facing each other. Blaney explains that he has no other place to go and that once Bob had promised him if he ever needed something . . . Rusk interrupts him: "All right, but you did take a hell of a chance coming down here at this time, the place is swarming with cops." Rusk checks out the situation by stepping close to the camera into an ominous frontal close-up, then steps back to the medium two-shot. Rusk offers to hole Blaney up for a night or two (28 sec.). Cut to a close-up of Blaney in profile. There are two exchanges between Rusk and Blaney, both in close-ups. Blaney assures him that he is innocent: "You know me. I wouldn't get involved in anything like that." Rusk: "Of course you wouldn't, Dick. The police as usual has got everything ass about face. I know these killings boggle the mind. That man must be a sexual maniac. Mind you there are some women who ask for everything they get. But you? You're not the type. Don't worry, you've done the right thing" (19 sec.). Cut back to the medium two-shot (as before). Rusk offers to take his bag: "It will be less conspicuous that way." Blaney should follow him to his flat, taking an alley toward the Strand (11 sec.). Cut to a medium shot of Rusk with a bag walking forward; then, turning left with camera panning after him, he walks down the busy market street (7 sec.). Cut to a close-up of Blaney, who makes a move forward while looking around nervously (2 1/2 sec.). Cut to a medium shot of Blaney walking out of the warehouse. Camera pans after him as he crosses the street between parked trucks and cars in long shot (13 sec.). Cut back to Rusk moving fast with Blaney's bag across the street between the traffic, also in long shot (12 sec.). Cut on action to a medium shot of Rusk entering his house; another cut to him mounting the stairs with camera craning and following as he enters his flat (7 sec.). The framing of the latter shot is exactly the same as in his ascent with Babs the day before. Cut to a medium long shot of Blaney walking away toward Rusk's house (6 sec.). Cut to a medium high shot of him entering the corridor of the house (4 sec.). Cut on action to a very high medium long shot of Blaney walking to the stairway and up toward the camera (thus becoming a medium shot as he climbs up to the door). The framing (and camera craning) is exactly the same as the one with Rusk (and also with Babs) (12 sec.).

The significance of these repeated shots (on the stairway) cannot be overestimated. They obviously were planned; they could not have been improvised considering the complex camera movements. In addition to giving unity to the film and heightening the drama, they are a personal cinesthetic statement of Hitchcock, to whom stairways are always a central, almost architectural pivot for a film.

In the next shot Blaney enters the flat and is greeted by Rusk, in a medium long two-shot. Blaney remarks: "It is very cozy" (10 sec.). Cut to a medium shot of Rusk with two framed (cheap art) reproductions of women on the wall behind him. He modestly says: "It's my little nest, my home. As my mom used to say, home is the place where if you have to go, they have to take you in. You met my mother, haven't you? A grand old lady." He walks out of the frame while the camera that has so far followed him now stops on Blaney at the window (10 sec.). Cut to Rusk in medium shot; he has to go to the shop; he tells Blaney to help himself to some food in the kitchen and feel at home; he walks over to the door (10 sec.). Rusk's walking back and forth shows him to be restless; at the same time, his movements create turbulence in the frame, giving it a certain nervousness needed before the climax.

Cut to low medium shot of Blaney, at the window, expressing his gratitude for Rusk's help (4 sec.). Cut back to Rusk at the door: "Think nothing of it" (2 sec.). Cut back to Blaney at the window (1 1/2 sec.). Cut back to Rusk: "Do me a favor, stay away from the window, will you." Cut back to Blaney: "Oh yes, of course, sorry"; he walks away (2 1/2 sec.). Cut back to Rusk (same shot) as he bids him good bye and exits the room (2 1/2 sec.). Note that the above repeated, brief shots again keep the scene on the edge. Cut to Blaney walking to the table with drinks, pouring himself one, taking a sip, then with his bag walking to the chest at the other end of the room. He starts opening drawer after drawer, apparently looking for an empty one for his own things (25 sec.). Note that this shot, in contrast to the previous ones, is leisurely and of comparatively long duration; the fact that it is also a silent one makes it even more quiet before the storm.

Cut to the door as a group of policemen with dogs on leashes burst into the room with a detective calling out: "Are you Richard A. Blaney?" (1/2 sec.). Cut to a medium shot of Blaney at the moment the police get hold of him: "You're under arrest." Blaney mutters: "What is it? What is it all about?" They leave the frame (2 1/2 sec.). Cut to a high medium shot as the group with Blaney in the middle runs down the stairs (5 1/2 sec.). Cut to a high medium shot of them entering the door of a police car (only the rear part of the car is on the screen); the car quickly moves out of the frame. Cut to a medium two-shot of Rusk standing by the wall. Partially hidden next to him stands the helmeted policeman whom we have seen before. The shot is from the side; it seems as though the police car's movement wiped the present shot into existence or, putting it in more realistic terms, as if the police car had been covering Rusk and the helmeted policeman so that, when it moved away, it appeared to disclose them (which, of course, was not the case). It is a minor item, but it shows how elegantly and fittingly Hitchcock can make a transition to a shot of significance: Rusk in the role of Judas. The policeman thanks Rusk for the help, even though there is no reward. Rusk's answer: "Oh, you know what they say Sarge, virtue has its own rewards." Then, ready to leave, he tells the sergeant that if they want him he will be in his shop (14 sec.). Cut to a reverse medium long shot of Rusk crossing the busy market (2 1/2 sec.). The scene lasts 6 minutes, 10 seconds.

Scene 21. Starts with Blaney at police headquarters charged with the necktie murders. After the high-pitch trigger (his arrest at the end of the previous scene) this one is most definitely a release. It is not a typical Hitchcockian construction since it starts with a full exposition in a long shot as Chief Inspector Oxford enters the crowded room full of detectives and formally charges Blaney. One of the detectives goes over to Blaney's bag and calls Inspector Oxford to see it; camera moves in closer (30 sec.). Cut on action to a close shot of the bag being unzipped. Camera pulls back and lifts to a medium group shot of inspector Oxford, Blaney, and a couple of detectives. The bag contains Babs' personal possessions. Blaney, amazed and shocked, suddenly understands and shouts out: "Rusk. It's Rusk"; the inspector gives the order to restrain him. They also find Babs' identity card inside Blaney's bag. The inspector reads it aloud looking into Blaney's eyes (30 sec.). As we see, the first shot is practically a proscenium set-up. Yet there is wisdom in this; the above two shots, in addition to being a release, also form a transition to the next trigger which will take place during the sentencing. Note the time deletions that are introduced at each consecutive episode.

The court episode, unlike the one in the police station, starts with a series of slow disclosures. First a close-up of a heavy door with the inscription: Court No. 1 (2 sec.). Cut to medium long shot of two barristers, in court attire, coming through a pair of glass doors (2 1/2 sec.). Cut to a medium shot of a uniformed court attendant letting the two barristers in to the court room in session through another pair of glass

doors. As they enter we hear a judge addressing a jury foreman: "Do you find the defendant Richard A. Blaney guilty or not guilty of the murder of Brenda . . ." The attendant just then closes the glass doors, thus cutting off the sound, and places himself, as before, at the right side of them. We are left hanging with this silent image for sixteen seconds, so reminiscent of the court scene in *Notorious*. After the long wait the attendant, in a close-up, leans forward to hear the procedure inside the court room (1 1/2 sec.). Cut back to the previous medium long shot (second repeat) as he opens the door slightly and we hear the judge announcing that Blaney has been found guilty of the ghastly crime and is sentenced for life, with no less than twenty-five years in jail— the door closes again when our attendant is interrupted (20 sec.). Cut to a medium shot of a uniformed court porter handing the attendant a written message (3 sec.). Offscreen we still hear part of the judge's summation. Cut to a medium shot of our court attendant taking the message and putting it in his pocket (2 sec.). Cut back to the porter leaving (1 1/2 sec.). Cut back to the medium long shot of the glass door (3rd repeat) with the view of the court; we hear a commotion inside. Our attendant enters the court; Blaney is struggling, with two policemen restraining him (6 sec.). Cut to a close-up of our attendant looking (1 1/2 sec.). Cut to a high medium shot of Blaney being dragged away by the policemen. He shouts: "Rusk . . . I told you all along it's Rusk" (6 sec.). Cut to a low long shot of Blaney with the policemen coming down another set of stairs, close to the camera. They turn into

a corridor, struggling with him all the time (12 1/2 sec.). Cut to a very high shot of a cage-like cell, looking down (from the point of view of a nonexisting ceiling), with the four walls in view into which Blaney is suddenly pushed. He touches each wall, tossing from one to the other, a most stylized climactic shot that perfectly projects the pathos of the moment (12 sec.). This shot belongs to the pattern of shock and release after the peak (as here after the sentencing) that we have noticed in other scenes of this film. We sense a closure, yet the scene continues. Cut to a high long shot of the empty courtroom, the lonely Inspector Oxford sitting on a bench. We hear only distant steps (10 sec.). Cut to a low medium close shot of the chief inspector buried in thought, listening to the reverberating voice of Blaney: "It's Rusk, I told you all along. Where are you, Rusk, I'll kill you. I've nothing to lose. I may as well do what I'm being put away for" (20 sec.). Note that this audio flashback evokes the visual flashback Rusk had of Babs struggling and getting his tie pin. Both flashbacks reach back in style to an old tradition in early cinema, now hardly ever used.

Looking back over the scene, one can only admire how Hitchcock, after a mild release shot (of Blaney being charged at the police station), is able to quickly whip up, with his high vernacular, an electrifying sequence of shots leading to the climax in the cell. To better understand Hitchcock's language I would like to comment on a small item in this sequence, the image of the court attendant at the glass door. The shot, repeated three times and held at one point for sixteen seconds, functions as the element of structure I call familiar image. The court attendant is also the onlooker thanks to whom the viewer can hear the proceedings inside the court, whenever he opens the door, ever so slightly. Inversely, whenever the attendant keeps the glass doors closed, the viewer is cut off from the proceedings. The incident of the message he receives is an annoying interruption since we want him to open the door rather than attend to court business. Finally, when the commotion inside starts, the attendant opens the doors and enters the court, thus finally letting the viewer in, to witness the forced exit of Blaney. All of the above requires the right kind of repeats of the stable familiar image (attendant at the door) and the proper amount of satellite shots in between, where even deep deletions of time pass smoothly without notice.

The scene continues with the Chief Inspector following up on his suspicions: in a long shot we see a London cab driving through the Covent Garden market (2 sec.). Cut to a medium two-shot of Inspector Oxford and a police photographer riding inside. The Inspector points out a fellow in a brown suit (Rusk) whom he wants photographed (3 1/2 sec.). Cut to a moving long shot (from the taxi) of Rusk talking to a helper in front of his warehouse. Cut back to the two-shot in the taxi; Inspector Oxford wants the taxi driver to go around once more to get a good close shot of Rusk (9 sec.). Cut to a close-up of a black-and-white photo of Rusk and his helper in a setting we have just seen from the taxi. Offscreen we hear the familiar voice of Monica of the matrimonial agency: "Yes Inspector, he came here on two occasions" (4 1/2 sec.). Cut on action, as she starts handing the photo back, to a medium two-shot of Monica and Inspector Oxford standing next to her desk. Monica tells him that Mr. Robinson was a special case and hard to get rid of (7 sec.). Cut to a medium close shot of the inspector who takes notice of the name Mr. Robinson. Monica: "Yes, Mr. Robinson; that is the man's name." She gets up and walks past the inspector with the file. A twelve-shot separation begins. Monica, in a medium close shot, with the file in hand, explains that Mr. Robinson had certain peculiarities in his tastes for women and that's why the agency refused to help him, but he kept coming back. Inspector Oxford, in a medium close shot, slightly tighter than Monica's, asks if this means that

Robinson liked women with sadomasochistic tendencies, women who like to be hurt. Monica answers in the affirmative, adding: "Men like this would leave no stone unturned in the search for their disgusting gratifications." She asks if the inspector has any special reason to inquire after Mr. Robinson. He: "Yes, we do, we do. And I would like you to keep my visit confidential." Monica, with her special air of a model secretary: "Yes, of course." This is the last shot of the scene; the separation remains without a resolution, as in the majority of Hitchcock's separations. This scene (21) lasts five minutes. Things start looking better for Blaney, except for the complications that are in store.

Scene 22. Starts with a night long shot of the gate to the prison (2 sec.). Cut to a low long shot of the interior hallway of the prison. A prisoner is led on the upper level (3 sec.). Cut on action to a medium shot of the same; we see that the prisoner is Blaney. He makes a sudden move forward (2 1/2 sec.). Cut to a low long shot. We see Blaney throw himself down a metal stairway to the lower level; he tumbles once on the stairway and lands on the cement floor (3 sec.). Cut to a close-up of his face with a narrow stream of blood coming down his temple. We hear the guards talk about getting a doctor and an ambulance (6 sec.). Cut to the same (as before) long shot of the exterior of the prison with a screaming ambulance rushing forward. There are two shots of this ambulance; more screen time is given to it than to Blaney's accident (25 sec. versus 17 for the latter). Evidently, Hitchcock needed a screaming siren as a transition to the next scene. The scene lasts 43 seconds.

Scene 23. A medium long two shot: takes us from the noise of the ambulance to the tranquillity of Inspector Oxford's home at dinner time: part of the dinner table in the foreground and the kitchen in the background. We see Mrs. Oxford ready to bring a serving dish to the table. Her first words are: "I told you it wasn't Blaney. I told you you were on the wrong track." The inspector is sitting humbly at his side of the table. He asks her: "So you think it is Rusk?" She replies: "Oh yes," and starts enumerating her reasons. He retorts: "But we have no evidence. What makes you so sure? Is it intuition? What is intuition telling you I want tonight for dinner?" She assuredly says: "Steak and potatoes, and you're getting pieds de porc." The scene, as expected, is comedic; its construction is simple. It is again a rest and a delay before the closure. The first shot lasts one minute, ten seconds, one of the longest without a cut in the film. Using Mrs. Oxford's cuisine as the running joke, Hitchcock "vindicates" her in this scene by showing that she knew all along that Blaney was innocent. After seeing the pork feet in close-up, Inspector Oxford settles down in resignation to the meal, but delays it by telling his wife all the details that led to the inquiry at the truck stop, adding that he expects Sergeant Spearman, with the evidence of Rusk's visit to that restaurant, at any minute. The wife is delighted. This part of the scene is executed in a series of high and low angle over-the-shoulder shots, twenty in all, interlaced with two close-ups of the pork feet on the inspector's plate. It is extremely funny to see him holding a cheek full of food, chipmunk fashion, not daring to swallow, while at the same time talking about the truck stop from where the evidence is to come. The moment his wife turns toward the kitchen he manages to spit out a chunk of pig's feet into his plate. Just then the entrance doorbell rings (the above sequence lasts 3 min., 20 sec.).

Hearing the doorbell, the inspector rises and the camera adjusts with him. He goes to the door and lets the sergeant in. The length of the shot (from the time Mrs. Oxford left for the kitchen) is 14 seconds. Cut to a medium shot of Mrs. Oxford coming forward from the kitchen; camera follows her with a pan as she greets Sergeant Spearman in a medium three-shot, with her husband looking on. She offers the guest a Marguerita. The sergeant silently shows that he has never heard of it (15 sec.). Cut to a tight close-up of her face; she starts enumerating the ingredients of a Marguerita (2 1/2 sec.). Cut to a less tight close shot of her husband listening, his eyes turning to the ceiling (2 1/2 sec.). Cut to a close shot of the sergeant with a dead-pan look, listening in a stupor (6 sec.). Cut back to the same close-up of Mrs. Oxford, who turns to go back to the kitchen (1 1/2 sec.). Cut to a side medium two-shot of the sergeant and the inspector who implores him to divulge the results of his inquiry. The sergeant calmly explains that the waitress in the truck stop recognized Rusk from the photo as the man who stopped there the night the woman was discovered. And what's more, she gave him a clothes brush Rusk borrowed that night to tidy himself up. The sergeant reaches for the brush, neatly wrapped in newspaper, and shows it to the inspector (the camera follows his movements). The inspector examines and even smells the brush, saying: "What do you say Spearman, potato dust?" The sergeant nods (49 sec.). Cut to a medium long shot of Mrs. Oxford coming out of her kitchen with the drink for Sergeant Spearman. Camera follows her as she reaches the two men. Sergeant Spearman politely takes the drink and tastes it. Inspector Oxford asks her if she heard the good news (8 sec.). Cut to a close-up of Spearman tasting the drink with an air of fear and expectation. Offscreen we hear her voice assuring her husband that she heard, but knew it all along (5 1/2 sec.). Cut back to the medium three-shot. The inspector insists that the brush go immediately to the lab for a test; the sergeant puts away the drink and takes his things. The inspector remarks that they have put away the wrong man. This time Mrs. Oxford retorts: "What do you mean they? You put him away." The inspector goes to see the sergeant to the door (the camera pans to them in a long shot). The inspector congratulates Mr. Spearman for the good work; Mrs. Oxford regrets that he didn't finish his drink; the sergeant leaves with apologies.

The inspector and his wife come over to the soft chair where she sits down with Spearman's drink in her hand. She sympathizes with poor Blaney. The inspector promises to start proceedings for reopening the case to free him as soon as possible. She asks if there will be compensation (47 sec.). Cut to a low medium close-up of the inspector who thinks that they may give Blaney some money, but that total compensation is never possible (5 sec.). This shot begins an eight-shot separation between his low and her high medium close-ups. Mrs. Oxford

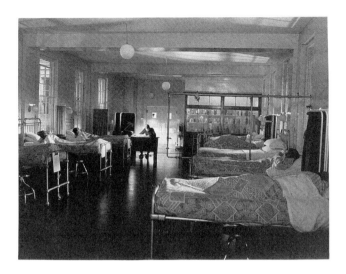

proposes that the least they can do is to invite Blaney for a nice dinner. He reacts with apprehension. She has a menu in mind: duck in a cherry sauce (with a French name). Oxford, horrified, makes the most biting remark about her cooking so far: "Well, I guess after the prison food he will eat anything." In the last shot of the separation Mrs. Oxford, quite hurt by the remark, lifts the glass containing Mr. Spearman's Marguerita and downs it in one gulp. Immediately feeling the effects of the drink, she gets up with some difficulty and walks out with a slight sway toward the kitchen as camera follows her. This last shot is 14 1/2 seconds long, the length of the other seven shots is around 5 seconds each. The total for the scene is 7 minutes, 10 seconds.

The ending of the last separation with Mrs. Oxford literally walking out of it (with camera following her) is an ingenious and elegant substitute for a resolution. It makes the last accent of the scene a humorous one and at the same time it vindicates her in the "duel" with her husband, since the camera never comes back on him to see his reaction. He, in other words, is eliminated (pictorially, that is).

Scene 24. Brings us back to the center of the drama: Blaney in the hospital and his daring escape, a serious enough matter yet interwoven with humor. A slow disclosure at the start is followed by a short separation and then by longer duration shots at the end. After an establishing long shot of the huge hospital room in dim light (6 sec.) there are three moving camera medium shots, dollying from bed to bed, each in the opposite direction: first to the right, then to the left, and again to the right, the last disclosing Blaney in his bed (the total for the three is 23 sec.). The above shots (as if searching for Blaney) introduce a certain amount of nervousness that is eventually released by a medium two-shot of Blaney's bed and his neighbors. Blaney asks: "Hey, are the pills working?" (4 sec.). This begins a 14-shot separation. It starts dramatically with an extreme close-up of a hand reaching for a hospital grip (1 1/2 sec.). Cut on action to a close-up of Blaney's neighbor hanging onto the grip and looking (2 sec.). Cut to a long shot of what he sees: a policeman slumped on the night desk (3 sec.). Close-up of the neighbor saying: "He's sleeping like a baby" (2 1/2 sec.). Close-up Blaney: "Do you think we gave him enough?" (1 1/2 sec.). Close-up of the neighbor: "Christ, mate, he's had a dozen" (2 1/2 sec.). Close-up of Blaney lifting himself up to get out of bed: "Good. Now I'm off to get that bastard Rusk" (3 1/2 sec.). Close-up of the neighbor: "All right. Let's make sure" (2 sec.). Close-up of Blaney: "It's now or never! I'm due back inside tomorrow" (3 sec.). Close-up of the neighbor calling out to another prisoner: "George, George! All right, George" (2 sec.). The rhythm of the brief shots is presently interrupted by a longer duration long shot of George, a middle-aged, funny prisoner getting out of his bed and, to appropriate music, creeping over to the guard at the desk, as camera follows him with a pan (18 sec.). Cut to a medium two-shot of Blaney and his neighbor watching George (2 1/2 sec.). Cut to a medium two-shot of George standing over the sleeping guard. He smiles in the direction of Blaney, then with two fingers of his right hand pushes over the guard who falls on the floor (with the accompaniment of music), with camera following; the shot ends with a high medium shot of the guard curled up on the floor (8 1/2 sec.). Cut to a medium two-shot of Blaney getting ready to leave and his neighbor handing him a piece of mica, saying that it may be handy to open doors; Blaney puts on a doctor's white coat (10 sec.). Cut back to the medium shot of George who by eye contact gets a signal to go ahead (from Blaney). He knocks at the window pane to alert the other guards to what happened; a commotion starts; a doctor and nurse are called; the frame fills out with a crowd of guards and medical personnel as well as some inmates with George smiling behind. The camera adjusts to a high medium shot (35 sec.). Cut to a very high long shot. We see the

group with a doctor examining the guard on the floor; in the background Blaney comes closer, buttoning his white coat; camera starts zooming into a close-up of him and follows him from overhead as he walks past and out of the door. We hear offscreen the doctor's instructions. The suspense starts mounting. The separation is resolved (10 1/2 sec.). Cut to a high medium shot of the attending doctor looking to the side (3 sec.). Cut to close-up of an empty coffee cup. We see the doctor's hand tilting it, revealing a few undissolved pills. We hear the doctor's voice: "Sleeping pills. They've given him their sleeping pills!" (4 sec.). Close-up of a guard looking, as if down a corridor; this 1/2 second shot is a strong trigger in the suspense, since the viewer is not certain if the guard sees Blaney or not. Cut to a long shot of Blaney walking along an empty corridor toward camera (into a medium shot); turning left with camera panning with him, he goes past a guard, to whom he nonchalantly bids good night and walks out the last set of doors (11 sec.). Cut to an outdoor high long shot. Blaney comes out of the big doors; the music gets stronger. He walks toward camera which starts following him as he tries the doors of several cars; he finds one open, then walks to the trunk (37 sec., the longest shot in the scene). Cut on action to a medium shot of Blaney opening the trunk (5 sec.). Cut to a high close shot of Blaney's arms taking from the trunk a large metal bar (2 1/2 sec.). Cut back to the medium shot of Blaney as he, bar in hand, closes the trunk, walks over to the side door and gets into the seat, reaching down for the wires. Offscreen we hear the alarm bells (13 sec.). Cut to a close-up of Blaney's hands knowingly manipulating the wires; we see a spark; the connection is made and the engine starts roaring (the music stops) as tension mounts, with alarms ringing in the background (10 1/2 sec.). Cut to a medium shot of the car moving away into a dark alley, camera pans with it (10 sec.). The total for the scene is 4 minutes.

The last scene in *Frenzy* follows two transitional but related shots: Inspector Oxford receives a call at his home about Blaney's escape. He rushes out, shouting to his wife (unseen) that: "Blaney has escaped and I have a pretty good idea where he went." A police car is to meet him downstairs (7 sec.). The second shot is inside a moving car, a medium two-shot of Sergeant Spearman sitting next to Inspector Oxford who shares with him his apprehension about Blaney's so-called suicide attempt, which, as it turns out it, was a part of a plan to escape (7 sec.).

Scene 25. Starts with (shot 1) a medium long shot of Blaney coming out of the stolen car, bar in hand, walking in the dark street toward Rusk's house. The familiarity with locale is essential here since it permits Hitchcock to accomplish his most complex fragmentation ever, without undue exposition. Blaney walks away; (the camera pans with him but remains stationary, 20 sec.). The music increases in intensity. Cut to (shot 2) a medium shot of Blaney walking by the iron fence, the one we remember from the night shot of Rusk wheeling out the body of Babs (8 sec.). This subtle symmetry sharpens the rationale of Blaney's revenge. Cut to (shot 3) a reverse shot of the downstairs door with, at first, Blaney's hand (opening it), then his shadow, and finally his face coming into a medium close-up; he looks in, intensely (4 1/2 sec.). (This energy-generating reverse shot is already part of a visual crescendo—a series of fifteen shots—2 to 16—during which Blaney climbs the familiar steps and that reaches its climax when he gets to the top.) Cut to (shot 4) what Blaney sees: a long, empty corridor leading to the stairway (familiar from the spectacular camera dolly down the stairs after Rusk took Babs up to his room) (2 1/2 sec.). Cut (shot 5) back to the medium close shot of Blaney closing the door and starting to walk four steps forward. Camera dollies back, keeping him in low close-up (10 sec.). Music again intensifies. Cut (shot 6) to a medium long shot of the stairs as camera dollies forward, simulating Blaney's next three steps (3 sec.). Cut to (shot 7) a high close shot of Blaney's feet climbing up three steps, iron bar in hand (3 1/2 sec.). Cut to (shot 8) a close-up of Blaney's angry face in movement as he goes up another three steps (2 1/2 sec.). Cut to (shot 9) a close-up of Blaney's hands moving up the railing (camera follows) (2 1/2 sec.). Cut to (shot 10) a high close shot of Blaney's mid-section, iron bar in hand, mounting another three steps as camera lifts with him (2 1/2 sec.). Cut to (shot 11) a high medium close shot of Blaney's face and shoulder; he begins turning to three-quarter profile (2 1/2 sec.). Cut to (shot 12) a high close-up of his hand sliding on the rail. Since he made a turn at the first landing, the hand follows the turn of the railing; his fingers now point down (camera follows) (4 1/3 sec.). Cut to (shot 13) medium close-up of Blaney's face in left profile; because of the turn, he now walks up to the left (2 1/2 sec.). Cut to (shot 14) a close-up of his hand on the railing, moving left and up (reverse symmetry with shot 9) (2 sec.). Music stops. Cut to (shot 15) a close shot of his feet going up also to the left. The dark railing studs are silhouetted sharply against his white pants (2 1/2 sec.). Cut to a medium shot of Blaney as he arrives at the door. Music again intensifies. The staccato rhythm stops here. He turns around to a right profile, part of the iron bar is seen in the bottom of the frame; he takes out the mica card to open the door, then changes his mind. Music stops (until shot 52); (15 sec.). Cut to (shot 17) a close-up of his hand at the knob, slowly trying to turn it. It works. He cautiously starts opening the door. A light crack appears (12 sec.). Cut to (shot 18) a medium close reverse shot (from the inside). The door continues opening as Blaney's face comes in (in perfect symmetry to shot 3, the entry down-stairs) and looks (6 1/2 sec.). And again as in the previous case (shot 3) we see what he sees (shot 19): in a slow disclosure long shot the camera pans from Rusk's couch to his bed (all familiar). It looks as if someone is sleeping in the bed (9 sec.). Cut to (shot 20) a medium close shot of Blaney as he enters further into the room, quietly closes the door, and starts walking forward. Camera dollies back with him; he takes three steps in the direction of the bed (8 1/2 sec.). The series of six shots that follow is a repeat symmetry to the chain of shots up the stairs (also with a few steps at a time). Cut to (shot 21) a long shot of the bed as the camera moves in, simulating Blaney's next three steps (2 1/2 sec.). Shot 22, medium shot of Blaney's two steps forward. Shot 23, close-up of iron bar in Blaney's hand, two steps forward. Shot 24, medium shot of Blaney's two steps forward, curving to the right. Shot 25, medium close shot of his feet (with iron bar seen), two steps forward. Shot 26, medium shot of the bed, camera moving in for two steps, each shot about two seconds in length.

Cut to (shot 27) a low medium shot of Blaney. He raises his arms with the iron bar and strikes down three times, each time his face coming to a close-up. The long duration of this shot (5 1/2 sec.) breaks the fast rhythm of Blaney's approach to the bed and also allows the viewer to absorb the implications of this climax: Blaney, the poor victim seeking revenge, yet, at the same time, Blaney the brutal killer. Now comes another slow disclosure. Cut to (shot 28) a medium shot of a woman's arm sliding out from under the cover of the bed and hanging down lifelessly. A few metallic bracelets slide down her arm (1 1/3 sec.). The slow disclosure is thus partially completed. Cut to (shot 29) a close shot of Blaney looking down, stupified (1 1/2 sec.). Cut back (shot 30) to the same shot of the woman's arm (1 1/2 sec.). Cut to (shot 31) a close-up of Blaney as he reaches down, presumably to the corner of the bed (2 sec.). Cut on action (shot 32) as Blaney's hand pulls away the bed cover and reveals, in a medium long shot, the corpse of a naked woman (2 1/2 sec.). The above shot is part of a double triad (of 6 shots) during which we see three shots of the naked woman, each time closer (long, close, and extreme close-up of her neck with a necktie around it, 2 seconds in length each, intercut with 3 close-ups of the stunned Blaney, 1 1/2 seconds each). In shot 37, the last of this series, Blaney turns suddenly in the direction of the door (this shot lasts only 1/2 sec.).

Cut to (shot 38) a long shot of the door opening, Inspector Oxford entering the room (2 sec.). Note the speed of these shots: the viewer has little time to think. Cut to (shot 39) a medium shot of Blaney, stunned. He shifts from leg to leg (2 sec.). Cut back to (shot 40) Inspector Oxford, this time in medium shot; he looks searchingly (2 1/2 sec.). Cut to (shot 41) a medium long shot of the bed with the naked woman, Blaney's midsection is on the left (2 sec.). Cut back (shot 42) to the Inspector (same shot) who examines what he sees; he seems momentarily to suspect Blaney for this murder too (5 1/2 sec.). Cut back to the same shot of Blaney (shot 43), who mumbles: "No, no, it's not . . ." (2 1/2 sec.). Cut to (shot 44) the same medium shot of the inspector who suddenly turns to the door, in reaction to thumps heard on the stairway (2 sec.). Cut back (shot 45) to the same shot of Blaney who also hears the loud thumps (1 1/2 sec.). Cut back (shot 46) to the inspector who closes the door and gestures to Blaney to stay quiet. He places himself to the side of the door waiting, while the thumps get louder (7 1/2 sec.). Cut back (shot 47) to a closer medium shot of Blaney (the picture of Rusk's mom is seen behind him) (2 1/3 sec.). Cut to (shot 48) a long shot toward the door as it opens slowly. The inspector hides next to it. Rusk enters backward with a heavy trunk on a dolly. He notices Blaney and the inspector; horrified, he breathes heavily (7 sec.). Cut back to the same medium shot of Rusk and the inspector who closes the door and looks at Rusk (camera adjusts and moves a little closer). The inspector leans against the door, dropping his arms and lacing his fingers; finally he slowly addresses Rusk, with a touch of irony: "Why Mr. Rusk, you're not wearing your tie." Rusk tries to say something, but his voice is gone (20 1/2 sec.). Cut to a reverse long three-shot from the back, of Rusk leaning on the trunk, Blaney still by the bed, and the dead woman in the background. Rusk looks at Blaney, a perfect wind-down shot before the final closure. Rusk starts letting the trunk go (3 3/4 sec.). Cut on action (shot 51) as the trunk, in close-up, falls to the floor, filling the whole frame (4 1/2 sec.). Credits start rolling up, superimposed over the trunk, in symmetry with the opening credits superimposed over the introductory shot of the river Thames.

Reviewing again Blaney's entry into Rusk's house (15 shots) and his actual ingress to the room (10 shots), one can easily see in Hitchcock's design a preference for the use of symmetries, both internal ones within the scene and those reaching by recall to earlier scenes. He arrives at a gentle crescendo by using elaborate and elegant visual rhetoric, rather than by seeking effects that generate only fear. The dramatic material here contains the potential for more fearsome moments; the actor's face, for example, could have conveyed fright, but it is not seen often or long enough. Hitchcock uses Blaney's face instead as a part of a chain of shots, equal in importance to his feet and hands; the latter, in fact, are of higher importance (the sliding on the balustrade during the walk up) as the most expressive in the chain. Hitchcock was aiming at an aesthetic mix without appealing to the lowest denominator.

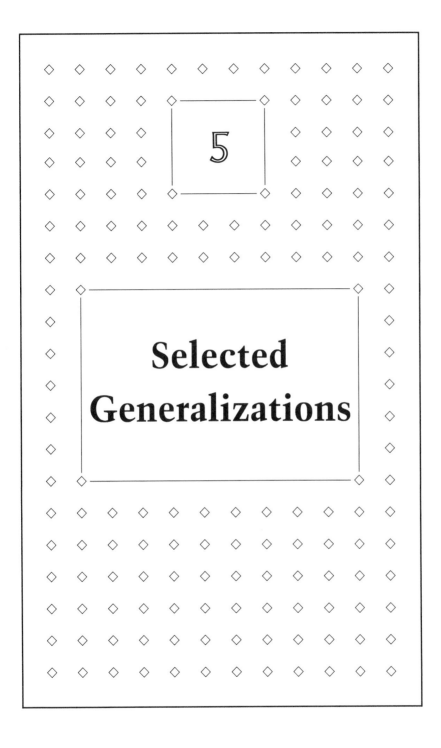

5

Selected Generalizations

A S PROMISED in the introduction, my obligation, at this stage, is to confront Hitchcock's forms with the "fundamental properties of the medium." It is apparent from the preceeding analyses that Hitchcock was far from imitating the theater or the novel and was miles away from cinema verité; on the contrary, what clearly transpires is Hitchcock as the preserver as well as the innovator and definer of the medium. Considering his penchant for stylization, the most surprising feature in all three films is the consistent linear continuity; even though often complicated by ingenious parallelism, the films remain basically linear. Curiously enough, this fact alone helps Hitchcock keep a neutral ground versus reality, with which he otherwise plays havoc.

The elements of structure he most often uses take considerable liberties with the naturalistic view of the world. Accordingly, in the three films analyzed here there is not a single shot (of longer duration) that would qualify as a "deep focus shot" as defined by Bazin, in itself an outrageous example of nonconformity with "reality." Hitchcock's fragmentations are the chief offenders in this area, mainly because they facilitate maneuvers with real time via occasional, and often hidden, deletions or elongations. Examples of the former are more than numerous; the most striking can be seen in *Frenzy* in the scene inside the potato truck when Rusk searches the dead body of Babs for his missing tie pin; also in the downhill car ride without brakes, in *Family Plot*. Elongations have two memorable representations: one in the final scene of *Notorious*, when Devlin descends the grand stairway with the ailing Alicia. It takes them a whole minute to walk down twenty-three steps, at a more or less steady pace. The other example is in *Frenzy*, also in the last scene, when Blaney goes up resolutely to Rusk's flat to seek revenge, a minutely fragmented ascent that is elongated to 30 seconds (for the eleven steps up). The director's fragmentations impinge upon reality in yet another aspect, an important one to Hitchcock, namely opposite movement and opposite graphics, a form he uses more often than anyone—since Eisenstein. One example that comes to mind is the scene in the wine cellar in *Notorious*. The scene ends in a classical Hitchcockian triad of consecutive closer shots of a wine bottle in Alex's hands, the neck of which is facing at first to the right, then left, and finally, in an extreme close-up, to center screen. The above contrapuntal arrangement hardly adheres to Aristotelian logic on a reality level; however, it is dramatically effective and cinematically elegant, conveying in a silent way Alex's thinking and his trauma. Such juxtapositions, opposites of all sorts, left after right, high after low, cross diagonals, etc., fill Hitchcock's films in such profusion that not a single page of the analysis passes without a mention of such forms. Through those fragmentations Hitchcock arrives at a rhythmic beat, a sort of cinematic meter that pulsates throughout his films.

In his Preface to the *Lyrical Ballads*, Wordsworth spoke of "the tendancy of meter to divest language of its reality in a certain degree." The same idea can be applied to cinema. Hitchcock's fictionality avoids a slavish devotion to mirrored reality; instead he builds a cinema-specific reality with rhythms and harmonies. Like a superb virtuoso he attenuates his meter here, accentuates it there, sometimes by a matter of a few frames or so, and thus arrives at a living and vibrating chain of minute differentiations, waves of intensity and calm, delicately attended to.

Hitchcock's separations, his primary element of structure, account for the majority of the fragmented scenes in the three films. The element of separation plays on the screen nearly in real time, since by its own laws it can seldom accommodate deletions; however, it tampers with reality by breaking up the deep focus space into separate spaces. It is only during the introduction and/or the resolution (to the separation) that the viewer can see the real space in toto. And, as we have seen, Hitchcock often bypasses introductions and resolutions altogether; in those cases the viewer has to fill in his own notion of the geography, usually by recall from previous scenes, made easy by Hitchcock with planted full shots in anticipation of such needs.

Whenever a narrative situation comes close to the edge of credibility (usually when for the sake of economy he has to bypass lengthy expositions), Hitchcock introduces extreme and sometimes unexpected camera angles. A good example can be found in *Notorious* in the turning, upside down shots of Devlin, as seen by Alicia Huberman after a night of alcoholic overconsumption. The spectacular and unusual shot succeeds in turning the viewer's attention away from the shaky veracity of the narrative (two minutes later Alicia, till now rebellious and negative, agrees to become an American agent).

In general, Hitchcock devotes very little time to external geography or the atmosphere of the places where his stories occur. In *Notorious*, Rio is hardly shown, except for a couple of aerial shots, a distant view of the beaches, as seen from Miss Huberman's high-rise balcony, and a glimpse of a few passersby in a city park, where our protagonists meet regularly. The same is true of *Family Plot* where one can hardly guess in which city the action takes place. In *Frenzy* we see a distant view of London and the bridge over the river Thames, but only under the superimposed titles; later we are given a few shots of the Covent Garden fruit and vegetable market, and occasional medium shots of workers carrying crates or pushing trolleys with merchandise; in sum, a rather niggardly attention to matters of the most accessible physical reality, an almost cranky dislike for background shooting and complete trust in a studio-made environment that can be minutely controlled. Even in such a magnificently constructed scene in *Family Plot* as the winding, downhill ride, without brakes, which was shot outdoors on a real location, there is not a single full exposition shot of Blanche's crippled car together with the other cars (or motorcycles) they passed or avoided. Hitchcock's total reliance on a separation type of fragmentation in the above scene points again to the fact that he is building a cinema-specific reality, constantly requiring a participatory viewer.

In the area of separation, Hitchcock introduced severel embellishments to its accepted usage: first his brief teaser mini-separations, usually four shots in A, B, A, B singles that preceed the introduction to the actual multishot main body of the separation. He started using this form in *Notorious* and has practiced it since in his other films, notably *Psycho*, as well as in *Frenzy* and *Family Plot*. Such teasers ease in the longer separations in a gentle way, presenting its iconography first in a shorter form. Second, Hitchcock introduced in *Frenzy* a perfected separation that is a combination of stationary and/or fragmented shots with a complex moving camera mise-en-scène. In such separations the framing of one of the participants remains stable while the other is in constant movement, resulting in changes in size and positioning. In

Frenzy, in the scene of rape and murder, Mrs. Blaney sits at her desk while Rusk is stalking around her in semicircles, slowly moving toward her, with camera following (this part of the separation contains thirty-five alternating shots between Mrs. Blaney and Rusk). In *Family Plot* one example is the scene at the gas station (Scene 11) between George (stable image) and Maloney (in constant movement). In *Notorious* there is an early precursor (30 years before) to the above combination, although that separation instead of camera movements contains juxtapositions of a stable image A against the B, with changes in camera angles. In the magnificently constructed separation in Scene 28, where Alex confesses to his mother that his wife is a spy, the mother is the stable image while Alex's shots change each time, the camera angle getting higher and higher. One should keep in mind, however, that in the majority of separations the A and B images are usually stable.

The traditional arrangement for separation is to film the participants in A and B single close shots face on (or nearly so). Hitchcock succeeds in injecting an occasional unexpected profile close-up of one of the actors in the chain of shots, without disturbing the special relationship. He does so, for example, in *Notorious*, Scene 28, at the race track. He seems to have been fascinated with profiles, especially in close-up. He uses them profusely in *Notorious* and to a lesser degree in *Family Plot* and *Frenzy*.

Another Hitchcock pattern is the reverse shot, including the taboo-ridden crossing of the axis. Reverse shots are usually part of his multiangular arrangements; they are also contrapuntal since, by their nature, reverse angles involve an opposition to that which is reversed. In Scene 11 in *Frenzy*, for example, Blaney, in a medium long shot, starts to enter a taxi from right to left and in the next shot, in a closer medium shot, completes his entry into the interior of the taxi from left to right. We witness a strong reverse shot and at the same time a crossing of the axis, a movement that is full of energy. Examples of Hitchcock's reverse shots are numerous; he avails himself of this mode in practically each scene and especially when someone enters a door or penetrates a given space. Hitchcock seems to be in search of a cinematic solution to the three-dimensionality of the flat screen. He also has a real need, and this has enormous theoretical implication, to show the *"fourth wall"* at every location, interior or exterior, literally and philosophically. This alone puts him outside the realm of the theater. The fourth wall in film is not a small matter; many filmmakers forget about it and therefore fall into the trap of proscenium arrangements which in turn corners them in a theatrical mode. Hitchcock's fourth walls are not conspicuous; he sneaks them in here and there. As in many of his structures, the viewer, almost on the subliminal level, gets the sense of a world that has order, organization, and balance, that is habitable and ready for human experience of all sort, a world of facts and acts (in the Wittgensteinian sense).

I must emphasize that the notion of a fourth wall in Hitchcockian practice is rarely concerned with information or exposition, since very often his reverse shots are closer and therefore, as in all close-ups, contain little background, hence less information. Yet they carry an emotional and cinesthetic impact. Still, in instances when the fourth wall is informational, the result is a gratifying feeling of either familiarity or reassuring acceptance of a missing link. I refer to familiarity in cases where the fourth wall has been physically seen but not in context of the total environment; the missing link would cover cases when Hitchcock delayed its disclosure. The delayed disclosure of Devlin's face during the party scene at the beginning of *Notorious*, after we have seen only the back of his head for a long time, is within the realm of the "fourth wall." Whatever the complexity of that realm might be, Hitchcock's aim is to encompass a total world as complete as human perception will permit. The most striking statement on the subject is Hitchcock's shot of the interior of the jail cell in *Frenzy*, where all four walls are seen in a most stylized (and even unrealistic) way.

Another Hitchcockian pattern can be found in his transitions. Hitchcock recognizes the paramount importance of transitions in cinema as the principal connectors as well as the brackets between segments in the story. He invests them with superior pictorial originality and a deeper meaning. They are multi-hierarchical; they bridge; they close; they forewarn. Judging from the three films analyzed here, representing an almost forty-year span, Hitchcock assigns a particular form of transition to each film. In *Notorious* it is the close-up of a protagonist placed at the end of the outgoing scene, a meaningful, thoughtful moment of meditation, often carrying a strong after image. Such close-ups, when the iconography is already established, signal closures of scenes and at the same time permit the viewer some thinking time.

In *Family Plot* it is the very high long shot that forms the transition, either in the outgoing or the incoming scene. Needless to say, the transition from Scene 2 to 3, the high shot of the taxi that carries George and Blanche, is a magnificent example. This is probably the most outrageously original bridge between two parallel actions. The visual effect is much ahead of the viewer's comprehension of the narrative consequences. Even though unsettling, or because of this, the transition provokes the viewer to follow the action of the scene with intensified interest. Such a transition is typical of Hitchcock's ability to stimulate interest in the narrative with means that are outside the narrative itself. There are many other high shot transitions that function in the same manner, notably the extremely high view of Blanche's car on the highway that is also symmetrical with the other high shots of cars, some of which signal trouble. A magnificent high shot of the cathedral as George runs up the steps to it begins the tragicomic scene of the bishop's kidnapping. Eventually in *Family Plot*, high shots become a signal of important happenings to come, and are not limited to transitions only.

In *Frenzy* transitions are more eclectic yet tend to be smooth connectors between scenes rather than startling beginnings or endings. The majority have compatible movements; some are similes. An example of the latter is the transition from Scene 1: in the last shot we saw a close-up of a dead woman floating by the river's edge with a man's tie around her neck; the next shot (start of Scene 2) is a close-up of Blaney in front of a mirror tying his tie. The connection here is ominous and casts a shadow, for a while at least, over Blaney as the possible killer. The former transitions, between compatible movements, are also elegant. After the long duration dolly shot retreating from Rusk's stairway into the street, a technical tour de force, there follows a shot of Inspector Oxford entering his apartment and walking toward the camera in the same direction as the dolly in the previous scene. This transition has a touch of irony in it, since we know that the first dolly shot signifies the rape and murder of poor Babs, while the inspector's walk reflects his mistaken assurance that Blaney is the guilty man. There is irony as well in the transition to the next scene: cut from the close-up of the tiny roasted quail on Inspector Oxford's plate to a shot of Rusk wheeling out the body of Babs packed into a potato bag. Without question these transitions are an important strand in Hitchcock's design and he weaves them into the fabric of the entire film with determination. Their very existence proves that Hitchcock's films are planned with precision since transitions of such magnitude could not be improvised or decided upon post factum.

Hitchcock also creates some minor patterns that, as always with him, are not just casual occurrences. First is the use of the zoom. As I have already elaborated, the zoom in Hitchcock's hand is cleansed from its usual vulgarity and grossness by the manner in which it is used. As far as *Notorious* goes, it should be noted that zooms at that time (1946) were very seldom used. The many zooms in this film could be considered practically avant-guardist, or at least experimental, with a touch of modernity. Hitchcock considered the zoom as a useful tool, not as a trick, and used it with precision. Let's consider the first instance of its use in *Notorious*, during the dinner in the Sebastian mansion: the dolly in focuses attention on the bottle of wine, an important "actor" in this drama; it connects this form with Alicia, and all future zooms will follow suit; and, the zoom ends the scene and is faded out, making it more of a closure than a statement, consequently softening the impact. The zooms to come are much bolder and more functional, like the one to the key before Alicia steals it, or the one from far above into Alicia's hand in which the key rests. Once introduced in the dinner scene, the other zooms become familiar movements. In *Family Plot* the few zooms are omni-functional; some, like the one into Blanche's eye, are jokes; others, like the zoom into the needle about to be inserted into Blanche's arm, are threatening. *Frenzy* has only a few zooms.

Another minor pattern of Hitchcock's is his singular mise-en-scène where unexpected images suddenly intrude. A perfect example can be found at the end of Scene 5 in *Notorious*, in Alicia's apartment, when Devlin is leaving the room. There are three surprising events here: an unexpected close-up of Alicia, the unexpected passing of Devlin behind her, and then Devlin's unexpected passing in front of her. As always in such cases, the viewer has to decode the positioning of the characters: most likely Devlin had to follow an S-shaped path around the table to the door, thus the rationale for his passing once behind Alicia and then in front of her. The impact of the images comes ahead of such a rationalization, and the impact is strong; it has the modality of a surprise, intriguing yet visceral and at the same time mystifying. Hitchcock uses such passages (in front) in all three films.

There is also an excellent unexpected image in *Frenzy* when Babs walks out of Forsythe's pub (Scene 14). The camera moves in on her face to a very tight close shot. Suddenly, upon hearing a question from behind her, she moves to the side and Rusk's threatening face unexpectedly appears. Such images, in addition to the strength and energy they generate, are also within Hitchcock's strategy to emphasize the three-dimensionality of the screen whenever possible.

As we know, Hitchcock likes close shots and as a result he populates his scenes with familiar images in close-up, another repeated pattern. Many of his scenes, even those with minute fragmentation, contain only a minimal amount of shots repeated generously and in different combinations. Central to these repetitions is the familiar image that usually has the function of glueing the mosaic together. Hitchcock also used a pattern of familiar movement, such as his craning shots in *Notorious* and *Family Plot*, and his forward and back dollying in *Frenzy*. They become the vivid iconography of the films.

The fundamental pattern of Hitchcock's work belongs to his orchestration of the total film. He checkerboards the scenes: those with quick cuts are followed by ones with minimal fragmentation or no cuts at all; scenes of high intensity are followed by relaxed scenes; humorous ones by dramatic ones, always on the principle of trigger-release, trigger-release, always enhanced with an abundance of symmetries. His structures invite the viewer to pay close attention. The incitement to attentive watching is one of his achievements.

The examples I have given to illustrate some of the patterns are mostly from important scenes, yet it is characteristic of Hitchcock's precise lacework that many gratifying examples of these forms can be found in insignificant corners of a scene. Therefore it should be repeated over and over that his most constant pattern is this precision enhanced by a scrupulous attention to details. Adherence to a proper cinema-specific grammar is not enough; Hitchcock's form is the sum total of his superb syntax, his originality, and most of all his exactitude. From the three films analyzed here it is clear that Hitchcock has grasped the structures of the language of cinema and has practiced them with exquisite artistry; they are the foundation of his craft and he uses them with determination, as artifacts made out of moving pictures (and not as slices of life). His knowledge of cinema's rules, however tacit, is evidence of his acute cultural competence in the medium. His spiritual depth is apparent in the way he throws light upon what amounts to base life and turns it into these exquisite masterpieces. By displaying the utmost linguistic variety he gives us delightful proof of his genius, and lifts cinema language to the high vernacular in his eloquent and often flamboyant way.

Glossary

Terms in capitals are cross references defined alphabetically. All terms are explained in reference to their screen effect unless otherwise specified.

ACCELERATED MOTION: A stuffy term for FAST MOTION.

AFTER-IMAGE: An image so graphically strong that the mind's eye retains it even though a new shot has appeared on the screen.

ASPECT RATIO: The shape of the overall picture—so-called because screen shape is identified by the ratio of the screen's width to its height. Screen shapes vary from the normal, nearly square, ratio of 1.33:1 to very long rectangles. (The ratio of most of today's wide screens is 1.85:1.) In the 1950s Hollywood began to compete with various kinds of wide-screen systems, such as Cinemascope, Cinerama, and Vistavision. If a director is preparing a scene which will not look good in a wide-screen format, he may use natural blocking to reframe the image. For example, he may shoot through curtains or doorways that are ostensibly part of the set but appear dark in the foreground.

AVAILABLE LIGHTING: see LIGHTING.

CINEMA VÉRITE: An approach to film-making that tries not to interfere with reality. It plays down the technical and formal means of production (script, special lighting, etc.) at the director's disposal and emphasizes the circumstantial reality of the scenes. It often uses natural sound, AVAILABLE LIGHTING, and conspicuous camera work (e.g. ZOOM and HAND-HELD SHOTS), since flexibility is considered more essential than perfection of technique. The term is applied to the documentary work of Jean Rouch, the Maysles, Richard Leacock and others.

CIRCULAR CAMERA MOVEMENT: see SHOT.

CLOSE-UP: see SHOT.

CONTINUITY CUTTING: A style of editing marked by its emphasis on maintaining the continuous and seemingly uninterrupted flow of action in a story. However, the continuous time is apparent, not REAL TIME (as within the long TAKES OF CINEMA VÉRITÉ, for example). Contrasted with DYNAMIC CUTTING.

CROSS-CUTTING: Switching back and forth between two or more scenes—for example, a serial episode that alternately shows the heroine nearing the waterfall and the hero galloping to the rescue. Cross-cutting can create PARALLEL ACTION, time, and space. In cases like the above last-minute rescue, excitement and tension are often increased by shortening the shots and accelerating the rhythm of the cross-cutting.

CROSSING THE AXIS: If we draw a line (axis) through the main action of a scene, any camera position on one side of the line will preserve screen direction. If a car is traveling left to right and the camera were to CROSS THE AXIS and shoot from side B, the car would appear to travel right to left. Crossing the axis is a beginner's "no-no" because the results can be ambiguous. However, any number of great directors have proven that they can preserve our sense of a single direction despite the *opposite movements*.

CUT: A TRANSITION made by splicing two pieces of film together. Types of cutting defined in this glossary include: CONTINUITY CUTTING, CROSS-CUTTING, CUTAWAY, CUTTING ON ACTION, DYNAMIC CUTTING, FORM CUT, HIDDEN CUT, JUMP-CUT, SEPARATION.

CUTAWAY: A shot of short duration that supposedly takes place at the same time as the main action, but not directly involved in the main action. For examples of cutaways, see REACTION SHOT and INSERT SHOT. Cutaways are sometimes used less for artistic purposes than to overcome continuity gaps when some footage is bad or missing. If Bush picked his teeth while speaking, a sympathetic editor would keep the sound but visually cut away to a shot of someone listening that was taken earlier to cover up such routine mishaps.

CUTTING ON ACTION: Cutting from one shot to another view that "matches" it in action and gives the impression of a continuous time span. Example: the actor begins to sit down in a MEDIUM SHOT and finishes in a CLOSE-UP. By having an actor begin a gesture in one shot and carry it through to completion in the next, the director creates a visual bridge which distracts us from noticing the cut.

DECELERATED MOTION: A stuffy term for SLOW MOTION.

DEEP FOCUS: see FOCUS.

DISSOLVE: see TRANSITIONS.

DOLLY SHOT: see SHOT.

DYNAMIC CUTTING: A type of editing which, by the juxtaposition of contrasting shots or sequences, generates ideas in the viewer's mind which were not latent in the shots themselves. Simplified example: shot of man + shot of peacock = idea of egomaniac. Eisenstein thought of MONTAGE as this kind of creative editing.

ESTABLISHING SHOT: see SHOT.

EXPRESSIONISM: A mode of shooting developed in Germany during the 1920s (e.g. *The Cabinet of Dr. Caligari*) which used highly unnaturalistic lighting, sets, makeup, acting, etc., to give a dramatic, larger-than-life effect. Its influence on American films can be seen in Ford's *The Informer* and Welles' *Citizen Kane*.

EXTREME CLOSE-UP: see SHOT.

EYE-LEVEL SHOT: see SHOT.

FADE: see TRANSITIONS.

FAMILIAR IMAGE: A graphically strong shot that repeats itself with little change during a film. The repetition has a subliminal effect, creating a visual abstract thought. A familiar image both serves as a stabilizing bridge to the action and accrues meaning as the film progresses. Examples include the "cradle endlessly rocking" in *Intolerance* and the LOW-ANGLE SHOT of Patton against the sky, in *Patton*.

FAST MOTION: Action that appears faster on the screen than it could in reality. Frequently used in the silent film chase. This special effect is shot by running the camera more slowly than usual (e.g., at 12 frames per second instead of the normal 24 for sound films). Since camera and projection speeds were not standardized until the silent era was almost over, we now often see silent films at a much faster speed than we were meant to. Thus we find an unintentional comic effect.

FLAT LIGHTING: see LIGHTING.

FOCUS: An object in focus has a sharp and well-defined image. If it is out of focus it appears blurred. Focus is mainly affected by the lens of the camera, the projector, and your eye.

DEEP FOCUS: In deep focus, objects in the immediate foreground and at great distance appear in equally sharp focus at the same time.

SELECTIVE FOCUS: In selective focus, the main object of interest is in focus, the remainder of the objects are out of focus. It is (too) often used when the two lovers gamboling in focus through the fields are photographed through a foreground of out-of-focus flowers.

SOFT FOCUS: In soft focus, often used for romantic effects, all objects appear blurred because none are perfectly in focus. This diffused effect is often used to photograph aging leading ladies. Soft focus can be obtained with filters as well as lenses.

FOLLOW FOCUS: If the camera or the subject moves during the shot, the camera may have to be refocused during the take in order to keep the subject in focus. The procedure is called follow-focus.

SEARCH FOCUS: Also called "rack focus." The switching of focus within a shot from one person or thing to another. For instance, in filming a conversation between two people, the director can place them in the same frame, one in the foreground and one in the background, and alternately keep one in focus, the other out of focus. This is a popular TV effect.

FORM CUT: Framing in a successive shot an object which has a shape or contour similar to an image in the immediately preceding shot. In Griffith's *Intolerance*, for example, the camera cuts from Belshazzar's round shield to the round end of a battering ram pounding the city gates. The circumference and location in the frame of the two circles are identical.

FRAME: see UNITS OF FILM LENGTH.

FREEZE FRAME: The effect in which action appears to come to a dead stop. This is accomplished by printing one frame many times. TV's instant replay sometimes "freezes" a crucial action to let us get a better look at it (but this is done electronically, not with film). Freezes are a popular way to end today's movies, to give an existential feeling rather than a sense of finality. Among the better examples are the zoom-freezes that end *The 400 Blows* and *Wanda*.

GRAPHICS: The formal structured content of the cine-image, as opposed to the haphazard arrangement of the narrative contents.

HAND-HELD SHOT: A shot made with the camera not mounted on a tripod or other stabilizing fixture. Since it gains flexibility while it loses stability, it is often used for CINEMA VÉRITÉ.

HIDDEN CUT: An inconspicuous cut, usually used in a fast-action scene, with which the director accelerates the action without significantly shifting the angle or distance as required for a more noticeable cut.

HIGH-ANGLE SHOT: see SHOT.

INSERT SHOT: A CUTAWAY shot inserted for the purpose of giving the audience a closer look at what the character on the screen is seeing or doing; e.g., we see a MEDIUM SHOT of the actor raising his wrist and looking at his watch; then an EXTREME CLOSE-UP shot of the watch face; then a medium shot of the actor finishing looking at the watch and lowering his wrist.

IRIS: see TRANSITIONS.

JUMP-CUT: A cut that jumps forward from one part of an action to another separated from the first by an interval of time. It thus creates geographical dislocation within a unity of space. It usually connects the beginning and ending of an action, leaving out the middle. Godard's *Breathless* created a 60s vogue for jump-cuts.

LIGHTING: The distribution of light and how it models the subjects and affects the graphics is the main aesthetic element of film other than composition.

Light can be *natural* (sunlit) or *artificial* (electric). It can be *flat* (not highly contrasted in brights and darks) or *highlight*. Highlights create dramatic graphic effects. Low-key lighting is recognized by the absence of a strong source of light from a defined direction which creates highlights.

When extra lights are not brought along for shooting, as is often the case with CINEMA VÉRITÉ, AVAILABLE LIGHTING (whatever is normally there) is used.

Most film stocks are not "fast" enough to shoot an ordinary outdoor night scene. So the scene is shot in the daylight and filters are added to darken the scene to look like night. This is called shooting *day for night.* Similarly, there are aesthetic reasons for shooting *night for day, exterior for interior,* and *interior for exterior.*

LOCATION: Any place, other than the studio or studio lot, where a film is shot.

LONG SHOT: see SHOT.

LOW-ANGLE SHOT: see SHOT.

LOW-KEY LIGHTING: see LIGHTING.

MASTER SHOT: see SHOT.

MATTE: A mask which obstructs some of the light passing through the camera lens. It can be of a specific shape (e.g. a keyhole) which is imposed on the film as a blank area while the photographic images are being exposed. In silent days it was often left blank. Nowadays mattes are more often produced with laboratory techniques than with camera-mounted masks. See TRAVELING MATTE.

MEDIUM SHOT: see SHOT.

MISE-EN-SCÈNE: A term generally used in reference to the staging of a play or a film production—in considering as a whole the settings, the arrangements of the actors in relation to the setting, lighting, etc. Some critics use the concept of mise-en-scène to describe what goes on *within the frame* in contrast with cutting, as the two key approaches to filmmakers' styles.

MONTAGE: In Russia, montage meant DYNAMIC CUTTING; in Europe, the term is equivalent to editing; in Hollywood, it is used more specifically to describe a sequence using rapid SUPERIMPOSITIONS, JUMP-CUTS, and DISSOLVES in order to create a kind of kaleidoscopic effect.

MOVING SHOT: see SHOT.

OPTICALS: SPECIAL EFFECTS usually created in the laboratory with an optical printer, but most of them can also be created in the camera. These include most TRANSITIONS (dissolve, fade, iris, wipe). See, for example, MATTE, SUPERIMPOSITION, and TRAVELING MATTE.

PAN SHOT: see SHOT.

PARALLEL ACTION: An effect created by CROSS-CUTTING, which enables the viewer to be two or more places concurrently. Using parallel action, a filmmaker can extend or condense REAL TIME and create a SCREEN TIME with a logic of its own. For instance, if the filmmaker wants to lengthen the suspense while the heroine has one minute to answer a question on a TV quiz show, he can cut between the homes of anxious friends watching in four different cities.

REACTION SHOT: A CUTAWAY shot of a person reacting to the main action as listener or spectator. Some comedians have planned reaction shots to jokes in order to give the audience a chance to laugh without missing the next line.

REAL TIME: The actual time an action would need to occur; as opposed to SCREEN TIME, a principal aesthetic effect created by filmmakers in transforming reality into art. Real time is preserved within the scenes of a play but (usually) only within the individual shots of a film.

REAR PROJECTION: A technique whereby the actors, sets, and props in front of the camera are combined with a background which consists of a transulcent screen on which a picture (moving or still) is projected from behind. Almost always used when a scene takes place inside a moving vehicle. The actors sit still and the scenery they are supposedly passing by is projected behind them. Sometimes called "back projection" or "process shot."

REVERSE-ANGLE SHOT: see SHOT.

SCENE: see UNITS OF FILM LENGTH.

SCREEN DIRECTION: Whichever direction, left or right, the actor or object is looking at or moving toward, described from the *audience point of view.*

SCREEN TIME: Duration of an action as manipulated through editing, as opposed to REAL TIME. A principal aesthetic effect by which the filmmaker transforms reality into art. CUTAWAYS and INSERT SHOTS are two ways of stretching or condensing real time to give the film different time. If we cut between a race and the spectators' reactions, we often lengthen the actual time of the race. If we cut away for part of a movement, when we cut back we may have cut out a large chunk of the action. For other ways of manipulating time see: FAST and SLOW MOTION, CROSS-CUTTING, HIDDEN CUT, JUMP-CUTS, and PARALLEL ACTION.

SEPARATION: Shooting people in separate shots who are actually quite close together. A conversation may be filmed with one person looking right in MEDIUM SHOT and the other looking left in CLOSE-

UP (probably after a TWO-SHOT establishing their nearness). A unique tool of cinema which can bring people in closer relation than if they were in the same shot.

SEQUENCE: see UNITS OF FILM LENGTH.

SHOT: A piece of film that has been exposed, without cuts or interruptions, in a single running of the camera. The shot is the elemental division of a film. Shots may be categorized: (1) according to the *distance* between the camera and its subject (e.g., a long shot)—these designations vary among directors and are relative to the size of the subject filmed and the way distances have been established in the film; (2) according to the *angle* of the camera in relation to the subject (e.g., a high-angle shot); (3) according to the *content*, nature or subject matter of what is being filmed (e.g., a reaction shot or a two-shot); or (4) according to the *means* by which the shot is accomplished physically (e.g., a tracking shot).

(1) LONG SHOT (LS): The camera seems to be at a distance from the subject being filmed.

MEDIUM SHOT (MS): A shot intermediate in distance between a long and a close shot.

CLOSE-UP (CU): The camera seems very close to the subject, so that when the image is projected most of the screen will be taken up with revealing a face and its expressions, or a plate of stew.

EXTREME CLOSE-UP (ECU): The camera seems very close to what would ordinarily be a mere detail in a close-up. For example, the whole screen is taken up with a shot of a tear welling up in an eye.

(2) HIGH-ANGLE SHOT: A shot which looks down on the subject from a height.

LOW-ANGLE SHOT: A shot which looks up at the subject.

EYE-LEVEL SHOT: Guess.

REVERSE-ANGLE SHOT: Shot taken by a camera positioned opposite (about 180°) from where the previous shot was taken. A reverse angle of a dog walking toward the camera would be a shot of it walking directly away from the camera. If a reverse-angle is made of two people in a TWO-SHOT, the rules of CROSSING THE AXIS have to be observed by reversing their positions.

(3) ESTABLISHING SHOT: Often the opening shot of a sequence,

showing the location of a scene or the arrangement of its characters. Usually a LONG SHOT. For example, if the story jumps from lover's lane, where an athelete is breaking training on the night before the big game, to his disastrous fumble at the championship, we will probably see the stadium and teams from a HIGH-ANGLE LONG SHOT before we close in on the hero's actions. Compare SLOW DISCLOSURE.

MASTER SHOT: Single shot of an entire piece of dramatic action. A standard Hollywood practice that facilitates the editing of a scene. For example, a conversation is likely to be photographed first as one lengthy TWO-SHOT; then it will be reshot in pieces at the different distances and angles needed to construct the scene.

TWO-SHOT. Two persons in the same frame.

THREE-SHOT. Three persons in the same frame.

(4) CIRCULAR CAMERA MOVEMENT: A camera movement that travels around its more or less stationary subject.

DOLLY OR TRUCKING SHOT: One in which the camera *moves bodily* from one place to another. (Compare pan and tracking shots.)

MOVING SHOT: One taken from some normally moving object such as a plane or a car.

PAN SHOT: One during which the camera stays in one place but *rotates horizontally* on its axis.

SWISH PAN: A pan so rapid that the image appears blurred. It usually begins and ends at rest.

TILT SHOT: One in which the camera pivots along a *vertical* plane.

TRACKING SHOT: A dolly shot in which the camera moves *parallel* with its moving subject. If the camera moves in on a seated person, that is a dolly-in; if it travels alongside of a person walking down the block, that is a tracking shot.

ZOOM SHOT: A shot taken with a zoom lens (i.e., a lens which makes it possible to move visually toward or away from a subject without moving the camera). We can get closer to a subject with either a dolly or zoom shot. When we dolly into a subject, objects pass by the camera, giving a feeling of depth. When we zoom, the sensation is two-dimensional, much like coming close to a still photograph. Zooms are used a lot in covering football games.

SLOW DISCLOSURE: A shot starting in CLOSE-UP that does not reveal the location of the subject at first. It then moves back or cuts to a full revelation of the geography, which comes as a surprise. A shot typical of cartoons would show an animal sleeping comfortably and then zoom out to reveal that his enemy is lowering an axe over his head.

SLOW MOTION: Opposite of FAST MOTION. The action appears slower on the screen than it could in reality. Popular for dream and romantic effects, and to show the gracefulness of athletes.

SOFT FOCUS: see FOCUS.

SPECIAL EFFECTS: Visual special effects are OPTICALS.

STOCK FOOTAGE: Footage borrowed from previous films or a stock library. It is often newsreel footage of famous people and events or battle scenes and other hard to shoot footage.

STOP MOTION: The method by which trick photography is effected; the film is exposed one frame at a time, allowing time for rearrangement of models, etc., between shots and thus giving the illusion of motion by something normally inanimate. This is how *King Kong* was filmed and also how flowers can grow, bloom, and die within a few minutes. Stop motion applied to objects is *animation*, applied to people is *pixilation*.

SUBJECTIVE SHOT: Shot that seems to represent the point of view of a character in the story. It may be what he sees (e.g., a shot through the keyhole he is peeking through into the next room), or how he sees it (e.g., a blurred shot looking up at the surgeon from the operating table as the character awakes from anaesthesia). In *The Cabinet of Dr. Caligari*, we learn at the end of the film that the distorted, EXPRESSIONISTIC MISE-EN-SCÈNE reflects the fact that the film's narrator is a mental patient.

SUPERIMPOSITION: An OPTICAL effect in which two or more images are on one piece of film, so that there appears to be a multiple exposure. Can be used when two characters played by the same actor have to meet; also for DISSOLVES, dream sequences, etc.

SWISH PAN: see SHOT.

SYNC OR SYNCHRONISM: The relation between picture and sound. If they don't match, the film is said to be "out of sync." Easiest to spot by watching a person's lips as speaks.

TAKE: see UNITS OF FILM LENGTH.

THREE-SHOT: see SHOT.

TILT SHOT: see SHOT.

TRACKING SHOT: see SHOT.

TRANSITIONS: Means of connecting two shots. The following transitions can be created either in the laboratory with an OPTICAL printer or in the camera.

DISSOLVE: The merging of the end of one shot with the beginning of the next; as the second shot becomes distinct, the first slowly fades away. Thus, for a while two images are SUPERIMPOSED. Also called "lap dissolves" and, in England, "mixes."

FADE: A fade-in shot begins in darkness and gradually assumes full brightness. A fade-out shot gradually gets darker.

IRIS: An iris-in shot opens from darkness into an expanding circle within which is the image. An iris-out is the opposite.

WIPE: A transition in which the second shot appears and "pushes" off the first one; usually they are separated by a visible vertical line, but the variations of wipes are many. Unlike an iris, there is a picture on both sides of the dividing line.

TRAVELING MATTE: A SPECIAL EFFECT used to blend actors in the studio with location or trick scenes. The actor is photographed against a dark background and this image can later be combined optically with the desired background. Thus actors can move among animated monsters, exploding shells, or cobras. The traveling matte is therefore unlike REAR PROJECTION.

TWO-SHOT: see SHOT.

UNITS OF FILM LENGTH:

FRAME: The individual picture on a strip of film. Sound films project 24 frames per second.

SHOT: A piece of film that has been exposed without cuts or interruptions. (Defined in detail under its own alphabetical listing.)

TAKE: Each performance of a piece of action in front of a camera (from "lights, camera, action!" to "cut!"). Each recording is numbered sequentially, until the director feels he has satisfactory results. From the takes he chooses one for each shot.

SCENE and SEQUENCE: Although the terms are used constantly, there is no agreement on what these units comprise. One definition is that a scene is determined by unity of time and place (like a dramatic scene) whereas a sequence is determined by unity of action (a more filmic unit).

WIPE: see TRANSITIONS.

ZOOM SHOT: see SHOT.